BUDU

or

TWENTY YEARS IN SARAWAK

by

JOHN K. WILSON

Drawings by ARTHUR THWAITES

TANTALLON PRESS LTD.
NORTH BERWICK

2.

B. WIL

ACKNOWLEDGEMENTS

While I was still in Sarawak, Borneo, the Nuffield Foundation gave me a grant to enable me to write an account of my work over the last twenty years. I would like to acknowledge this grant with very sincere thanks, since without it this account would never have been written.

To those who have helped me and contributed to it, also my sincere thanks.

Very special thanks are due to A. A., a lifelong friend, who undertook the wearisome task of correction and in the dark days following my banishment from Sarawak, by her unfailing encouragement and advice, so made it possible for this story to be completed.

CONTENTS

BOOK 1

BOOK 2

A unique set of Drawings depicting some aspects of
the life of the Sea Dyaks.

By

Arthur Thwaites

ERRATA

Page 7, para. 3, line one,
for "concrete hut" read "concert hut".

For page 259 read page 264
For page 264 read page 259

PROLOGUE

The Author

John K. Wilson was born in Glasgow in 1914, completing his Primary School education at Newlands Public School. His Secondary Education was completed at Dunoon Grammar School. He then proceeded to Glasgow University where in 1935 he graduated as a B.Sc. with hons. in Chemistry. At Jordanhill Teachers' Training College, he became qualified to teach both in a Primary School and a Secondary School. He gained experience as a teacher both in a Primary School in the Gorbals District of Glasgow and at Glasgow Academy, and subsequently after the war at Campbeltown Public School.

In 1937, realising that war was inevitable, he joined the Royal Air Force Volunteer Reserve and by 1939 had been awarded his wings, having learned to fly at weekends at the Elementary Flying Training School at Prestwick. He completed his advanced training in Salisbury, Rhodesia, early in 1940, and subsequently saw active service as a pilot in Aden, Western Desert, Greece, Crete, Jordan and Iraq. He was shot down by rifle fire and as a result of this fractured his spine in the ensuing crash. Determined not to end up in a wheelchair, he dumbfounded the medical authorities when after more than a year in a plaster cast, having secretly but painfully kept himself mobile by dancing in his plaster cast, he was pronounced fit to resume light flying duties in an Elementary Flying Training School as an instructor. Just a year later, he returned to active service flying duty on heavy bombers over Germany. He was awarded both the D.F.C. and the A.F.C.

It was not surprising that when he returned to teaching he felt quite out of tune with the then concepts of pure academic teaching and he could find no satisfaction in his chosen profession. His many hours of earnest thought while lying in his plaster cast and his subsequent experiences bombing German cities, had indeed changed his whole philosophy of life and he was determined to seek a new challenge. Teaching, he was certain, should embrace a far wider concept—that of the Community and not just as something that happened inside four walls.

So, in 1949, he joined the Colonial Education Service, and found himself in Sarawak, Borneo, as the Principal of the Teacher Training College in Kuching. As Principal, he travelled extensively but it soon became apparent to him that merely to open schools in areas of backward and primitive peoples was not enough. He saw for himself that while the policy of opening a school in a remote area was a necessary step, this defeated its own object since all the clever pupils left their home areas, never to return. Thus, unless there was some parallel development within the area of the new school, a school, rather than bringing progress, brought depopulation.

With some regrets at leaving the comforts of civilisation, he resigned as Principal of the Batu Lintang Teachers' Training College and accepted an appointment as an ordinary teacher at Budu, right in the heart of the Dyak Communities, remote and inaccessible. It seemed to him just essential to study at first hand the whole problem of helping backward people. For fifteen years he, as leader of a team of Community Development Officers, recruited and trained by him, sought the solutions and in so doing established beyond doubt new basic principles to raise the standard of living of backward peoples. In recognition of his services he was awarded the O.B.E.

It is not surprising that, known to the Dyaks as Tuan Tuai, or Tuan Budu, his name is already legend. Refusing steadfastly to become a political influence under the Malaysian Federal Government when Sarawak gained its Independence within this Federation in 1963, John Wilson was banished by this Government in June 1968 and ordered never to return to the land he had come to love.

BOOK I

The Budu Community Development Centre as seen from the hill

CHAPTER ONE

INTRODUCTION

Write not your diary on the day itself,
For it takes longer than that to know what really happened.

WITH ONLY AN IDEA, but an idea born from many hours of earnest thought, John Wilson resigned as Principal of the Batu Lintang Teachers' Training College, Kuching, Sarawak, Borneo, and became a teacher in a small Primary school at Budu. He chose Budu primarily because it was in an area untouched by any religious, political or economic missions. It was new territory and it contained particularly challenging problems of inaccessibility, a high prevalence of disease and an unfortunate attitude on the part of the Sea Dyaks to many new ideas.

To reach Budu from Saratok the nearest port was then, even under excellent conditions, a four days' journey. Goods were transported in open longboats about thirty feet in length, made locally from large tree trunks. After a day, the lower reaches of the River Krian were left behind and the journey then became both dangerous and exhausting for all concerned. Were the bow of the canoe to be as much as a few inches wrongly set to the swift current, disaster would have resulted. Travel between Budu and other Dyak communities was by foot, along jungle paths where snakes abounded, not to mention leeches. If the rain came on, as it almost always did in the afternoon, small streams became torrents, small rivers floods. Being caught in underwater branches was frequent. Journeys were exhausting since the paths just went up and down, up and down, often slippery or criss-crossed with tree roots, painful on bare feet which was the usual form of travel.

It was to this kind of situation that John Wilson went, knowing or hoping that if he could successfully institute a new way of life for the Dyaks at Budu, then other districts would be more easily influenced. For more than a year he was completely alone, seeking no outside contacts, no other European company, only determined to master the Dyak language, understand and learn the Dyak customs. As his affection for his pupils grew so did his certainty that among them were a few whose intelligence far exceeded his own. Their insatiable zest to learn, their natural charm, their open frankness, their qualities of character and above all their smiles and gurgling laughter as they toiled and sweated to build their new school or prepare vegetable patches, made John Wilson more determined than ever to find a way to help. Slowly but surely, hazy ideas took the form of concrete plans dependent primarily as to whether it would be possible to form and train a team of Community Development Officers, capable to assist in a planned adult education programme, to provide medical coverage of the area, to open up co-operative trading and marketing concerns, to initiate some form of agricultural extension work both at a main centre and on the land near to Dyak communities, to select and train potential leaders from the local

1

communities, to open new Primary schools at selected places, to convene an elected Committee of Progress to administer a well-defined area and above all capable to bring a spirit of co-operation among the Sea Dyaks to work towards a common aim.

The response to Wilson's efforts to recruit his team was more than encouraging and from well over a hundred applicants he chose Mr Thomas McBride of Maybole, Mr Arthur Thwaites of Warrington, and a little later, Dr Ronald Lees of Banff, all of whom volunteered to leave the comforts of civilisation for a mere fraction of the salary they could normally expect, to undertake arduous work under very difficult conditions of inadequate accommodation, of danger in the remote regions of Sarawak in Borneo. Perhaps initially they just wanted to get away from a mere existence offering no challenge or excitement. They remained to help John Wilson for as long as they were needed or as circumstances allowed. Fifteen years or so can be a long time but perhaps not long enough to indulge and assuage the inner longing to help a backward people to bridge the gap which separated the Dyak peoples from twentieth-century thoughts, ideas and technology. Unaware probably of their unique qualities of leadership, of compassion, of dedication, of determination that all three possessed, they gave without thought to themselves or their own future, but certainly in return they gained the loyalty and affection of the Sea Dyak peoples among whom they lived and worked for so many years.

When John Wilson went first to Budu in January 1953, Budu was not even marked on the map, but was just a few acres of unproductive hilly land across the river from a Dyak longhouse or village, called Rumah Gelau. By 1963 it was more than a place marked on many new maps of Sarawak. It was a centre of thought and Dyak Culture, from which emanated a realisation that the decline of the Sea Dyak peoples, a once virile and determined race, was due not to the lack of the qualities which make men great, but to the high incidence of disease which ravaged the body physically and brought about a mental hiatus, to the lack of fundamental education which made them feel so utterly helpless in the urban or near urban areas far down the rivers. Without hope for the future, it was probably that they had ceased to make any effort at all and found comfort only in the drinking of cheap arak, as a solace against the wants and needs of tomorrow. Slowly but surely over the years a new virility, a new hope, a new faith in the future of themselves and their children emerged. Just as small stones can create ripples in a pool and grow in magnitude to the edge, so from Budu and the Dyaks of the Krian, the Awas, the Grenjang, the Paku, the Entaih, the Entebai, the Kanowit, the Btang Lupar, the Rejang rivers and regions, began to feel a just pride once again in their own splendid abilities inherent in their race. Above all the Dyaks had begun to believe that they could play a major part in their own development and progress and so prepare themselves to play a vital role in the actual government of their country, Sarawak, and be an equal partner in this government, working amicably with the other major races of Chinese and Malays to ensure a better destiny and provide a heritage of strength to their children whom they loved so much.

In all nine main centres were opened up, giving Community Development coverage to about twenty thousand Dyaks. Many adjoining areas, while not directly receiving help, followed so far as they could, some of the ways of progress. The map will allow readers to orientate themselves as the story unfolds. Names underlined are actual main centres in the full meaning of the word. Small crosses indicate positions of Primary schools, opened up as the need arose to act as feeder schools to main centres.

Basically, the approach was the same at all nine centres. Self help was always the theme song in the establishment of any centre. This by its very demands on the community, involved the people and as time passed and things could be seen actually taking shape, there was an awareness that progress could only come from their own efforts. The wide and unique coverage in adult education ensured that the emerging child from school did not become the master in family thought and planning just because he could read and write. Through this very adult education, parents realised the necessity to provide and plan medical help, economic development and long-term improvements to their very homes, if they were to keep their children with them. Through understanding and explanations, most realised that all their children could not become nurses, teachers or agricultural assistants. They were well content when, as the years passed, those whom all had helped to study abroad in Nairn, Glasgow, London and Auckland to become teachers, nurses, administrative officers, engineers and co-operative assistants, returned capable and willing to carry on the process of development and progress. That one of their boys became a qualified doctor, gaining his degree at Aberdeen University, was indeed a source of pride, incapable of expression. This alone made all their efforts worth while and at one stroke proved the potential in a Dyak child, given the opportunity.

It was clearly defined that for any area to be helped there had to be a *Phase One* of establishment. This consisted of opening up a school both for adults and children, a clinic, a co-operative shop, agricultural extension work with gardens at each centre, owned by the respective Committee of Progress. This took from three to four years.

Phase Two, one of consolidation, with emphasis on selection and training of potential leaders. This took a further three years.

Phase Three, the handing over phase after each centre had as its administrative hub an elected Committee of Progress with a trained local secretary whose general education had reached that of the fourth or fifth year in a Secondary school.

There had also been planned a *Phase Four*, the establishment in the more progressive areas of some form of Secondary Education with a vocational bias. In 1963, however, Sarawak gained its independence within the Federation of Malaysia. Government, being much too busy with other plans for rural development, felt that no help should be given to the establishment of any form of Secondary Education in any remote places. Undaunted, John Wilson, through help from such organisations as Oxfam, Asia Foundation, Scottish General Co-operatives, and the people, opened Vocational Private Secondary Schools at Budu and Ng. Entebai. They were substantial schools and did provide what was needed since by this time over twenty-six Primary Schools had been established and the output from them fully justified these two schools. It seemed vital to John Wilson, for the ultimate success of the project, that this form of education was provided to ensure continued development at the village level and to ensure that a few could carry on to higher and more technical education.

Mr McBride, in his evaluation report, writes: "The raw material of all Community Development is human. People and their attitudes to their surroundings and life in general, are the targets of Community Development. The primary purpose is not material, it is abstract. The real test is not what is visible at the end of a project but what path the community, left to its own resources and initiative, decides to follow. Only time can provide this answer."

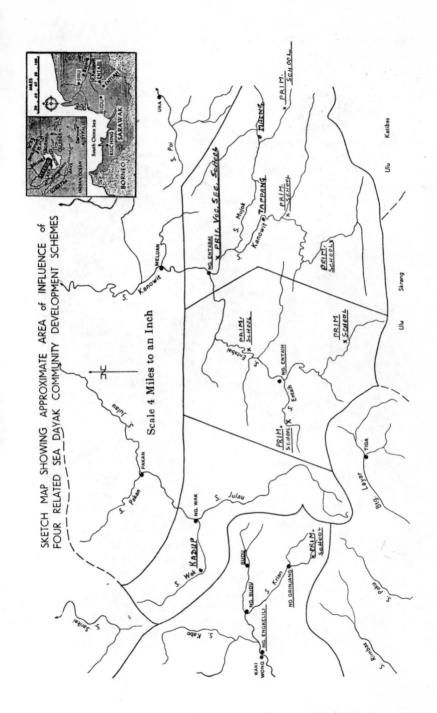

SKETCH MAP SHOWING APPROXIMATE AREA of INFLUENCE of FOUR RELATED SEA-DAYAK COMMUNITY DEVELOPMENT SCHEMES

Scale 4 Miles to an Inch

5

The Muas rapids on the way to Budu

CHAPTER TWO

From sleek contentment, keep me free. — L.U.

AND SO TO BUDU

The graduation ceremony at Batu Lintang Teachers' College was and still is a very happy occasion. In those days there were no brightly decorated or substantial buildings as there are now. During the war, Batu Lintang was a prisoner-of-war camp and the Japanese had incarcerated most of the Europeans. It was almost fitting that from the miseries and sufferings of those who had lived and died there, a clean and hopeful new generation should be trained to become teachers with a spirit of determination and dedication.

There were about twenty-five long wooden huts with leaf roofing and wooden floors. Some were dormitories, some were made into classrooms, some used for offices and administration. One was reserved for concerts and meetings. Each was about ninety feet long. The huts had not been built in long lines but were scattered over a fairly large area. Flowers and green shrubs were growing in abundance. Neat paths from hut to hut gave one the feeling of always knowing that there was something to see at the end of them. Almost every hut had been decorated inside with some form of native design on the rafters and main beams. Handcraft had been encouraged and suspended here, there and everywhere, there was evidence of the real skill of the students. There were shields with intricate designs, blow pipes, hand-woven baskets, ratan trays, finely carved spears and hunting knives. Murray Dickson, its first Principal, had given it this character and I was not loath to follow his ideas. Slowly but surely the ghosts of the war years were laid to rest. Instead of the clammerings for food, drink and medicine, there could be heard in the evenings groups of students singing their own native songs. There were Malays, Kayans, Muruts, Land Dyaks, Sea Dyaks, Melanaus, Kenyahs, Kelabits, Chinese, and they were all joined in happy comradeship.

The Graduation ceremony always took place in the concrete hut. The signal for assembly was the slow beating of a very large gong. Inside the hut, beams had been garlanded with greenery and yet the native designs in bright colours could still be seen. The many visitors were seated and all waited expectantly for the procession of graduating students to enter. It was colourful since all students wore traditional dress.

On that November day in 1952 after the songs had been sung and the certificates awarded, I took my place on the small raised stage to make my last address to the students whom, in my teaching of them, I had come almost to love. Very few people knew that I had resigned as Principal and certainly not the students. I had more than enjoyed my job. It had become part of me and the thought of leaving Batu Lintang was as though I were abandoning a well loved ship. It was imperative that the students should not

7

feel that I had quarrelled with the Director of Education. Nor had I in fact. Throughout the months of indecision Mr Barnshaw, the then Director, could not have been more kind, more patient in trying to make me realise that there was greater need of me at Batu Lintang as Principal than in some remote spot in the interior, however laudable might be the reasons. So in language as simple as I could find, I explained that for some four years I had been teaching students to become teachers and that another fifty would in a few days leave the college to take up their appointed places in one school or another, some to urban areas and some to remote areas. That, as they all knew, I had done much travelling in all parts of Sarawak and particularly in remote places to visit former students, now headmasters. That I had come to the conclusion that I had still much to learn myself about how a small four-class, one-teacher school should be run. That it had been agreed that I could leave Batu Lintang and, like them, become sole teacher in a remote school. That I too had become just an ordinary Local Authority teacher just as they were going to be.

This was something the students could understand, since I had often told them that a good teacher should never ask a pupil to do anything that he or she would not also do. With this approach I could almost feel that they were in agreement and I was satisfied that there would be no wrong rumours as to my reasons for leaving Batu Lintang.

They were not to know and must not know that for months I had argued that much more was needed than just to train a teacher, wave him goodbye as he left to do at that time an almost impossible job, and then forget about him altogether. My conscience simply rebelled. There were no heroics intended at my resignation, just a simple determination that someone had to go out into the remote parts to find out some of the answers and if no one else was prepared to do it, then it would just have to be me.

How could I have done otherwise? I had visited almost every teacher who had been trained at Batu Lintang to find out just how they were getting on. Those in the more urban areas were doing a splendid job on the whole. Those teachers, however, in the more remote regions were finding that it was almost impossible to teach and organise their schools as had been laid down or suggested. It was not my practice ever to give notice of my visit. First it was difficult to give definite dates since often schedules went by the board for mere weather reasons. I had, not once but several times, been storm bound for several days at a time. Also I particularly wanted to see the schools in actual operation. Above all I wanted no incurrence of expense on behalf of the people to entertain me as they were so wont to do, spending much that could have been put to better use in buying things like cement or cupboards. I am, I make haste to say, not naturally austere. I like my comforts just like anyone else. It was this attitude, however, that gave me the reputation of being austere when in fact I was only helping them to save money.

So more often than not, my arrivals were unheralded. I usually had a guide but made a point of carrying my own haversack. I wanted no large entourage to upset the work of the day. In any case two or three can travel much faster than twenty and it is so to this day. It was not uncommon for me to find in the schools, not pupils but two or three cows. It was not uncommon for me to be hastily welcomed to the singing of God Save the King, sung in parts to the tune of John Brown's Body or Clementine. Diminutive pupils ranging from four to twenty years of age were seldom in any ordered seating. Sleeping accommodation varied from sleeping on the earth to sleeping on old sacks in tumbledown huts that certainly did not keep out the rain. What had been vegetable gardens were more often destroyed by the pigs living around the longhouse and there was nothing the teacher could do about it. Worst of all was the certain evidence that the children had skin diseases because they had no soap. Sickness was common because, while the trained teacher had been given the rudiments of first aid and knowledge of simple medicine and its use, he had no medicine. Desks varied from bits of wood stuck into the ground with a smooth part of a tree on top for writing on, to the occasional normal type desk bought by a more wealthy parent in the bazaar. When the child left school such desks were always taken away. The teacher's quarters were seldom better than what we would normally keep pigs in.

Threats to the school committee that if they did not co-operate more with the teacher, steps would be taken to remove the teacher, brought temporary obedience. Pigs would be taken further away, hens would be cooped. I often used to delay my departure until at least a start was made to make life just that fraction easier for the teacher.

Of books there was little evidence. There was no money. Teaching apparatus that the teacher had painstakingly made when at Batu Lintang was often found lying around broken, and useless. This was not quite the fault of the teacher. After all he had four classes to teach and Dyak children have few inhibitions. If they want to talk, they talk; if they want to play, they play.

I realised and admitted to myself that all those things were purely material and that time could set them right, given a few more teachers, more money to buy the necessities and tolerant supervision from more experienced teachers. What worried me most was the attitude of both parents and pupils alike to the real meaning of education. Almost without exception, all believed that the purpose of the school was to provide education to enable the child to get a Government job. Though I argued that this, instead of bringing progress to the area would mean that in time the population would gradually decrease, to them it seemed just a lot of nonsense. "Why should a child go to school if not to get a job at the end of it?" He didn't need to know how to read and write to farm his paddi or get fish from the river.

It appeared to me then, even as it does now some fifteen years later, that it was almost being dishonest, almost cheating, to continue training teachers to open schools in remote parts if no parallel development could be initiated with the school as the focal point. The teacher, I argued, had to be a member of a team or at least organise the work of visiting teams to bring enlightenment to the people and initiate some form of development that would and could provide a living for the child as he left school. Without this, I was having no part in this business of training teachers.

It was all just as simple as that, and, having finally decided that I would have to go myself, since it seemed that no one else would, I set about preparations. In addition to buying all the things that I thought would be necessary, in the few weeks that remained to me before going to Budu, I had to take crash courses in the main dispensary in Kuching, in the main agricultural station at Tarat. Without knowledge I might as well not go. Everyone, seeing that I was determined, was very helpful and most heads of departments went out of their way to ensure that I had every facility to gain that essential knowledge. It has proved of course very useful but I had much to learn the hard way.

I was human enough to wonder at my own decision, in that it, in effect, meant that any future security was lost for all time, that I had now no pension to look forward to, that instead of a thousand dollars a month job, I would have only a quarter of this to live on. My own savings had had to be used to buy what I thought was needed. I was, however, putting no halo around my head. The decision was my own and what I was doing, I wanted to do. Although a few, very few, nodded their heads wisely and said that they thought I intended to go native, the great majority tried at least to understand and did give me both moral and practical support for which I was very grateful. I was further heartened when, just before I left Kuching, the then Acting Chief Secretary, Mr Ellis, wrote me an encouraging letter and informed me that there were good prospects that a sum of £5,000 would be put at my disposal to help in this research. Even then it was beginning to be realised that my going to Budu was basically to find out certain answers and not to cause upsets nor let the flag down!

The 1st of January 1953 dawned bright and clear. Three lorries turned up as ordered at Batu Lintang when it was still dark as the launch I had arranged for was to sail at seven a.m., just as the tide turned. To miss the tide down the river meant waiting another day. There was no lack of helpers. Many former students turned up even at that early hour and within a twinkling the lorries were loaded and down we went to the wharf. There, too, were many to give a helping hand to load and by seven all was on board, cement, wire netting, three small pigs, a dozen hens, boxes and boxes of this and that, baskets and baskets of seedlings of one sort or another which had been given to me by my old friend Mr Ong Kee Chong, who to this day never sees me stuck. So I climbed aboard after making my farewells with Empeni Ikum. Empeni had come to Batu Lintang a year or so before but could not enter any of the recognised classes to become a teacher owing to his standard of education. Nevertheless, I had helped him by allowing him to attend classes to try and catch up for himself although I was primarily employing him as my gardener. He was very trustworthy, strong, sturdy and had made a special plea that I would take him with me. I readily consented and I have much to thank Empeni for. In quiet unobtrusive ways he made life for me in those early days at Budu, if not comfortable, certainly much more comfortable than it would have been had I been completely alone.

My thoughts, as we sailed down the river to the sea, were peaceful and though I had qualms as to my own ability not only as regards finding out what I wanted to find out, but as to living alone so far from my own kind, I comforted myself by remembering that I had at any rate enough food to last for a few months no matter what happened.

I gave thought to my basic plan which I had at least worked out, though I did not know whether it was feasible or even possible. The establishment of a good and properly equipped village school seemed to be the first priority. I hoped that such a school would, in a period of five to ten years, become reasonably self-supporting from cash crops such as coco, tea, coffee, kapok oil, palm and rubber. That by penning in good quality pigs and by breeding, the local people could also gradually improve their own livestock. By the time I had come to the mouth of the river I had dreams that all around Budu, beautiful pigsties had been built. No, I knew it would not be as easy as that.

The next priority would be to find a way to bring knowledge and education in its broad sense to the twenty-forty age group, so that parallel to progress in the village school, economic progress could be obtained throughout the area of which the school was a centre, thus creating openings in that area for children leaving school.

A way had to be found to reduce sickness, to clean up the longhouses, to show the people that only by co-operation could progress be obtained—thus ensuring that the lessons learned by the children on hygiene and on a cleaner way of life would have some practical meaning and that they would less and less seek to leave their homes for the lights of the bazaar.

Last but certainly not least, it was vital to ensure that any plan for progress came from the people themselves and that it was a plan in which all could take part from the youngest to the oldest. The plan must emerge from the people so that none could say in the future that it had been imposed on them.

The sea was calm and all was peaceful as we approached Kabong where we were to anchor for the night. There ahead of me lay the river Krian, up which we would go the next day. Beyond that I could not venture to guess. My boats were burned and I certainly could not go back to Kuching, defeated at the start. I slept soundly. At dawn the next day the anchor was brought up and on we chugged up the river to Saratok. I began to wonder if Philip Bedus and Nicholas Rangkap, two former students now teachers, would as promised meet me in Saratok. I began to wonder if some twelve of the Budu men would meet me also as promised, or would I find myself at Saratok with all my pigs, hens and plants and just nowhere to put them and with nowhere to take them. Empeni was a great comfort with his stolid assertions that all would be well.

By mid-day on the 2nd of January we were tying up at the small jetty at Saratok. Neither Philip nor Nicholas could be seen, only the District Officer whom I knew slightly, having met him the previous year at Saratok when recruiting teachers. It was quite obvious that he resented my arrival and resented still more that I, a European, was going to Budu where he, presumably, could not keep his eye on me. He was an unusual type of District Officer. Most District Officers were keen on their job and many went out of their way to help up-river peoples in any way they could. The previous year we had had differences of opinion on selection but I was certainly surprised when without even the normal courtesies of shaking hands, he informed me in a loud voice, "Now, you are no longer Principal of Batu Lintang so don't expect me to arrange transport up river nor indeed can I store your goods here in the Government store".

Luckily at that precise moment I spied Philip and Nicholas arriving and although I burned inside me since his remarks were quite uncalled for and certainly in the very worst taste I kept my temper and contented myself by saying quietly, "Good morning, Mr . . . , I am not aware that I have made any request for transport, nor indeed have I asked for space in the Government store".

I turned to meet Philip and Nicholas. Both were standing close by and obviously had heard the conversation between us. Philip's mouth was wide open with sheer amazement on his face. However, I managed a smile and greeted them both warmly and asked if the Budu people had arrived. "Yes," said Philip, "they are in the bazaar and are following down."

I breathed a heartfelt sigh of relief. My pride alone would have prevented me from asking for even the slightest help from the District Officer. I have said he was an unusual type of person, a poet. During the next few months we agreed, one might say, to co-operate, but it was clearly understood that I in return would have to listen to his poems.

As though the people wanted to make amends for the very obvious show of bad manners, there were many helpers in addition to the Dyaks from Budu, to transfer all my equipment from the larger Kuching launch to a small Chinese launch owned by Alun. Alun had quietly brought it alongside the bigger launch. Throughout the years Alun never failed to help and often at great risk to his boat he would, for us, travel up the river at night.

Alun's launch had been arranged for by Philip since we both knew that the first step was to get everything up to Kaki Wong, the farthest part of tidal reach, some two to three hours up river. It had also been arranged that the canoes from Budu would be at Kaki Wong and this was confirmed by Philip. Philip was a great help. I had always had a lot of time for Philip and Nicholas. They had been excellent students and I knew them well. Philip's staff work was superb.

As Alun said that it was too late to go up that day, he tied up for the night and we arranged to go aboard ourselves the following day when we saw the tide moving up. The river flows quite fast and tidal help is needed as well, to give enough depth over the rapids to Kaki Wong. We all made our way to the bazaar and round a table with about a dozen cups of coffee I was introduced to the Dyaks from Budu. Most I remember to this day. There was Lium, Janggat, Nyabong, Emperak, Kelangan, Buda, Gambang, Amis, and Kirch. They were all strong and fine looking Dyaks. As I tried to size them up, I felt a feeling of confidence come over me and I knew I could work with them.

I met for the first time Chin Thai who owned one of the shops, indeed the shop we were drinking coffee in. During the war, Chin Thai, often at great danger to himself, saw to it that the Dyaks received a share of the salt and tobacco or semekau as it is locally called. Chin Thai to this day is one of my firm friends. He was kind, considerate and always obliging, often going to great trouble to find the things that I needed. He often sent up bread as though he knew I would want it, as I did. He is old now and retired but I would never dream of going to Saratok without paying him a visit to talk about old times and drink a cup of coffee.

The evening in Saratok was a happy one. There were many ex-students there and all were interested in what I was going to do.

Then came the question of where to sleep. Usually a European visitor stayed with the District Officer but I was adamant that I would sleep wherever the Budu Dyaks were going to sleep. Philip was quite put out at that decision but I explained that I was in fact no longer a Government servant and that I was just like the Dyaks from Budu. Where they slept, there I would sleep. I must confess when it came to the bit and I saw just where, I nearly had second thoughts. "No," I said to myself, "it has to be this way and no other." However I gave my first lesson in hygiene and before lying down on a mat that I had bought, I swept up all the dirty litter of paper, empty tins, cigarette ends and old clothes. Although I had a deep and concentrated hatred for rats, after having once at Aden, during the war, found one inside the leg of my pyjamas and actually running up my leg, I slept soundly despite them.

Somehow or another we all got on to Alun's small launch but we must have looked quite a sight sprawled over everything I had brought from Kuching. Dunggat did tell me that he thought it would be slightly difficult to get everything to Budu. He told me, through Nicholas, since I as yet did not know any Dyak, that they had only twenty canoes at Kaki Wong and he thought that fifty would be needed. He smiled, however, and said that some of them would do two trips. As events turned out they all had to do two trips.

By the time we reached Kaki Wong it was around three o'clock. Here Philip's staff work again showed itself. He had arranged with the people from Rh Numpang to have a small hut ready to store the goods in overnight. I silently blessed Philip. By the time we had unloaded it was dark. It was then I first met Entamin, a wise old Dyak who was looking after the one and only shop at Kaki Wong. I could only see, however, a few tins of fish and cornbeef, some dried fish and a few other quite revolting looking things that I certainly did not relish eating. Apai Paul, as Entamin came to be known, was resourceful and in next to no time a hen had been killed and was cooking in the pot on the wood fire behind the shop. So also was a large pot of rice. How delicious that meal tasted. I think I had been too anxious to be able to eat in Saratok. After eating we all just curled up on the floor and slept. No, we had no pillows nor blankets. Ah well, I had chosen this kind of life so why should I begin to wonder about it?

Next morning, the day dawned bright and clear. The river seemed just right for the canoes which had to be paddled far up the river to Budu. Pausing only to point out this and that which I said I needed earliest at Budu, I left Kaki Wong to walk to Budu with Lium. He had been my shadow since I had arrived in Saratok. From that day to this I have a warm feeling inside me when I think of Lium. A grand man.

Our path took us along the bank of the river in its early stage and I was able to see the first canoes setting off. My heart was in my mouth; granted the canoes were being handled expertly by the Dyaks, their bodies gleaming in the early sunlight, but they looked as though they would be swamped at any moment.

"Surely," I said to Philip and Nicholas, who were walking with me to Budu, "the canoes are too heavily laden!"

Philip just smiled and said that I must not worry. They would get to Budu but even he could not say when. "Probably in two days time," was all he ventured. "It so much depends on the water and whether there will be more rain today."

We did not talk much on the way. Single file is hardly conducive to conversation and in any case I was much too busy preventing myself from slipping. Luckily I had done a bit of jungle travelling and I felt quite confident that we would reach Budu that day, even though it was some six hours walk. It was not to be.

Lium, apparently, had had his instructions. So on reaching a longhouse, into it we had to go to pay our respects, sit for a while and tell our news. When I knew that the Budu people were not expecting me till the following day, I was quite content to take it easy. Then there were schools on the way and as the headmasters were more often old pupils, I could not but stop and wish them well. We slept the night at Rh Jacob. Jacob was an unusual Dyak in that he had some way or another been to school. He could speak fair English also and this was an unexpected treat for me. We sat far into the night talking about this and that. I learned much from Jacob that was to stand me in good stead. He also had a relation called Edwin who lived somewhere up the Krian River. He was at Rh Jacob that night too. Both Edwin and Jacob became two of my most trustworthy supporters.

By mid afternoon the next day, the 5th of January 1953, I had reached Rh Gelau, just opposite Budu School where I was to spend many years.

That evening a ceremonious welcome was accorded me, complete with all the trimmings of gongs, Dyak dancing and speeches of welcome which I understood only through Nicholas's or Philip's translations. I was very moved, however, by the sincerity of the welcome, especially when I was blessed with the traditional white cock being waved over my head to the mutterings of, I supposed, prayers for my safety and good luck to my work.

It was an evening to remember.

Early next day, I said goodbye to Philip and Nicholas who had to return to Saratok. I saw them go with a sinking feeling in my stomach but it had to be. So with Empeni I crossed the river to the school to start work. I sat down on the steps of my little house that had been built ready for me and I must have sat for hours just wondering where to make a start. I was quickly brought out of my reveries, however, by Empeni telling me that the pupils were in the school and they seemed to expect me to start teaching them. How right they were. I think though the pupils were a bit upset when I told them that it would be a week or so before we would need pencils or jotters. I can still see Jawie giving one of those delightful smiles. Possibly even then he had an inkling of the future.

I was aware even on that first day of Luke who in the later years played such an important part in the work. Generally more serious, Luke could, however, display a real sense of humour, not common among Dyak children. His eyes were intelligent and deep. Although obviously undernourished, he had a bearing and a natural grace that made him almost automatically the leader.

I remember also Bilun, with his round chubby face and dazzling white teeth. He was smaller than Luke or Jawie but strong and sturdy. There was Chundie, lithe, with large round eyes which were like those of a deer being hunted. There was Kunchie, Kalong, Chuk, all eager to be helpful and nothing seemed to be too great a trouble although occasionally they did look quizzically at me as much as to say, "What on earth is that for?"

It was fortuitous that much had to be done before formal lessons could start. We were all hard at work from dawn till dusk and at the end of a week, at least I was certain that at Budu there was character in the children and a willingness to work, even though they were hungry, tired, ill-nourished and with little or no decent clothing. I am fairly sure that this was the reason that from the beginning I rarely wore much else than a pair of small pants, rather like swimming trunks. At least, I said to myself, if I dressed in those, no pupil could feel ashamed about his own dress. To this day I follow that custom. Both Mac and Arthur, realising that to dress in formal shorts, shirt, shoes and socks meant only creating a barrier between themselves and the pupils in the sense that there would be class distinction dependent on the clothes one wore, decided also to follow my example. It had the virtue anyway of showing quite clearly that to learn, or teach, one did not actually need to be dressed in white shorts and shirt. I am fairly sure that this relatively small detail of dress had and still has a tremendous influence on the very character and outlook of the Budu pupils. Above all it made very clear that the wearing of smart white clothes was not a hallmark of either intelligence or learning. That I, their teacher, could also dirty his hands and share even in the gathering up of pig dung was, too, the first lesson in the real meaning of education, and that an educated man was not always walking around with books in his hand and a pencil in his mouth. So the only rule about dress was that it had to be clean even though it was tattered and torn. I had long thought in any case that a Community Development worker to do his work would have to lower his own standard of living to be able to merge with the standard of living of the people with whom he was working. One has to take care though that a fine balance is realised. It must not be too low, but just that little bit above theirs so that the people can feel it is attainable and not a condition that they could never reach. If, for instance, someone had offered to build a substantial house for me at Budu, on the lines of a Government house complete with its own water supply, bathroom, modern kitchen, bedroom, beds, chairs, tables and other furniture I would have had to decline. Not, mind you, because I liked to sleep on the floor, or eat at a table made from strands of bamboo, or sit on a kind of stool made from branches of trees, but because I considered it vital to live as they had to live. When their standards of living gradually improved, as improve they did, when they themselves were beginning to buy beds, chairs, tables, then and then only could I rise with them. I am fairly sure I have been right but I would not be dogmatic about it. Comfort is not actually to be despised nor would I decline it under normal circumstances. A great deal depends on how that comfort is obtained and on the whole one should create it for oneself, not have it handed to one on a plate. I rather envied Empeni who knew how to make a simple basket chair from jungle rotan and I certainly liked Empeni more for his determination to make a little comfort for himself. Especially when he gave me his and made another one for himself. Many actually followed his example.

One thing is certain, that were I able to turn back the clock and though I were given an opportunity to take a different path, do different work than I had done at Budu and Entebai, I would without question decide to go to Budu and just become an ordinary teacher in the village school. That throughout the years there has been hardship, struggles for this and that, goes without saying. How could it have been otherwise? There have been occasions, however, when all the hardships were forgotten, all the cares and worries of no account and times when an inner thankfulness was in my heart that I had been privileged to do the work that I have done.

With whom could I exchange the deep happiness that came over me as I read Jawie's letter on the 7th of July 1966. In this letter he wrote that he was so delighted to tell me that he had passed his medical degree at Aberdeen University and that he was now Dr Jawie Masing, M.B., Ch.B., I was not ashamed of the tears in my eyes when I read it. They were tears of sheer absolute happiness, a state that is to be envied. All the tiredness of my fifteen years' work just disappeared. Even if I had accomplished nothing else, Jawie, my own delightful pupil at Budu in those early days, had qualified as a doctor. The first Sea Dyak to become a doctor and who had obtained his medical degree from a Scottish University. One of the many things that I had prayed, hoped for, planned for had come to pass.

No, it is not given to many to have some of their dreams come true.

I could picture Jawie as he wrote the letter. Now tall, handsome, who without even speaking stood out as a man above other men. When he spoke there would still be that boyish touch about him, a touch he has never lost and makes him dear to all. He used to pucker up his nose when in deep thought and having gained a solution a huge grin would appear on his face and his eyes would light up. Indeed I felt proud of him.

I wrote him, of course, immediately to congratulate him. Never had a boy, I am sure, made such a supreme effort, and effort that had ended with this degree. He well deserved the praise that showered on him from all who knew him and of his determination to succeed. Naturally enough, my only regret was that I could not be present at his graduation. Nevertheless, he had close friends there to see him shyly but proudly walk up to the dais to receive his parchment. Eddie and Auntie Jean were there to share in his great day. Jawie, apparently, in a way that is just Jawie somehow unwittingly gave a little comic relief to the solemn occasion because as he turned to go back to his seat, with his parchment in his hand and the other clutching his gown from under his feet, his cap with tassel went askew. In his own inimitable way he kept blowing the tassel from his eyes so that he could see where to go. There was much happy laughter in which no doubt Jawie joined. Jawie could always enjoy a joke and his deep throated chuckle was infectious. He was and still is a great mimic, as I learned in the first days at Budu when Radio Sarawak came into being. The school radio was only allowed to be used at certain times, but one evening I heard the voice of the announcer giving the daily news. It was at least an hour early and I ran up to the school, fully determined to punish the culprit. As I dashed in the whole class went into fits of laughter and there was Jawie, with a piece of wood in his hand to act as a microphone, giving a truly great performance. I had to laugh too.

When I wrote to Jawie I casually asked him that, if he could find a moment, I would greatly appreciate his own story from his own recollections. A few weeks later I received what follows. More and more was I convinced that I had been right to go to Budu.

Jawie, as Dr Jawie Masing, M.B., Ch.B., wrote the following:

WHAT I SAW AS A SMALL BOY

"As a small boy I was unfortunately often unwell. When I was sick my grandmother would invite one of the local medicinemen to visit me. He would come along with his brown bas, an equivalent of the modern doctor's black bag, and after listening to my grandmother concerning my complaints and symptoms he would proceed to examine me. If the presence of air in my tummy was diagnosed he would massage it with coconut oil as lubricant or instruct a member of the family to do so. When there was no obvious cause found, he would explain that these manifestations were the work of the evil spirits requiring to be undone in a night-long incantation.

"I can only recall seeing a government dresser once in my village. He came late one evening and that evening I witnessed a minor operation being performed under the light of a paraffin lamp, on a rubber tapper who had a boil on his thigh threatening to burst and it was very painful. Here was the first opportunity for ninety-nine per cent of the villagers to see a demonstration of modern medicine and a large number of people turned up. The pus of the boil was released by piercing it with the hot point of a needle. There was a jerk and a grunt, but there was also a smile of gratitude on the patient's face when it was all over.

"At school we were taught hygiene. Some of us were very dirty, so dirty that the schoolmaster thought that ordinary soap would be of no avail. A paraffin bath was recommended and this was to be followed by a thorough scrubbing. These operations were performed by the bigger boys under the direct supervision of the schoolmaster.

"At about the age of eleven years I witnessed a smallpox epidemic. The disease is locally known as 'tampok engkala' as the pockpits produced on the skin resemble that left on a detached fruit of that name. There was a team of vaccinators, but many people did not come forward because of ignorance and unfounded fears. There was never any health education among the general population.

"The second schoolmaster we had at Budu School had a severe attack of 'cold-and-hot' disease as it is locally known. To the medical world this disease is known as malaria. How strange it was to see this man shivering vigorously in the heat of the mid-afternoon tropical sun. When the hot stage came he would roll on the floor until he could find a place where the gentle breeze would soothe him a little. There was no medicine, but fortunately he survived after many days of the illness.

"The above are only a few examples of what I saw as a small boy. It would be unusual for a small boy like myself not to have seen more in a community where health service or public health hardly existed. Suffice to say that the health service of the whole district consisted of a dresser and a box of medicines and equipment put together. But I must confess that it did not occur to me that what I saw was related to the career of a modern doctor, let alone think that I would be one to embrace it.

"One bright afternoon, when everyone was busy with lessons in earnest, a well-known local guide suddenly appeared in front of our school and bombastically commanded the schoolmaster to meet the 'Principal' up the river. There was a stir in the class. We gathered from the guide that a distinguished visitor had come to see us from the capital, no less than the Principal of the only Teachers' Training College in the state. The schoolmaster asked some of the bigger boys to accompany him and the rest of us were told to continue with our lessons. Most of us were good students, but we were too excited to continue with our work. Twenty minutes later we saw approaching the school a red-haired European of medium height, apparently busy talking to the schoolmaster. He entered the class and we stood up to wish him 'Good afternoon', and after returning our greetings he politely asked us to sit down. My English was too poor for me to understand the ensuing conversation between him and the schoolmaster. But I had the impression that he seemed to like us. We were told later that he was going to spend the night with us in the school.

"That evening the school dormitory was much quieter than usual at first. Instead of doing our homework we went upon invitation to spend the evening with the Principal. Conversation was a little difficult because of our poor command of English. Always encouraging and interested in us, the visitor suggested that we should sing and he asked if we knew any songs. We knew a few, one of which was 'John Brown's body . . .'. So few were the songs we knew that evening 'John Brown' was glorified many times! Nevertheless these songs brought us closer to him.

"The following day the distinguished visitor left as quietly as he had come with the few who accompanied him. Nobody knew why he had come. The journey to Budu and back to the capital meant trudging many miles of rough jungle paths, and we wondered the more at his simplicity and unassuming presence. The few other Europeans who had come before him were always accompanied by sizeable entourages and bands of servants. There were rumours in the village after his departure. Some said that he had come to inspect the school and others, thinking that he was on a recruiting campaign, suspected that he was preparing the way for a second arrival. We, the school boys, knew least. But we were quite sure that he liked us. None, however, thought that he would come to teach us.

"School life in Budu was as usual during the following four months. Then news came that the Principal of the State's Teachers' Training College had resigned and that he had offered to teach at Budu Primary School as a Local Authority teacher. The Kaloka District Council had accepted. Budu School Committee was most glad and was quick to agree to his appointment. The thought of having a highly qualified teacher was most desirable so far as the committee was concerned. But, some community elders had reservations and doubts, mainly on the ground that he would bring problems, foremost of which was that of his safety. Life in Kuching, the capital, was safe, easy and comfortable. In contrast, life in Budu was rough, with rapids, floods, and uncontrollable diseases to think of. However, the majority opinion was that a man who had sacrificed so much should not be rejected and besides something good for the community might come out of it. Soon after this, in the beginning of 1953, our European schoolmaster arrived. There was a reception in his honour at Bumah Golau that evening.

"Our new teacher was anxious to learn about the people and on the other hand, the community was anxious to know what was behind his mind. I remember very well sitting almost directly opposite him near my grandfather. At one point in the evening my grandfather ventured to ask him in the Malay tongue if there'was someone else coming to stay with him at Budu. He begged my grandfather to speak in Dayak, the language of the community, explaining that he was anxious to learn it. The general impression was that he had come not to displace things but perhaps to enrich the community.

"In the following six months school work proceeded in earnest. My English improved a great deal and with some encouragement I could conduct a simple conversation in English. Mr Wilson by now was quite fluent in Dayak and he could discuss local affairs with the community elders with increasing confidence. At the end of June he took the initiative and called for a general meeting of the community elders in which he threw a series of challenges to the community, among which were the calls for the establishment of a Committee of Progress, co-operative shop, payment of annual rate for a community fund, adult education, and labour contribution for the building of the necessary centre. In return he promised he would try to raise their standard of living, to improve their health, and to train their young men to take over from the expatriates. The last of those concerned me, but I did not see how I would fit in. Would I be selected for training? Did I have the ability? Three and a half years passed by and like many others I helped in the shops and offices two and a half days a week and the rest of the week was for the books. Life was hard but I was always looking forward to learning more, and never really felt tired. Then, one evening I was asked to attend an interview. Little did I realise that I was to be selected for further training abroad.

"The setting for the interview was a dark room with three chairs and a round table, on top of which was a paraffin lamp fitted with a reflector. There were two men occupying two of the chairs and one of them asked me to sit on the other chair facing them. I knew both my interviewers. Normally they would smile to me, but that evening they looked serious and earnest, not unkindly. The lamp was shone on me and the interview began. One of them asked me in a quiet, firm voice if I wanted to be a doctor. I was a little taken aback and after a few thoughtful seconds I raised my eyes and answered in the affirmative. The other then asked if I was prepared to go abroad, to be away from home for anything up to eleven years, and to tolerate loneliness. This time it took me more than just a few thoughtful seconds to say 'Yes'. Then, there was a further explanation that during these eleven years I would have to study hard, sacrifice a lot, and have very little money to spend. Five seconds elapsed during which a few thoughts passed in my mind. Hard work I had always done, and as for sacrifice, I had nothing to sacrifice. As for money, I never had any. There was nothing to lose, but everything to gain in this venture. I firmly said 'Yes'. The interview ended after one of them explained that they were contemplating sending me to a school in Scotland. I left in somewhat ill-concealed excitement.

THE YEARS AT NAIRN ACADEMY

"Early in the beginning of 1957 I was informed that there was a place for me at Nairn Academy, a school in the northern county of Scotland. I would not be alone. Three of my classmates were coming. In April 1957 we found ourselves in Scotland. It was early spring and the air was still cold. After three months in Glasgow we were brought up to Nairn, a small town in the north of Scotland. There we were accommodated in a large house called 'Grianach', run by Mr and Mrs Mactaggart, whom we knew later as Aunty Jean and who suddenly turned to me and said in a note of welcome and assurance, 'Well, my lad, this will be your home for the next few years'.

"Aunty Jean was right. 'Grianach' provided a happy home for us for the following four years. It was, also, a home for ten other boys and girls. Later, as more Dayaks came from Budu to join us at Nairn Academy, the Dayaks became almost the majority residents.

"Our presence in Nairn put Budu and Sarawak on the map for most of the people in the town. The reaction of the influential people in the town was favourable. They were anxious to help Mr Robertson, the Rector of Nairn Academy, and so was the teaching staff of Nairn Academy, some of whom used some of their non-teaching time for giving us free tutorials. The pupils of Nairn Academy accepted us as one of them and we took part in school activities each according to his talent. One of the young men of Nairn, by the name of Peter Gordon, volunteered to go out to Budu and gave one year's service to the Budu Community. The press of the north of Scotland took a sensational interest, and thus we read in the *Press and Journal* such headlines as 'From the Jungle of Borneo to Nairn'.

"During school terms at Nairn Academy I was so preoccupied with ordinary school subjects that the thought of doing medicine sank into the background and so did the nostalgia for home. It was different during the cold winters and the long vacations. I missed then the warmth of the tropics and there was time to think of home. Fortunately I never felt any loneliness as I always had the other Dayaks for company. Besides, Mr Wilson had bought a flat in Glasgow where Aunt Ella looked after us and a caravan was placed on Loch Lomondside, all for our use during the vacations. These bring back many happy memories to me.

"At the end of my fourth year at Nairn Academy I was told that there was a place for me at Aberdeen University Medical School. This was great news to me. I knew I had a long way to go yet but at least the door was open for me to study medicine. In July that year I returned home after being in Scotland for four years. It was a very happy reunion with my family and friends. I had not lost the love for life in the ULU (interior) of Sarawak and spent my vacation with my family in the interior.

THE YEARS AT ABERDEEN UNIVERSITY

"At the end of September 1961, I left Sarawak again to commence my medical course at Aberdeen University as a Sarawak Government scholar. I worked hard at university but it was not altogether unenjoyable. In my first year I confined myself very much to studying and did not take part much in university activities. Having made the first year a success I felt more settled and confident and began to take active interest in some of the university associations, among which were the Aberdeen University United Nations Association and the Aberdeen University Asian Students Association, of which I later became President. Those associations provided me with opportunities to meet and work with students who were not in my class. Besides, they gave me a sense of belonging, and this is a great asset to a foreign student far away from home.

"My last year at Aberdeen University, although one of the busiest, was a rewarding one. Perhaps one of the happiest moments I have ever had in my life came when I met a group of classmates on my way to see the final examination results. They congratulated me with wild enthusiasm and with a short explanation that I had passed. I had acquired what I had come for!

IN RETROSPECT

"For almost eleven years now I have been away from home except for two summer vacations. It is a price I was prepared to pay and I have no regrets. I realised that I owe my education to the efforts of many people with charitable and dedicated minds, not least of all to Mr John K. Wilson. To them I owe a debt which cannot be repaid and I very much hope that my conduct in my chosen professions will be worthy of them. At the time of writing I am serving as House Officer at Hairmyres Hospital, near Glasgow, Scotland. I am looking forward to returning home soon to serve as a Medical Officer in Sarawak.

JAWIE ANAK MASING.

CHAPTER THREE

HOW THE PROJECTS GOT UNDER WAY

Looking back, I certainly cannot say that one day I was just the Local Authority teacher at Budu School and the next one Community Development Officer. It was indeed a gradual process of becoming as it were merged within the community, involved with their problems and, like the people, seeking a way in which conditions could be improved.

I remember leaving Kuching on New Year's Day 1953 and I arrived at Budu on the 5th of January. The same evening a ceremonious welcome was given me in Rh Golau, just opposite Budu School. On the next day I started to repair the school with the older boys such as Jawie and Luke to help me. This took several days but it was worth it. In the process I learned a few important words of Dyak and so when the school officially opened I could at least ask the pupils to stand up or sit down or open their jotters. Much of my teaching in those early days was by signs and as each action was completed I quickly wrote down the Dyak for it. In the evenings I learned and relearned all that I had managed to write down. As I made the school my first priority I had little contact with the people. Indeed I remember telling them that they must not come around the school during school hours since it was not only distracting to me but to the pupils, their children; that if they wanted their children to learn quickly they must not disturb; I think actually they were just curious and wanted to help me in case any of their children misbehaved. When they saw that everybody was studying hard, they obeyed and went about their own work. In the school there were no disciplinary problems at all. Without exception the pupils were obedient and mannerly. In all the years that I have taught Dyaks I have never once had to punish any pupil beyond raising my voice a little. I was, however, determined to make them catch up with the syllabus and by using every dodge that an experienced teacher knows of, they quickly understood that I was only fierce if I saw them wasting their time. Actions in any case often spoke louder than words and occasionally I would throw their jotters out of the—I was going to write windows but there were none—telling them to look for a grass-hopper which could certainly write better than they could.

By the middle of February I felt quite confident that I had everything mostly under control in the school and that the pupils were making splendid progress. I have little doubt that they told their parents this and I feel certain that this was the first bond of trust between me and the people. In the evenings, helped by me, my faithful follower from Kuching, Empeni Ikum, began to teach the older Dyaks to read and write. Empeni never tired and in those early days he was a tremendous help in every way. Although Empeni did not go to Nairn Academy, he with Paul, another stalwart, spent a year in Scotland mostly at farms and with the Scottish General Co-operative in

Glasgow. Empeni now is a headmaster in his own right at one of the centres, Kadup.

At the weekends my small house became the dispensary and from early Saturday morning till late Sunday I was kept busy. Before leaving Kuching, I had spent several weeks as an ordinary attendant in the main Kuching dispensary. At Batu Lintang also, over the four years, I had looked after our small sick room. Although far from knowing much, I could recognise most of the common diseases and I had plenty of medicine given me by the Director of Medical Services. He had more faith in me than I had in myself. He used, jokingly perhaps, to say to me that I would probably cure 98 patients and kill the other two. His attitude was that it was better to do something than nothing and I have much to be grateful to him for. He was quick to answer any medical problems which I found from time to time and could not understand. I learned a great deal this way. I must however have done some good, since the numbers increased alarmingly and often there was little time for food. It was not unusual that the pot of rice cooked by Empeni for me would be eaten by patients who had come from a distant longhouse and were hungry. So a second bond of trust was formed and it certainly looked as though I had come to help them and sought no personal reward.

By April, green shoots were beginning to appear on the planting material which I had brought from Kuching. This planting material had been given to me by a very old friend, Mr Ong Kee Chong, who to this day never fails to help me. Most of the coffee plants had been transplanted and most of the fruit trees. Pineapple shoots began to sprout. Kapok seeds began to grow. On the hills behind the school, on what had been overgrown with lalong, useless shrubs and small trees, there were appearing orderly terraces that followed the contour. In the evenings there would be spirals of smoke from burnt earth piles, to give the plants a good start. As it was quite obvious to the people I could not take away the trees, a third bond of trust was formed.

Then about this time a most important incident took place. The then Director of Agriculture for some reason best known to himself had decreed that Dyaks were not allowed to plant pepper vines. Many had disregarded this edict. Frankly I could not myself see why they should not be encouraged to plant pepper far less to be told that they must not. The Director, however, decided that it was time for him to put his foot down and instructed the Agricultural Assistant, Saratok, to summon several Dyaks for disobeying the law.

A number of the Budu Dyaks received summonses, among them one by name of Janggat Lium whom I got to know and liked very much. His pepper garden was well looked after and he was just about to get his first crop. It was indeed an interesting evening listening to some twelve really angry Dyaks, determined on some form of civil disobedience. I realised that this was the first test of my ability as a Community Development Officer and on what I did would depend a lot. Again and again I explained that the law was the law and to fight the law physically in any way was certainly going to make matters worse not better. "Surely" I said to myself, "there must be some way to help!" Janggat then quite calmly asked me to defend him at his case. I don't suppose he realised just what he was asking. Would Government understand my reasons were I to do so or would my action be taken as European support for the Dyaks against Government? After all it was not so long ago that Rajah Brooke had had to be firm. However, I reasoned to myself that an important part of the job of any Community Development Officer was to help the people of the community that one became involved in, and that if a scheme of Community Development was to begin, here then was at least an opportunity not only to help the Dyaks in a matter that I in any case felt sympathy with but also to ensure that Government, in any Community Development Officer, had to accept that, no matter the consequences, he would with no thought for his own personal job or because of the need of a salary to live on, take such action as he felt on conscience grounds that he must. So I agreed to defend Janggat as a test case. This decision at least meant that tempers grew less fiery and the rest of the Dyaks were persuaded quite easily to return home to await the outcome of Janggat's case.

It was listed for the following week. I confess I did not sleep well just previous to this but having decided, I knew I would do my best. News must have travelled fast since the courtroom was crowded, with hundreds sitting on steps leading up to it and a few more hundreds sitting under the shade of the large tree just outside the District Officer's office. I had never imagined myself as a lawyer but I suppose, certain in my own mind that the law was unjust, I brought out point after point. I felt actually sorry for the Agricultural Assistant putting forward the case for the Department. Apparently my voice could be heard quite some way off and in retrospect I must have looked like one of those red haired covenanters asking for normal justice. I certainly let myself go, for in for a penny in for a pound had always been one of my own sayings and I was living up to it. At the end I had a severe attack of cold feet wondering if this was to be the end of any attempt by me to help the Dyaks. Could Government forgive me this blatant usurpation of authority and accept the criticisms that I had loudly spoken in a court of law? Never before had a European defended a Dyak in a case of this sort. The magistrate hearing the case was obviously in a quandary. His sympathies were with Janggat but I did admire him in his judgment, which was that Janggat had in fact acted illegally and that he had no option but to fine Janggat. As he himself felt that the law was a little unjust the fine was nominal. So I lost the case, technically anyway, although morally I had won. Knowing that an appeal would be heard in a divisional court I asked for a stay of execution of the verdict and appealed on grounds that there was no clear evidence that Janggat had known of any written instructions that Dyaks were not allowed to plant pepper.

The District Officer must have made himself busy. There was no appeal but a telegram from Chief Secretary, informing the District Officer that the Director of Agriculture had now agreed that Dyaks could plant pepper so long as the land chosen could not be used for farming. I paid Janggat's fine with a light heart and we wended our way back to Budu by launch, canoe and by foot. Janggat and I were as one might expect firm friends and it is so to

The Ng. Entaih Community Development Centre

this day. Once again the news had travelled and although our return was not quite like a winning football team, it was near enough and we had a marvellous celebration that night in the longhouse. Not a drunken one but it was just that the whole atmosphere had changed. I was certainly one of them and it was clear that this bond of affection almost, between myself and Janggat, was all that was needed for the people really to begin thinking that there was a way somehow for progress to take place.

It was strikingly clear that evening that Government had gained a tremendous moral victory. As I said to them to back it up, "Government couldn't have known about this law. It must just have been something that the Director of Agriculture wanted and apparently hadn't known. When Government did know, of course, the law was changed. This is always how to make a wrong into a right, not by fighting and quarrelling but by being firm and determined." From then on, much of the antagonism which had been apparent towards Government faded and to this day the Budu Dyaks use talk and discussion to get what they believe to be right.

The last doubts had been dispelled and the Dyaks were now sure that I had come to help and with no thought for any personal reward. By the following week, two sunken pit latrines had been constructed and a third very large one was in the making. This one caused the next crisis. The pit was about ten foot by six and we had reached a depth of about ten feet. That night the rain came on, not just ordinary rain but heavy relentless rain. It rained and rained for a solid twelve hours—stopping just before dawn. All seemed to know that something had happened to the beginnings of the large pit latrine. Indeed it had. The sides had fallen in and it looked as though no hole had ever been dug. We were all silent as we looked at it but after a few minutes, the head of the longhouse said in a quiet voice with no emotion whatsoever; "Our Gods obviously did not like such a hole and so in their own way, have filled it in". No one else spoke and all turned away to get on with the day's work. It was so exasperating and I just did not know how to get round that one. In a sense they were right but didn't realise that if it had been covered over the night before the rain would not have caused the sides to fall in. Desperate, I shouted "Wait!" They stopped and slowly turned and came back. I knew by instinct that superstition had to be fought with superstition so in a grave voice I asked "How many people actually live in this longhouse?" Tuai Rumah Celau replied that there were about two to three hundred when everyone was at home. I then made a tremendous effort and smiled broadly and in a loud voice said: "Of course your Gods didn't like this hole that we made yesterday and have clearly shown their dislike but I am sure it is because your Gods do not think it big enough!" I saw belief in their eyes because I think they too wanted to complete the latrine, and before anyone else could say anything, I jumped in with a changkol and basket and started to dig away the earth that had fallen in, muttering aloud that instead of ten foot wide we would make it twelve foot wide so that two hundred could use it. Within minutes several had jumped in beside me to help, Janggat one of them. Breathing a great sigh of sheer relief I carried on for a few minutes and then left them to finish it. This latrine worked for many years.

As though all clouds were beginning to blow away, by great luck three of my beautiful white pigs had little ones, making nineteen in all. This was tremendous. From the time that I had arrived and stied them in a wired off, cement pig sty, very few Dyaks had any belief that my pigs would live far less breed. Now they could see for themselves. As I needed money to help pay for food, I sold them to the Dyaks for a very nominal sum but only if they penned them. Most did.

There were many other contributing factors, all intended to stimulate the people, not by talk but by something they could see. The pigs were kept clean by washing them morning and evening, using a small alcon pump. All the pupils took it in turn to look after the engine. Many people often came just to watch. In odd moments also I had managed to wire both the school and my own small house with a 12 or 250 volt supply, electric light. I could charge a 12 volt battery from this engine and it was of tremendous use. I preferred reading by a small reflector type of paraffin lamp since this did not bring the multitude of insects. When any visitors came I just used to switch on and the room was flooded with light. It was a great delight to the Dyaks but I always carefully explained that it was not just wires and bulbs, showing them the battery or the engine. It had happened that when I visited a longhouse when I was Principal of Batu Lintang, I was called in to visit someone and he asked my help to put light in the house. He told me he had been to Kuching and having seen people just touching a switch, he had bought wires, bulbs and sockets. He was most upset when I told him he would need to buy a great deal more but it does prove the simplicity of the Dyaks. Then, too, I had a large radio and although there were at that time no programmes in Dyak, the people loved to hear the music and even listen to the news, since they knew that I would translate for them. I had also brought, gifted by the British Council, a simple but efficient projector, worked from a pressure lamp. Many a pleasant evening we spent showing films of educational and geographical interest. I had also brought with me a very good incubator, hoping that I could produce about sixty chicks at a time. I had no success with this at all. It just needed too much looking after and I gave up trying when all I could get out of my incubator was one little chick. Luckily I had not told them what it was all about. However by May we had some splendid vegetable gardens and I even had large juicy tomatoes. They were happy but busy days and I certainly never felt lonely or wished to return to Kuching.

Although the Dyaks had not approached me officially about how to make progress, I knew that they would and I just had to be patient.

I took every opportunity to rub their noses however. They became really alarmed when I casually mentioned that there was not much use in teaching their children although some of them were clever. The children, I said, were learning about hygiene in the school and if they carried on they would not like to go back to the smells of the longhouse with the cringgits (midges) and mosquitoes to keep them company.

Although I had no intention of giving up so easily, I kept telling them that my year with them would be up soon, and I would be returning to Kuching. That this would be just as well since there seemed no point in educating their children so that those children, seeking a better way of life not to be found in their own longhouses, would inevitably leave their homes to seek work somewhere else. I certainly was not going to help to do this since this would be bad for the area. Better that the children stopped school and carried on and worked with their parents. However, if the people were keen to make progress in their own areas, clean up the longhouses, make sunk pit latrines, raise pigs properly, plant things that could be sold then their educated children would not be in such a hurry to leave. It was the old song sung to a more intimate tune now. There had to be parallel progress around the longhouse with that of the school. That the seeds took root became more and more obvious in the general talks and discussions which by now were taking place almost every evening when I had finished work in the school.

I knew that if anything was going to happen it would happen just around June, when the harvest was safely in and the people had a few weeks before they needed to start all over again. I was not therefore surprised when the first official delegation came to see me to ask what I would do. I remember distinctly telling them that if they had come to ask me what I was going to do to help them, they had better go away back home and think again. Plans for progress just had to come from them. Although I knew I was taking a chance, the meeting was short and brief and the delegation left. A week later they returned and the conversation opened more or less on the lines that I wanted. I knew that a major battle had been won and it was now just a question of channelling the victory.

So in a few more weeks the Progress Society was formed and a working Committee of Progress elected, two members from each longhouse. Making sure that they knew what they were in for, I reminded them that a proper dispensary would have to be built, that a school for adults had to be built with sleeping accommodation, that a shop had to be built, and an office for administration. That this would have to be done by them, free. If they were prepared to promise that all this would be done, I said I would go to Kuching and see what help I could get, since I would need others to help me in all this. It had therefore taken me almost six months to ensure that a desire for progress had come from them and not been imposed.

It would seem essential therefore that the first requisite is not just to live in the area of the intended project but almost to become a part of it and be completely involved in its affairs to the exclusion of all else. Perhaps the people, but this will be found out from Tungku's own story, felt that I had really become one of them even though of a different race and that being so, they were prepared to be led and advised by me. Their own superstitions and folklore also helped me. The Dyaks, living in natural surroundings, even to this day fall back on real nature to provide signs as to what they should do and not do. Naturally enough, I seemed to come into many of the dreams of some of the older Dyaks. A vital one which I was quick to seize on to forward my own prospects with them was that of the small stone rolling down a hill and becoming bigger and bigger. I nodded wisely when I was told that the old men had concluded that the small stone at the top was the beginning of the way to progress and that they had no doubt that by the end there would be something quite large. I quietly crossed my fingers since at that time I was far from being optimistic that anything could be achieved. I learned however to respect their superstitions. I had plenty of my own and could see no reason why the Dyaks should not have them. The old men also told of stories that they knew one day a stranger would come to help them and it was evident that they had begun to believe that I was that stranger. I again nodded wisely but reminded them that I was only someone who liked work for its own sake and was not to be identified as someone sent by their Gods. This very negation, however, seemed to convince them that I had more than human powers. As the years passed I learned that their very politeness made negatives into positives. If they are hungry the true Dyak will not say he is hungry and even blithely state that he has eaten. One begins to know that he expects nevertheless to be invited to join in a meal just to help finish the food and to give no offence to their Gods.

I grant you life was hard. How could it be otherwise? Food consisted of rice and to a large extent salt fish with an occasional hen as a great luxury. There were no mattresses to sleep on but just hard floors. I was not trying to be cruel to myself. It was all part of the process of identifying with the community. It was just an essential part of the job which I had undertaken to do. Nevertheless I achieved a peace of mind and a serenity of outlook that could not be bought. It is true that I now have a good mattress, a very good one, but it is the more cosy and comfortable because of the ten years or so that I made do with sleeping on hard floors.

The teaching, too, I make haste to say, was not all one sided. I learned a great deal from the Dyaks. Although I knew a fair number of stars in the Northern Hemisphere from my own night flying experiences, I knew little or nothing about the stars in the Southern Hemisphere. In the early days I could never understand how the Dyaks knew approximately when the Chinese launch, Alun, would be at Kaki Wong, the farthest point up river of the tidal reach. In the end, of course, they explained that they knew the time by the shape and size of the moon. How stupid I had been not to realise this after all my education! So a full moon meant that the launch would be at Kaki Wong around six o'clock. Half moon, around mid-day and mid-night. Although it was not often, there were occasions when we came up river by night and so did Alun if it were urgent. Quarter moon was either about nine o'clock or three o'clock depending on the wane or the rise. I became fairly skilled in knowing just when the Dyaks would burn and plant, from the group of stars, the Pleiades. On most evenings, the sky was just a myriad of stars and certainly the senior pupils often with me had most enjoyable times seeking out this group or that. Orion's belt never failed to interest them. Taurus was another great favourite. The North Star could, during most months, be seen and often this came in very useful as did the Southern Cross. Gradually most of the young Dyaks of age between twenty and thirty began to speak of Grenjang as being West of Budu and not just a place over there where their hand or arm pointed. I learned too the greatest of all lessons, that distance should not really be measured in miles or furlongs or metres but in time. From my own bitter experience in travel when I used to estimate times of arrivals at certain places by measuring on the map and so arrive in the dark, a procedure not at all welcomed by Dyaks, I accepted their estimate of the distance according to time taken. It is so to this day. I learned that they were the wise ones when it came to river or jungle travel and that it was just sheer stupidity on the part of any European even to try to help. In helping, usually either I fell in and caused greater trouble or was so ungainly at it that they could not carry on for laughing. So I laughed with them and contented myself by being led. Their very politeness often caused me to be lost. I had to go in front. I liked this, mind you, since I could set my own pace, but often, although I had been over the path several times, I would be so preoccupied with my thoughts that I would take a wrong turning. Usually only after half an hour would they tell me that I had taken the wrong path.

Most of all I learned not to be as impetuous as I had been. That it was far better to ponder, discuss all angles before any final decisions could be taken. To this day, Mac and Arthur get quite obstinate with me when something has to be decided. They sit and bear it, knowing full well that by the next day I will have changed my mind. This is just not the case. I learned from the Dyaks that by talking, a possible solution was apparent, but that it should not be conclusive till after I had slept on it. I certainly do not profess to find solutions in dreams but when I wake up the morning following after an important decision is made, I know instinctively whether that decision is right. Possibly it is conscience that gives a sound sleep or the reverse, but it is true that on the day following, the final decision sometimes bears no relation at all to the previous one. Mac and Arthur will agree, however, that usually the final one has been the best, and the one that worked.

Certain dangers there were, but being a Scotsman, who had heard his Grannie saying so many times that "what's for ye, will no go past ye"! I took supreme comfort from this maxim. I think one had to believe in it anyway to survive so far away from so called civilisation. There were almost always the near shaves of breaking a leg or an arm or some other bone when one fell from a log laid to cross a small stream. I hardly remember one journey but that a snake was killed or I killed a snake. This latter pest often made me wish I was not the first on any path. Talking of snakes reminds me that the Dyaks are not loath to play a practical joke. On one trip from Budu to Entaih, very early in the morning, I found myself giving a mighty jump up. A huge, and it was huge, python had been curled up right on the path. As the colour was a vague green I could not be blamed for not noticing it till my foot was just above it. I cannot say I joined in the subsequent laughter. It had just been killed by the owner of the rubber garden through which we were passing. I certainly hate snakes as much as the Dyaks but I held to a firm conviction that snakes will only bite when attacked. I always travelled with a kind of walking stick and if this was not available a branch of wood. As I stepped out I would intentionally give the ground a thump ahead of me, just so that any snake would get out of the way. It worked many times. For myself, the gravest danger lay in crossing flooded rivers. When meetings had been arranged for certain days, no matter the weather, I went on since it was vital not to break a promise. Often we were caught in thunderstorms that caused rivers to rise, not just a few feet but twenty, thirty or even forty feet. To cross a fast flowing stream is one thing but to cross an angry looking fast flowing river with mighty logs on it is quite another. Whirlpools and currents follow no known pattern. Often there had been close shaves by being caught with one's legs under tree stumps with the force of the water pulling one under. To survive one must not fight the current although all one's instinct is to do just that. I learned from the Dyaks to curl up one's legs and let myself go with the flood till a convenient calm part made it comparatively easy to scramble up the bank. Being wet was the least of the worries. It made walking cool and one seemed to travel faster in rain than in hot sunshine. All, including myself, carried our own bags. One member of the party used to climb the highest tree and scramble along the branch that almost reached the other side and give the bags a mighty heave. Usually they fell on the other side, quite dry but not always. As I walked, how often did I think that all that I had done in my youth and before I came to Sarawak, had somehow prepared me for this work. I could swim well, I had learned to climb, both with ropes and ice axes. I could cook and look after myself and this I had learned at weekends on camping holidays and when I worked in hotels during the University holidays to help pay my own way. All my knowledge of engines and electric lighting had been gained during my training as a pilot. Most of all I think my flying experience taught me not to lose my head in a crisis.

So with the faith of the Dyaks and with their best wishes I set off to Kuching to see what help I could get to start a real planned scheme of Community Development. There is little need for me to repeat myself but briefly, a three-year, phase-one plan was in principle decided on by the Committee of Community Development in Kuching and I returned convinced that all would be well even though much had to be done. On my return to Budu, it was purely a matter of organisation to complete the buildings which the people had promised to build. I had just to be careful that everything was arranged fairly since Dyaks, like any other people, resent and rightly so, any unfair division be it of food or work. By this time there were over four hundred families in the Progress Society and to get the work completed meant, after careful calculations and the drawing up of plans, that one from each family would have to spend fourteen days in the jungle cutting the wood required. When all this was done, each had to give up to three days on the scheme site to help build. What fun it all was, although I used almost to be so tired at night that I often cannot remember going to sleep, or even eating.

By December 1957, the work was well in hand with roofs to be seen on the dispensary and shop, the adult school and mess room and dormitories. The question of staff was of the utmost priority. The estimates provided for myself as Officer in Charge, two teachers for adult teaching, one Agricultural Assistant, one Co-operative Assistant and a dresser. Moderate subsidies had been provided to buy materials unobtainable locally, such as cement and roofing. Efforts to recruit from Saratok, Kuching and Sibu brought many applicants but none came up to the standard I expected or wanted. I was determined to have good assistants who would do more than just a day's

32

work. It was vital that the example set by possible assistants had to be such that would give a good example not only to the pupils in school but to the people with whom they were to work. Several were tried on a month to month basis. As they were more often to be found even smoking in the classroom and spending far too much time on dressing themselves up in what I called bazaar clothes I quickly dispensed with their services. They were just not trainable. It was then that the idea of recruiting at least one European if not two, came to me. I knew if they could be found that there must be some young men who wanted a different kind of life than just a mere routine of catching the 7.50 train into the city and returning by the 5.20. The story of the recruitment of Mac and Arthur can be read elsewhere. There can be little doubt that had I not decided to try and find such young men, I doubt very much if the project could have got under way at all. I said nothing of course to anyone either in Kuching or Budu. I made plans to go home, ostensibly for a short holiday before commencing the three-year project, but actually my only concern during that holiday was to recruit, if possible, two young men, one qualified as a nurse, and the other as a kind of engineer cum agriculturalist cum jack of all trades. Having found them I thought little of paying their passage to Sarawak, hoping that if they turned out to be what was wanted, the Community Development Committee in Kuching would reimburse me. I was reimbursed in full. When the cheque arrived some months after our arrival at Budu I felt that there was a great deal to the saying that "never venture never win". Throughout the years I have repeatedly done this and paid for things myself first, not because I really wanted to jump fences or make a "fait accompli" but because there was just no time to go into long paper-work battles to get what was needed.

By the 4th of April 1954 I was back at Budu with Mac and Arthur. On the 5th of May the scheme as has been related elsewhere was opened officially by His Excellency the Governor, Sir Anthony Abel, who from that time on gave his maximum support both morally and physically.

There seems little point in me writing accounts of the project from then on since anyone interested can read Mr McBride's statistical report. It is an excellent report and gives a very clear and concise account of the work done over the years with an honest assessment of the results. This report will be an appendix to this story.

By 1955, much had been achieved at Budu and at that time began the trickle of people from other areas to see for themselves if what they had heard was true. A great deal of my time was spent in looking after such delegations, but I felt that this was worth while. I knew that it would be possible to open up other areas in a similar way given time and trained staff. To all I said that of course I would help, but they would have to do a great deal by themselves first. This was particularly true with the delegation from Entaih in the third division. It was led by one of the finest Dyaks I have ever met, Sirai Libau. He was determined that the people around Entaih would and could make progress, similar to that he had seen at Budu. We all agreed that if we were to start anywhere else, Entaih would be the first despite the fact that from Budu it could only be reached by walking some ten to twelve hours along paths that were in those days often overgrown. So I agreed to pay them a visit and find out for myself the spirit of the people and just what they themselves were prepared to do. I toured the Entaih area extensively, sleeping in almost every single longhouse since I was determined that the people should know that progress first depended on themselves. At the end of the tour I was convinced that there was every chance that a scheme, started at Entaih on some land to be decided later, would be successful. Presiding over a large meeting I merely said that I would try to help them but that they had better start first by building a small school somewhere convenient to most houses. If they did this, I would return a year later to see what they had done. I spent the day going round several suggested lands and finally decided on what is now called Ng. Entaih, land at the very junction of the Entebai River and the Entaih River. As events have turned out my decision was right despite the fact that at that time it looked a complete jungle.

The various deputations to visit Budu were of course always urged to talk to the people, for in this way the concepts that had taken me six months to get across when I first arrived at Budu could actually travel quite far without my having to be among the people. My tour of Entaih certainly convinced me that much had been passed on. There was no need to cajole or plead with the people of Entaih. They had made up their minds that no matter how hard or difficult they would do what was asked. I felt therefore confident that I could go to Kuching to plead the case of the Entaih Dyaks even as I had done for the Budu ones. Actually I had very little trouble in persuading Government to sponsor a new scheme at Entaih so long as I was sure that by doing a scheme at Entaih the Budu one could carry on as planned. So provisional estimates were drawn up and approved in principle and January 1958 was the starting date decided on. By this time both Mac and Arthur were fully capable in almost every aspect and I knew that they could be left at Budu, for at least a few months at a time.

News, however, from Entaih, namely that Sirai had been put into jail for opening a school without permission caused me to drop everything at Budu in October '57 and literally almost run to Entaih. I was indeed angry. The then District Officer at Kanowit, not having received my letter telling him of the proposal at Entaih, had acted in accordance with the law. However I got Sirai out of jail and this incident, rather like Janggat's trial seemed to cement a friendship between me and the people of Entaih that remains till this day. It seems ironical that before a Community Development Officer can really begin to work, he has in some way to win a point against bureaucracy. So long as the Community Development Officer does not play it up and explains, just as I did on Janggat's case that it was not by order of Government, that Sirai had been put in jail but because of a law that had got out of date, no great harm comes of this. I rather used the win as it were to enhance the real Government even though certain individuals in Government administration get the kick or the blow.

Entaih, being even further than Budu from any bazaar, and even more remote, with little or no communications with the nearest District Officer at Kanowit, some four days journey by canoe, if one was lucky enough to have an outboard engine and some six to seven days to get back, I had bitten off something that might be hard to swallow. Kuching, having been advised by the District Officer Kanowit that he could not recommend Entaih since by its very remoteness it would just be impossible to administer and extremely dangerous for any European working there, took I think cold feet and advised an enquiry before any final decision was taken. A Mr R. Bewsher, who knew me well and who had visited me at Budu, the District Officer Kanowit, and the chief of all the Dyaks in the area Pengara Dunyang, were asked to decide. The District Officer, I knew, wanted me to start at a place called Meluan—a lovely spot mark you and one that had buildings all ready and available. It had been a fort at one time in the not so distant past and it was substantially built. I had several reasons for not agreeing, chief of which I think was that buildings were there. How could a Community Development Officer inculcate in the minds of a developing people the need for their own work if buildings were to be given. Also Meluan had a Chinese bazaar very close to it and while in no way being anti-Chinese I knew that it would be next to impossible to run a co-operative shop successfully at Meluan. I think, too, I knew that if we opened at Meluan, there would never be a scheme at Entaih or further upriver than Meluan. I was determined that difficult though it might be the scheme, if any, would start at Entaih and in due course establish something at Meluan.

I agreed, however, that by all means there should be an enquiry but only if they agreed that such an enquiry would take place at Nh Sempurai, near Entaih. As the District Officer had not been up there at all, nor had Ro Bewsher, they all thought it was a good idea. I knew that if they listened to the people of Rh Sempurai, their many fears would fade and would give the green light to a scheme at Entaih. The Pengara I knew was on my side. So the day arrived for this most important meeting at Rh Sempurai. Luke and I left Budu that morning before dawn so that we would arrive during light and with a little time to spare. The D.O. and Ro Bewsher were not expected till late in the day. The rain however came on and the rivers rose in flood, not just a little flood but one of those frightening floods. We had many rivers to cross by swimming and it was just a few minutes before midnight that I arrived, but on the day promised. Sirai, I am sure will never forget this, since he certainly knew the tremendous effort it must have been to reach Rh Sempurai. Indeed I would have been justified in not arriving but there was a lot at stake. Snakes had to be forgotten about as we slushed and swam our way to Sempurai. In a sense it was lucky I did arrive late, since both the D.O. and Ro had long talks with the people without my being behind them and prodding them on. Also I think, because everybody knew that we had made a marathon effort for our cause, there was no further thought that the scheme should be anywhere but Entaih. Meluan hardly came into the conversation. By plodding on I had won a moral and tactical victory.

So it was arranged that the people would prepare, ready for occupation, three staff quarters, an office, and a store and that as soon as this was done I would arrive and start work at Entaih.

Mentally, the work proved much easier than at Budu. We had learned a great deal at Budu, both in the understanding of Dyaks and in knowing what was needed first. The plans of the buildings at Entaih were much improved upon and slowly but surely with the help of the people the jungle cleared and terraces made ready for planting. Physically however the work at Entaih was much harder than at Budu. The setting up of a kind of chain of essential supplies was extremely difficult owing to the very distance that Entaih was from even Meluan, the nearest place to buy even paraffin. Things became a bit easier when we had established a small base at Meluan where we could stay at night and store goods when awaiting good water. Outboard engines didn't seem to stand up to the gruelling work of some ten hours driving per day and to keep things moving at all we had to have about four outboard engines available. The river was very different from that on the Budu side and we had frequent sinkings with the loss of all goods, canoe and engine. Gradually however the trainees learned more and more and by the third year of the Entaih project we had our transport and communications under control. In the early days, two full days had to be allowed, and sometimes three for a journey from Entaih to Meluan. Now it is common practice to leave Entaih in the morning and return the same day with light to spare. We have of course some excellent drivers, capable and confident and able to undertake minor repairs en route. Experienced drivers, such as Jangga, Salang, Naga, Giman and of course Eddie kept on breaking records. My fastest trip to Entaih from Ng Entebai was just over an hour and a half. Those trips were always a great pleasure to me. My dog, Junie, with its white bushy tail up used to stand right at the bow with his nose in the air. He just loved this. People used to say that Junie told the driver by a turn of his head that a log of wood was ahead. To a certain extent this was true but his nod was only because he himself didn't quite know what he was seeing. He was an extraordinarily intelligent dog and loved by all. One could almost talk to him. Often, knowing that I was coming up river, children from every longhouse used to stand waiting to see us pass. Not to see me, I make haste to say, but to wave to Junie who used to wag his tail. The people often asked me how I trained Junie to stand at the bow. I didn't. Junie, I knew, was a hunting dog of good stock and being so, he had to be in front where he could best smell the scent of things that he wanted to hunt. So to the bow he always went, with his nostrils quivering, emitting now and then the excited whimper when he smelt something. He gave us a few frights, by disappearing over the side at some difficult rapids, but always we found him swimming after us. That he was intelligent was proved when, as he himself grew experienced, he would recognise rapids and crouch down till we were past. He was a grand dog. I went to Kuching for a week and when I returned, Junie could not be found. He was last seen swimming after my canoe. For many months I could still hear Junie barking but I would not seek another dog. Jugam, Mac's dog, however one day arrived at Entaih, having walked by herself. She is still at Entaih. She was probably looking for Mac, who had gone on a short holiday home. Jugam had pups and we kept one, and named it Elizabeth. Eddie named it Elizabeth, actually after the Queen. Gradually Elizabeth changed to Lassie. Lassie was as Junie, much loved and took her place at the bow also. We lost Lassie when I went home for a short leave. Luckily she had pups and

I had kept one of them who gradually has taken Lassie's place in my affection. She is called Brown Feet, but mostly Bruffit. She is still with me and has just had her first pups. A wonderful dog, to me anyway. She too travels in the bow just as Junie did. They are all from hunting stock though.

As I have said the opening at Entaih was in many ways easier because of what we had learned at Budu. Also it was possible to bring some of·the trainees, such as Jenuang and Henry Chuk to Entaih to help in all aspects of the work. Generally speaking the establishment of Entaih followed very much the same pattern as at Budu. There was a primary school, an adult school, a shop, a dispensary, an engine room and sleeping quarters. The statistical story of Entaih can also be read in Mr McBride's report and I need not dwell on the details. Mac's account is full and excellent, giving the good and the bad.

We had many more setbacks, however, at Entaih than we had had at Budu. I often wonder how we survived them. By this time I had recruited Dr Ronald Lees, whose story can be read under medical and a lad Bill Grafton. Doc. was recruited under the Entaih scheme to take over the medical work just as Arthur had done it on the Budu side. Bill was a kind of McBride, able to do lots of things such as wiring up for electricity, repairing engines and organising the shop side, not to mention teaching both adults and trainees.

All would have gone as planned but as I have explained in another chapter, Arthur took ill and was forced to be away for some two years nearly. Doc. manfully and without thought for himself undertook to look after both schemes. This was a terrific undertaking, since to do so meant that he had to undertake this travel to and from Budu almost every two months. He never complained. One good thing however came out of it and that was whether we liked it or not, trainees such as Rabing, Mapan, Enyang specialising in dispensary work had to be left in complete charge much sooner than was planned. It was surprising how well we coped, but of course Doc., like Arthur, was a meticulous teacher especially in meting out medicine. Bill Grafton did valiant work but I could not give him the same training as I had given Mac, since I too had to keep popping back to Budu, if only to let Mac go on holiday home. Bill, being just that little bit impatient and often in too much of a hurry to get things done, could never quite understand that our first job was to teach trainees and people how to do things and not to do it ourselves if we could avoid it. Bill loved to repair engines but was not like Mac, indefatigable in teaching the trainees. To Bill, however, must go the credit of keeping our engines going at Entaih and this was a major job in itself. Bill found the walk from Entaih to Budu a gruelling affair, only to be undertaken in an emergency. He must have known himself, although we certainly didn't, that there was something wrong with his heart. I often wonder if the physical energy expended by Bill on those journeys between Entaih and Budu was not partly, at least, responsible for his early death when at home on holiday. News of his death came as a great shock to us all. We remember him as he would have wished us to, and remain grateful that he gave so much of himself to help.

There were other setbacks too. Twice at Entaih, freak typhoons hit us and every single roof was blown off and even hailstones fell. It happened that at the time Doc and I were running an adult course of both women and men. Really it was frightening and had Doc not been there I question if I could have kept my head. Doc was superb and seemed unconcerned as he went here and there picking up small children who had received wounds from flying aluminium sheeting. The Dyaks were really afraid and I certainly did not blame them. Almost without exception they huddled together under tables, fortunately large ones. Even after some ten years, I can still picture Sirai under one of the tables, with tears streaming down his face asking help presumably from their Gods beseeching that all was not lost.

When the first fury had subsided I knew it was time for strong action. The devastation was unbelievable. Trees had been blown down, there were no roofs left and everything was just a sodden mess. Fortunately the rain stopped and the sun came out, late though it was. Frankly, I myself took this as a sign that all was not lost with an optimism that I certainly did not at the time believe. By cajoling, hectoring, I got them out from under the tables. "Of course we could get the roofs on or some of them", I said, although I didn't quite see how myself. I just knew we all had to do something to minimise the shock of it all. Soon, Doc and I had the kids picking up all the books that had blown away and being kids, their fears quickly went and soon they were running madly about running races picking this up and that up. Sirai, quick to follow me, took the lead and in fact we had several roofs on again before an hour had passed, sufficient anyway to be able to sleep that night. It put us back however by about two months.

Then on two occasions unusual floods hit Entaih, with levels about five feet higher than ever before experienced. To make matters worse it was during the night, around three o'clock. Flood waters during daylight are frightening enough but in the darkness, pitch darkness, the sound of rushing water all around is almost terrifying. Small children had to be rescued from attic dormitories since they were unaware of the flood and still sleeping. Valuable irreplaceable medicine had to be taken from the dispensary through which water was rushing as a waterfall. Vital foods had to be taken from the shop and engines taken to high ground. Apparently unconscious of the extreme danger, the trainees and staff alike worked ceaselessly till dawn, rescuing this and rescuing that. As I told them afterwards, they showed the true courage of their ancestors. Their reply was naive in that they just said that I had told them to do this or that and it never occurred to them to do otherwise. It confirmed what I had suspected all along that if Dyaks are led, they would follow through fire and water. I knew then that if the Nairn Dyaks returned with those essential qualities of leadership then all would be well. They did and if I were asked in what way we, the Europeans, helped most I would undoubtedly reply saying that through the examples given by Mac, Arthur, Doc, myself, we had managed to inculcate this quality of leadership in certain Dyaks.

Nevertheless, Entaih, despite the many setbacks caused by nature and illness, slowly but surely began to take on an appearance of solidity and permanence. Entaih to this day stands firm and is in addition a most beautiful spot. What had been jungle, there now grows orderly high yielding rubber trees in excellent condition. There are flowers, coconut trees and fruit trees in plenty. The buildings are well maintained and in the evening when the 5 h.p. Peter's diesel electric is started, Entaih provides a most beautiful scene. The shop is well looked after by Mr Enyang, a most faithful and conscientious Dyak, one of my oldest trainees. He teaches and looks after the dispensary with an assistant whom he trains as well. As Secretary of the Progress Society with Sirai still as Chairman, he conducts the business of meetings better I think than we did. With Henry, as Headmaster of the primary school, assisted by three teachers to look after more than 100 pupils, there seems little doubt that Entaih will grow from strength to strength. I consider Entaih my best work, but into it I put all the experience I gained the hard way at Budu.

As Entaih grew, more and more deputations came to ask for help in other areas. I felt however that we could not extend our resources of trained or semi-trained staff further at that time, since to do so would have weakened both Budu and Entaih. It was then I conceived the idea of the Iban Team Project. Briefly, it was a project which suggested that from certain selected areas, eight trainees would be chosen at as high a standard of education as was possible. Those trainees would then be brought either to Entaih or Budu to carry on their normal academic schooling and be absorbed in the general training to become Community Development Assistants. Eight trainees were therefore selected from the Mujok area, the Ulu Kanowit area, Ng Entebai and Meluan making a total of 24 trainees. Government agreed to provide food and transport. Parallel to this training, Committees of Progress would be set up at chosen places in the areas of recruitment. While the trainees were learning, the people would build what was necessary, plant what was needed and so by periodic visits from myself or Arthur, or Mac or Doc, four centres would gradually take shape. After about three years I considered that some of the senior staff such as Mac or Arthur or myself could leave the parent schemes at Budu or Entaih and give concentrated help in those four centres. So Ng Maong on the Mujok came into being, Tappang Punguu on the Ulu Kanowit, Ng Entebai at the junction of the Entebai and Kanowit rivers and Ng Kadup on the Waden river.

Physically the plan worked well but a tremendous effort had to be made by the senior members of the team. I doubt if we could do it twice. I need not go into the detailed planning and organisation since once again, all this can be read in Mr McBride's report. I would be the first to admit that none of the centres opened up under the Iban Team Project could be compared to either Budu or Entaih. We knew that the project was only a sop to certain areas, but like giving medicine, something was better than nothing. Those centres have not the financial stability of Budu or Entaih and it is possible as centres they will not survive. Nevertheless, much was and has been accomplished through the Iban Team Project. Were I to be asked again to start an Iban Team Project I would be inclined to say "No"! Experiences at Budu and Entaih have proved conclusively that there must be on the spot at any centre an example of good leadership and it must be possible to run as was done at Budu and Entaih a well planned adult education coverage. This was not possible under the Iban Team Project, for obvious reasons. It was not possible to give any of those four centres when they were handed over, fully qualified Community Development Assistants either in the shop or the dispensary, also for obvious reasons. There just was not the time to train Rabings with an SRN or Lukes or Limans to take over the administration of each centre, nor of course was there money. The Iban Team Project was pared down to a minimum, purely because the Sarawak Government just did not have the funds to be more generous at that time. Had each embryo centre been allocated the same funds for progress as Entaih or Budu, I am fairly sure that the result would have been worth it. Nevertheless, the project was worth while. I certainly learned a great deal as did Mac, Arthur and Doc. There is at least a spirit of development in those areas and without being too optimistic, it is possible for the Progress Societies in those four areas to make a considerable impact in the area as time passes.

With the advent of Malaysia, it was not possible to provide the follow up supervision which both Budu and Entaih received before all executive powers were handed over to locally born people. Also with the advent of Malaysia, a completely new concept of development was started. As most of the principles used were actually contrary to the principles under what I would call real Community Development, I have opposed the new plans and of course become very unpopular. It would be interesting to see who is proved right as time passes. I can say no more on this at this stage since as is often said, "The proof of the pudding is in the eating".

So the years from 1953 to 1965 passed busily and happily. In that year, the Iban Team Project had to stop and no further contracts were offered by Central Government to carry on the work of Community Development with Budu and Entaih as the pattern. Both Mac and Arthur, by virtue of having to live, accepted new contracts under the new plan of development, both hoping that they could influence the people concerned in those schemes with some, at least, of the real principles of Community Development as at Budu or Entaih. Time alone can tell what success each achieved.

I myself moved to private ground, up river from Ng Entebai to try and establish a Secondary School. Had Sarawak remained as a colony, I am sure I would have received the go ahead green light. It had always been accepted in principle that the establishment of a Secondary School was the final phase of any Community Development Scheme. How could it be otherwise? Three feeder schools had been established near Entaih and up river. Other feeder schools had been established near Tappang Punggu and Ng Entebai. In all by 1965 there were over twelve primary schools feeding the main centres at Entaih, Ng Entebai, Maong and Tappang. The output of pupils from the main centre schools was around 50 to 60 pupils a year and those pupils should have some opportunity for Secondary Education, albeit a biased one concentrating on new methods of agriculture, co-operative trading and general administration, not to mention care and maintenance of engines on which the very survival of the area depended.

Suffice it to say that no help at all was forthcoming from Central Government. Rather was I being persuaded to become the Principal of any Government Secondary School. I could not see myself leaving a job so nearly finished and decided that I would at least attempt to open a Private Vocational Secondary School on the land where I had built for myself a small house. It happens to be Eddie's land and so a Private Secondary was a possibility if I could find financial support to set it going. I knew that revenue from all the high yielding rubber trees at each centre, at Entaih, Maong, Ng Entebai and Tappang would be made available to me for long term running but a year or two was needed till the rubber trees could be tapped. The rubber had actually been planted with this in mind, namely to provide revenue for area progress in education, agriculture and medical coverage.

To register the school took me exactly three months and about two reams of typing paper but finally approval was given but I got the impression that no one really believed that this was possible without help. Asia Foundation and Oxfam were approached and came generously to the rescue. Without this help it would have been almost impossible. The former Director of Education, Mr M. G. Dickson, and his brother Alec. Dickson went to a great deal of trouble on my behalf for which I will always be grateful. In another Chapter can be read in more detail how those foundations and other foundations helped me. Suffice it to say here that by 1968, I had established the Private Vocational Secondary School here on Eddie's land. It is adequate although in no sense can it compare with a Government Secondary School. There are of course many economical difficulties not yet solved, particularly as the price of rubber has fallen to less than half its former value. The price is so low that it is not economical to tap the trees at Entaih or any centre. Nevertheless it survives but only with a very small nominal roll but all that would be needed to fill it would be a food and salary subsidy till such time as the rubber prices rose. Support from the people is there in full measure but the people too suffer from the fall of rubber prices.

At Budu, a private vocational school was also established. For the time being it is closed since there was evidence that political juggling was going to affect adversely almost every principle inculcated in the scheme. Rather than let this happen I advised Luke to close it temporarily, till such time as the position was made clear after the general elections. Budu must not become a battlefield for politics, of that I am determined. The scheme however generally carries on and no doubt time will bring its own enlightenment.

Luke and Arthur now help me here and it is quite like old times. We miss however very much the almost daily contacts with the people and the visits to longhouses to discuss this and that but with the political situation as it is and because of the known influence that we have, we confine ourselves entirely to the work in the school. Only Arthur manages to get around, but this he can do more easily than I since his great love is treatment of those who either cannot afford to go to a dispensary or who are too far away to make it worth while even. His motives in travelling can never be questioned. Mine would be, but wrongly, since I would never under any circumstances bring politics into a Community Development.

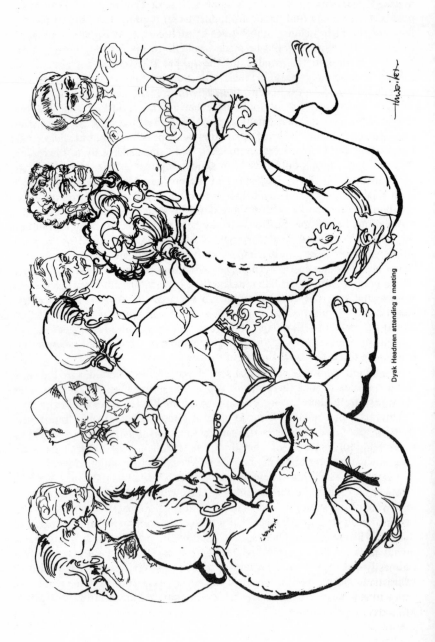

Dyak Headmen attending a meeting

CHAPTER FOUR
The Faith which stems from Authority is not Faith.

PROSELYTIZATION AND COMMUNITY DEVELOPMENT IN THE BUDU AND ENTEBAI SCHEMES

At varying times throughout the periods of the project, much uninformed criticism was levelled at me for my apparent opposition to any form of proselytization at any centre operating as a Community Development Centre.

Before I arrived in Sarawak, I was admittedly wary of the work of some missions and had at times questioned their work in Africa and Ceylon where I had travelled fairly extensively during the war. Being not such a full blooded Presbyterian from Scotland as a person who sincerely felt that everyone had the right to whatever religion they believed in, nevertheless I was very prepared to view the work of the various Missions in Sarawak with a completely open mind. It was very refreshing to find in Sarawak that while certain areas had been given over to this mission or that mission, the fact that there were in all some seven different denominations, meant automatically that each mission had to tread warily and survive by its own work. To a large extent, excellent work had been done by all missions. Only in small pockets did I find evidence of, shall I say, the wrong type of proselytization. This was not due to higher authority but to misguided parochial pride. Some locally trained priests or fathers counted the converts on paper as an indication of their prowess of christianisation and openly scorned those who would not become Christians. Even in the early days of my travel I found this to be an extraordinary attitude especially as most of the Dyaks, within the framework of their own customs, abided by and followed quite a number of the ten commandments. I have to this day, never regarded the Dyaks as Pagans, since this might imply that they had no religion when in fact most Dyaks are deeply religious in their own way.

Only within the school structure of each mission did I find cause for thought. In some mission schools, it seemed that schooling could only be given to those children who professed themselves to be Christians. This seemed very wrong to me at the time. Later on, however, and after a few years at Budu I began to realise that the Dyaks themselves had misinterpreted what had been offered by the Missions. I found that the Missions had quite honestly offered schooling but only to those who really wished to become Christians. Naturally enough, many Dyak parents, since there was no other way to get their children to school, became so-called Christians and are so to this day. They had the choice however. Now of course the Missions are much more careful and to a certain extent the Budu Scheme played its part in the enlightenment.

Another aspect which I found somehow to be wrong, was that in certain areas where missions worked, the people themselves had become divided. The Christians lived in one part and the non-Christians lived in another part. It was a co-existence which quite often worked but in death, troubles and famine it did not seem to. I recall one experience, arriving at a certain longhouse on Xmas Eve. It was only incidental to me that it was Xmas Eve but after a ceremonial entry to the longhouse, I quickly saw that I was walking on ice. I soon realised that half the Dyaks were Christians and half not. As the only Europeans who travelled at that time in this district were invariably Christian Fathers I was hailed by the Christian half with all ceremony. They were quite dismayed that I was not from any mission. I seemed then to be "oozed" along to the non-Christian portion by my guide, Sain, whom I remember so well to this day. Both halves, however, had obviously been celebrating, each in their own way. Voices became loud and there was much stirring around. It seemed certain that I could not speak to them on just a simple matter of trying to open a Government School with a trained teacher due out from Batu Lintang the following year. My guide grew quite anxious and soon after, led me into a room and without a word, lifted some floor boards. "This way, Sir! I am afraid for you and we must leave quickly". We did. As at that time I knew no Dyak language apart from a word or two, I did not know the reason but was prepared to trust my guide. We seemed to travel for hours in the dark, wet jungle but eventually we stopped to take shelter and rest in a small farm hut. It was the cosiest and nicest place I have ever found rest in. While we cooked our rice, my guide explained that the Christian half had become very angry with me because few of them had been able to understand that I was not a mission father and felt I should be punished for paying so much attention to the non-Christians. The latter, in their turn, had become angry with me also, since they too, having drunk copiously, failed to realise that I was not from any mission. Indeed they thought I was and regarded my "oozing" to their portion of longhouse as an attempt by me to persuade them to become Christians. Looking back, I am sure that it was this experience which made me decide that if at any time I found myself in a position to help an underdeveloped people, it would have to be in an area where no mission had operated. This decision should not imply that I was opposed to the work of missions but merely that the work of Community Development should if possible start where there were no divided loyalties.

And so we come to Budu and the Budu people. On my first visit there in 1952, I had been very impressed with the self efforts of the people of Rh Gelau. They themselves had built a small school, even though it was without walls, paid their own teacher albeit a teacher who could barely read or write. It seemed true that they preferred to do this, than send their children to the nearest mission school. Naturally I was interested and it was not surprising that, when the final break from Batu Lintang came, my thoughts turned to Budu.

Budu seemed to have an environment that would fit in very well with some of the dormant plans in my mind. That there was no mission operating there, was, it is true, a factor which helped me to decide on Budu but this does not mean that I was anti-mission. It meant simply that I was seeking a place where a different idea could be used experimentally. Budu was also remote and remote enough to provide the challenge. Communications were non-existent. There was at least a nucleus of people who already had shown a self help spirit and this being the basis of true Community Development I was optimistic that something could be done at Budu.

The journey to Budu and how the project got under way has already been dealt with in chapters two and three. In this chapter it is only necessary to give the reasons why no mission of any denomination was invited to help at any scheme centre. It arose in a curious way and rather unexpectedly. The Dyaks have a curious trait in that they will seldom proffer any information unless specifically asked about it. A perfect example of what I mean happened only a few months ago. News had been received that our Jawie Masing, one of the first trainees to go to Nairn Academy, had received the degree of M.B., Ch.B. Naturally enough I specifically sent someone up the river to inform people whom I knew to be interested. When he returned I asked him if they had been pleased to hear the news. The answer I should have expected, knowing them so well. It was simply "They did not ask me about Jawie so how could I tell them"! I realised it was my own fault since I should have sent a letter with him. Indeed the very politeness of Dyaks could well be their undoing.

Anyway, this day I was walking up the banks of the Budu river and as it was a hot day, naturally enough, when we came to an inviting pool I suggested we should stop, have a swim and eat the food which we had brought. It was obvious that I was not going to be allowed to swim in that particular pool but nobody seemed willing to tell me why. After exhausting the ordinary questions as to whether there were crocodiles in the pool, or whether it was too deep with unseen currents I realised that I would have to find out the reason the long way. By asking its name, they replied that it was called Lubok Tuan. I immediately asked the name of the Tuan but nobody was prepared to answer that one. Eventually after a long series of questions it emerged that a certain priest had been murdered and thrown into this particular pool. Apparently he had been murdered because he had tried to force some Christian customs on a nearby longhouse. This made it necessary for him to be removed completely and for all time. Only then did I realise the reasons for the suspicions of certain sections of the people. They were not sure whether I had come to make them into Christians or not.

So it was when the large numbers of people arrived for the meeting at Budu in June 1953 to decide whether a plan of progress could be formed, that at the very outset, I made it again quite clear that I was no Mission Father, that I had not come to force them to be Christians nor indeed had I come to try and change even their own particular customs. Some believed me and some did not and I knew then that to get over this first hurdle I had to do something very quickly. Luckily I knew that Dyaks believed in promises but the promise had to be made in a way that would brook no breaking of that promise.

I fell back on the well known custom introduced by the Rajah. So I prepared a letter of promise and in this letter I explained and promised that I would in no way proselytize the Dyaks nor would I try to change their own native customs. It was duly thumbprinted by me and witnessed by the thumb print of some six local chiefs. The document looked quite impressive. This was not enough since I also knew that for one promise there had to be an equal and binding promise from the other party. So underneath was written that the Dyaks promised on their part not to try and change any of my customs. This was also impressively signed by a representative of each longhouse.

The atmosphere seemed immediately to have cleared and the meeting got down to deciding whether or not a plan of progress could be evolved.

Throughout the years I have kept to that promise even though at times strong pressure was brought to bear that at least a building or two could be used by Mission Fathers to hold services. On no scheme ground and in no building built by the people under the scheme has there ever been held a religious service by any member of any mission. The various rumours that seeped down the river that I was opposed to the work of the missions were entirely false. Visits of priests to various longhouses were never opposed. It was not my affair but the affair only of the head of that house. To my certain knowledge at least one longhouse became Christian during the years of the project. Had I allowed religious gatherings to take place in any scheme building, it would certainly have been, to me anyway, breaking a promise that I had given. I was being no party to that.

The members of my team, knowing of the promises given, believing also in the concepts of the scheme and loyal to them gave full support that there would be no proselytization on any scheme ground or in any scheme building. So much so that when a certain Bishop arrived to visit Budu and asked if he could hold a service this was politely refused. The Bishop however was invited to go to the nearest longhouse and if the people so agreed, he could of course hold a service there. The Bishop was very angry. Returning to Kuching, he complained on the grounds that as Government money was being used, it was right and proper that a representative of a mission could hold a service at Budu. The Committee of Community Development supported our decision. Still not convinced, the Bishop appealed to London but again he received no support.

Many Christians have throughout the years visited Budu and indeed quite a number of priests and fathers from various denominations. They have been made very welcome. Each recognised that although no actual mission was represented, although there was no Church for any service of any denomination, a Christian work was going on. A people were being helped and they were being left alone to decide for themselves in the years to come as to whether Christianity would be accepted as a whole within the area.

This of course has always been the hope and there are signs that before many years have passed, the Budu people will accept Christianity as their religion. It will not however be piecemeal, a few here, a few there. When it comes, I think it will be complete or nearly complete. The boys who studied abroad and especially at Nairn, in Scotland, were given opportunities of a liberal education in all forms of Christian religions. Even now it is clear that those boys, now men, are having the influence which will in all probability produce this fundamental change. I would myself not be surprised if a new form of Christianity is developed, a form retaining that which has proved good in pure Dyak custom and interlacing in their own old customs, good Christian ethics.

Perhaps, therefore, a people will come to Christianity through their own beliefs and own volition. If not, let us not accede to the greatest of all wrongs and try to bribe a people to become Christian. Let example be the teacher and let the people follow what they believe to be right. Basically, the work at Budu and Entebai could be regarded as a Christian work in the sense that we, the members of the team, tried to inculcate Christian ethics although we represented no mission. Moral instruction took place daily but the teaching matter came mostly from actual incidents. For example in the early days, some trainees and older pupils, knowing who was detailed to go to Saratok, used to give money to the driver to buy what they wanted in Saratok.

This way they were saving approximately fifteen to twenty cents on every dollar purchase, this being the difference between the Saratok price and the price of the article at Budu. As we, the Europeans, made a particular point of never buying anything direct either from Kuching or Saratok, but only through the Budu stores, it was relatively easy to explain during the moral instruction lesson that those who bought direct, using shop transport, were actually cheating. It took several lessons however before we finally convinced everybody.

There is certainly no doubt in my own mind that I was neither opposed to Christianity nor any mission no matter its denomination. It was simply that the rules of the project forbade any prosyletization on any scheme ground or in any scheme building. As Principal of Batu Lintang, having as students a fair representation of the seven missions operating at that time in Sarawak I had learned in any case to be completely neutral. I could give no extra favours to the Seventh Day Adventists, nor the Methodists, nor the Borneo Evangelicals. As assistant principals I had a Roman Catholic priest as one, and a priest of the Anglican Faith as the other. This arrangement actually worked out very well and I remember no occasion when there was even a slight disagreement on general policy. They were excellent men and highly trained. Indeed to this day I look on them as very close friends in the real sense of the word.

In travelling to select students and listening to practice teaching, I met almost every father or priest, then in Sarawak. All without exception, were sincere and dedicated men although an odd one or two went astray. I am sure that it was their very sincerity, their very dedication which almost forced the missions to proselytize through schools. This was not so much their fault as the fault of their superiors at home. They were inadequately supplied with funds and much of their basic revenue for living, frugally as they did, came from ordinary school fees. Education was almost the only commodity the priests could sell to live. The touching devotion and loyalty of present day products from Mission schools to the priests and fathers who taught them in school makes very clear that a splendid job was done under very very difficult conditions.

Their knowledge of the people and the very district they lived in, made the priests or fathers the natural people from whom I could obtain the information I needed so much. At no time and nowhere was I made to feel an outsider. I was received hospitably and courteously anywhere I went. I can recall very many pleasant evenings discussing common problems with priests of all denominations. I am sure those very fathers and priests would be the first to uphold that I was certainly not anti-mission. I was quite well aware of their problems and they being the men they were, acknowledged mine in frankness and understanding. They realised, I am sure, that an honest sincere criticism of this or that in any school was based on purely professional experience.

The secular schools came in for equal, if not more, criticism. The Mission schools, as with the secular, had few if any trained teachers in the early days. Realising their own shortcomings as teachers and many of them in any case only taught because they could find no one else to do it, they welcomed wholeheartedly the prospect that trained teachers would one day become available. They were one and all co-operative and desirous of making their schools better.

I hope, therefore, I have laid to rest any doubts that I aligned myself with that body of people who condemned the work of the missions. I would be the last person to do so. I consider that it was a privilege to meet so many dedicated and sincere men and I would certainly go out of my way to meet once again those missionaries. They had to learn how not to run schools, even as I had to, and it is just as easy for me to be caught out by lip service to the principles of Community Development as the fathers were and possibly still are, by mere lip service to the ideals of Christianity.

That I could make a list of do's and don'ts is true. They would not be written to the fathers and priests who with no thought of personal comfort and under most difficult conditions give spiritual help to many who live in remote districts. My list would be meant for their superiors at home.

The Budu and Entebai Community Development Schemes were and are interesting experiments but it is much too early to draw broad conclusions. I just do not know that the purely secular teaching that went on over a period of ten years or so will give a permanent stability of wise and Christian action. One must be patient and wait to see what the second and third generations will do before a fruitful comparison can be made.

After all is said and done, the whole world is just a school of inquiry and the value of life lies, not in the length of days, but in the use we make of them. By holding very firmly to the promise I made to the Budu people, against often severe criticism, at least I have made it possible that some day an interesting and worthwhile study can be carried out by a social scientist. It would be a challenging study.

CHAPTER FIVE

Large streams from little fountains flow,
Tall oaks from little acorns grow.

THE DEVELOPMENT OF CO-OPERATIVES IN THE BUDU/ENTEBAI SCHEMES OF COMMUNITY DEVELOPMENT

It was of course imperative that I found someone whose main task would be the setting up and the administering of the co-operative trading and marketing ventures. There seemed no one suitable in Sarawak and, as I have already explained, I made up my mind to go home to Scotland to find if possible this someone.

I knew the kind of person I was seeking although I doubt if I could have described him to anyone. After interviewing sixty potential assistants to help me at Budu, I began to think that the kind of person I not only wanted but needed so badly, was just not around. At least there did not seem to be anybody who still felt the odd sense of adventure in going to Sarawak to live under hard conditions for what only amounted to a meagre living allowance. Then on a miserable night in February 1954, sitting round a more miserable fire in an hotel near Maybole, in walked Mr Thomas McBride, whom I had arranged to meet. I liked the look of him as soon as I saw him. Tall, fair-haired, slim, blue eyes, obviously healthy and intelligent looking. Over a cup of tea, we took the measure of each other. When I explained the kind of work, the kind of hard living conditions such as sleeping on floors, eating rice as a basic food, the meagre salary, the uncertainties, the difficult communications, the non-existent roads, the very remoteness of Budu, a three-day journey from Saratok and the nearest supply point, the kind of person the Dyak was and with whom he would be working, I saw that he was interested. I became certain that he was the man I wanted when in his questions, direct but polite, he was endeavouring to assess me as much as I was assessing him. Curiously enough, qualifications were the last thing we discussed. In Mac, as he has been called to this day, the basic essentials were there, a trained accountant, service as an engineer in transport under military service, a keen brain, unmarried, a zest for living and more important than all, a sincere desire to do something different. His innate honesty was apparent even at this first interview when he admitted quite frankly that he did not know whether he wanted to help an underdeveloped people. He gave the correct answer by saying that a lot would depend on the attitude of the people. However, I knew that if he were the man I thought him to be, he would quickly gain the respect of the Dyaks and knowing the Dyaks as I did, I knew that Mac would give to them a part of himself in this human service to help a people bridge the gap to progress.

As I myself was paying his passage to Sarawak in the first instance and

49

A Dyak climbs to his longhouse from the River

Thwaites

possibly might find myself paying his passage back if the Sarawak Government did not agree to his employment I had to be sure that he was the right type of person. I am sure Mac was quite well aware of my reasons for wanting to meet his mother and father, some of his friends and if possible anyone with whom he worked. This way seemed much more direct and decisive than writing to various people for a reference. Having met his mother, a charming motherly soul who was obviously going to miss Mac if he went to Sarawak, I was as certain as anyone could be that Mac was the right person and one who could play a full part in this, as yet a dream of helping a people. I was still more certain, having met his co-worker, that if Mac were still prepared to come with me I need not look further. Just as I had been given an opportunity to size Mac up from his home background, I kept the matter quite open till he himself had had the opportunity to size me up from my home background and from the people who knew me.

So final details were settled and by mid March, accompanied by Arthur Thwaites, we three set sail for Sarawak, each probably with unspoken qualms of the future in our minds. My only qualms were as to the reception both would receive from the Government of Sarawak since I had jumped, to put it mildly, quite a few fences to recruit them. The Crown Agents had not even been consulted and so in effect I had put myself above this authority. I knew I had been wilful but it was done with the complete acceptance that I would myself, from my own personal funds, stand the loss if necessary. To me it was essential to recruit the man or men I needed, the men who would have to live with each other for at least three years, men who would have little or no relaxation from work even on Sundays. I was not putting myself above Crown Agents, then solely responsible for all recruitment to a colony. I was just determined not to accept potential helpers chosen by paper qualifications. I was not without experience in selecting a particular man for a particular job. Apart from my own flying experience I had, during the war, commanded a flying training unit for just over a year. On my recommendations depended whether some forty lads, tested each week, would end up as pilots, bomb aimers, navigators or be returned redundant.

I was as confident as I could be that with Mac and Arthur helping me, the future of the project was at least now a good possibility. It was, as it turned out, a partnership that was to last fourteen years not three, and indeed although often separated by circumstances, a very strong bond still exists between us. How splendidly both Mac and Arthur adjusted themselves to the appalling conditions of living and work is a story in itself. Suffice to say that during the years, although we occasionally differed in small routine methods of approach to certain problems, never did we quarrel or have angry words together. Possibly because we were always busy with no time to let little hates become big ones. Nor from the outset did we actually live together and this was planned. We fed together or should I say we ate the cold rice together and when possible met in the evenings to cook a fried egg and chips. Each took it in turn to prepare something, even although more often than not, Arthur produced a burnt offering or caused a minor fire in the tiny room. Still we did not quarrel. Arthur, however, has always been regarded by both Mac and I as pure gold and blandly accepted our ribald comments.

Mac was only twenty-two and Arthur twenty-five. No words of mine could fittingly describe how splendidly each did their job. They became men in a few months, trusted completely by the people and myself alike. To this day that trust has not been broken by word or deed. When we all left Budu, as leave it we had to, I am sure Mac and Arthur left behind them a deep respect not only for themselves as individuals but for Europeans in general. At this stage it should be mentioned also, since it is to their lasting credit, that their attitudes to work, their ability to adapt themselves to hard conditions, young and all as they were, came to the notice of Mr A. Dickson, C.B.E., and because of it he was more than ever convinced that the young volunteer could make a contribution to helping the less fortunate in territories far from Britain. Mac and Arthur stand unique in that they were in fact the first two volunteers of this category. From it, as history tells us, the Voluntary Scheme of Service Overseas has grown from this mere two to more than two hundred a year, not to mention the Peace Corps and V.S.A. I doubt if Mac or Arthur actually realise the part their behaviour played in establishing such services.

To while away the time on board ship and because it was necessary even at the very beginning to inculcate that time was not on our side, for many reasons too complicated to discuss at this stage, Mac and Arthur began to learn the Dyak language. Thus it was possible that when both arrived at Budu they knew the essentials and very quickly became fluent. Indeed Mac is regarded now as an authority and is unsurpassed. Yes, both were apt pupils but more important it was possible to give them a fair briefing on Dyak customs and what they should do and not do, at least till they found their own feet.

As the ship neared Malaya and Port Swettenham as a port of call I began to realise the enormity of my "offence" in recruiting without prior permission. The matter of their reception in Kuching had to go well or not at all and so I made plans to leave them at Port Swettenham and fly to Kuching to see what kind of weather was to be expected. I vividly recall seeing Mac and Arthur standing close to the aircraft I was booked to fly on. In those days the airport at Kuala Lumpur was mostly grass and quite informal. By this time they also knew the chance I was taking, but I had assured them I would honour the provisional agreement I had signed with them. Nevertheless, neither by word nor deed, did either display what might have been a natural concern for their own future. After all I could have played the biggest practical joke on them by taking them out to Singapore, which was at least certain, but leaving them to find their own way back to Britain. No, as I watched them just before leaving I knew I had been given their trust and, because of it, I knew I too would have the courage to approach top officials and somehow clear a path for them to land. It had now become not a matter of mere money, although there was a considerable amount involved.

Using every minute of the five days grace I had won by flying on ahead, both Mac and Arthur were, if not cordially received (as many felt that this time I had gone too far and just could not believe that mere youngsters could do the job I would be asking them to do), received politely. Official contracts were drawn up and signed within a day and lingering only to introduce Mac and Arthur to some intimate friends in Kuching we set off for Budu.

We reached Saratok the following afternoon and were met by quite a number of people from Budu and other upriver places. Till now Mac and Arthur had been living under reasonably comfortable conditions. Now I know that Saratok, while attractive enough looking from the river and near approaches, was in fact dirty and unhygienic just behind the shop facades. I wondered how both would react to sleeping on dirty floors with probably rats running either over or beside the body and fulfilling normal functions of nature amid the hum of a hundred or so bluebottles disturbed from their wormy feast. I had warned them of course, but even so, to meet reality as it was, made them realise that all I had said was true. Being the lads they were I could virtually see them gritting their teeth and almost hear them say: "Well, we were told, but ...". I comforted them a little by telling them that although Budu was primitive and conditions were hard, it was clean and one could swim and bathe in the river beside our small huts which I had got ready. They brightened up considerably and were further heartened by the appearance of a very fine looking long boat, expertly driven by Empeni who greeted us with one of those wonderful open smiles which meant much more than words. Mac was tickled to death by the flag which Empeni, quite by his own volition, was flying at the back of the canoe, bright yellow background with the very distinctive Lion Rampant in bright red. Empeni, of course, in his enthusiasm to give us a welcome did not realise the significance of flying this flag and I was not surprised to receive a summons from the District Officer. He was, as I have said, an unusual District Officer and certainly without the sense of humour or tolerance one was accustomed to find in most District Officers. Empeni was the more difficult to pacify but smiled again when we raised a Union Jack at the stern.

The evening passed very pleasantly with Mac and Arthur buying this and that, which both knew would be needed. Little but important things such as soap, toothpaste, writing paper, stamps, pencils, pens, none of which could be found at Budu. After a meal of fried rice we lay down to sleep. We were all sufficiently tired not to bother much with the rats or other vermin. Such was to be the anodyne for most hardships in the coming months and, as it turned out, even for the next evening when by a series of unforeseen events both Mac and Arthur had to face probably their most gruelling and frightening journey.

Early next day we got aboard the canoe and travelled up river for about two hours. The river became shallower there and as it was fairly heavily laden all who could be spared, had now to walk.

Lium was once again our guide, a splendid Dyak, although getting up in years and one for whom I had the greatest respect and even affection. He took his time, realising that both Mac and Arthur would need all their energy if they were to arrive at Budu, some eight hours walk further on. Walk is not the right word since that implies a neat path or road. Our journey lay through almost deep jungle and Lium had from time to time to cut away overhanging branches. It was more a sliding, slipping, slithering, pulling journey rather than a walk. Even so, Mac and Arthur were coping spendidly and I had great hopes that we could make it without having an overnight stop somewhere. I was most anxious to arrive at Budu that day since I had promised the people that I would arrive on the 4th of April. I knew they would be expecting me and would have prepared food and a fitting reception for Mac and Arthur, all in Dyak custom.

We were held up however at Rh Bruang, a longhouse of some forty families, first because it would have been most impolite not to eat the food which they had prepared and still more impolite not to drink some of the "tuak" or Dyak wine which they also had prepared in readiness. The people in any case wanted to hear all the news which they knew I must have. This being Mac's and Arthur's first visit to any longhouse, it must have been quite a revelation and I am sure they must have wondered just what they had let themselves in for. By two o'clock, however, we were on our way again with the path getting steadily worse. Near Ng Budu we were met with bad news. The teacher I had left at Budu, a lad named Birai, a most loyal and devoted follower was, I knew, married. The news was that his wife had just died and please could I come to his longhouse. At the time I was so concerned and unhappy at the news and did not reckon the effect of the extra two hours journey on Mac and Arthur, we immediately set off on the detour. Lium said he knew a short cut. Shorter it was, but very very difficult and exhausting even to me; normally Dyaks follow the longer and less steep routes. Lium led us up hills and down hills and this during the hot part of the day, made the going very hard indeed. Mac and Arthur were beginning to tire. We reached Birai's house by five o'clock and paid our last respects to Birai's wife. This was all I could do and with a heavy heart, set off on the last leg. Mac and Arthur although feeling the journey by now, would not agree to following on the next day. It was plucky of them to wish to carry on with me and I did not force them to stay the night with Birai. It in any case would have been a strange introduction to the Dyaks, had they decided to spend their first night in a longhouse where a funeral was to take place. So we pressed on with Lium trying to make up for lost time since he was anxious to reach some shelter before darkness fell. The heavy going had ruined the sandshoes of both Mac and Arthur and as what was left of them was more a hindrance rather than a help, they both discarded their shoes and walked on stockinged feet. I had always travelled bare foot anyway, since with experience this is by far the best way.

I had always too, made a point of carrying my own haversack on my back, purely I think, because by doing so I identified myself with Dyak ways of living and incidentally made very clear that I was no District Officer on travel. Up till now both Mac and Arthur had also been carrying their own haversacks and being humanly young, had filled them to capacity with almost everything they thought they might need, rather like Boy Scouts. Lium and I persuaded them to give their bags to very willing and energetic Dyaks who accompanied us. This made the going easier but we still had an hour's journey ahead of us to the nearest longhouse, Rh Dasai, when darkness fell. This I thought was almost the stupidest thing I had ever done. Here were Mac and Arthur, young, energetic and healthy certainly, being thrown in to the deepest pool before learning how to swim. That they were still able to walk, or shall I say stagger into Rh Dasai at all, demonstrated that they had that certain something—real solid guts—so essential if they were to leave their mark at all. The people of Rh Dasai gave us a delightful welcome, plying Mac and Arthur with hot drinks and although desperately tired, both valiantly responded until they just dropped off to sleep sitting up. It was easy then for me to slip away for the last hour's journey and with a minute to spare I arrived at Rh Gelau on the date I had promised. There was of course no sleep that night at all. I was so exhilarated by coming home as it were, and seeing again all my old friends and the pupils whom I had been teaching the previous year, that all weariness dropped from me and I lasted the pace.

Next morning Mac and Arthur arrived none the worse for their gruelling experience of the day before. As we had much to do, even to get settled in, the day passed quickly as did all other days that were to follow. On the third day after our arrival at Budu, the canoe on which we had started the journey arrived and on it all our main stores and equipment although we found that half had had to be left at Ng. Budu owing to low water. Arthur immediately, still tired and all that he was, sorted out what medicine there was and began the work which was to absorb him for the next twelve years. I often wonder, had he known then just the trials and problems that were to face him from time to time, if he would choose to start again. I rather think so, but let's hope he will tell his own story.

Mac, knowing quite a bit about engines, immediately showed his worth by repairing two outboard motors. However, his specialist job was to establish the co-operative shop and as the Budu shop was scheduled to be opened within two weeks, he had therefore little time to spare. Four hundred members had each bought a ten dollar share. The Department of Co-operatives seemed helpless to assist with all the paper work involved. Forms were unobtainable in the quantities required. As the forms were so complicated and quite unintelligible to illiterate people and to a large extent ourselves, we shed no tears over this. Each form also took about twenty minutes to fill in, get signed and thrice witnessed. It all seemed a stupid waste of time to Mac and I couldn't have agreed more. So paper work was given a very low priority. Over this, there was much friction between the Department and ourselves. Nevertheless, convinced as Mac was, that the setting up of a supply chain was a more vital priority, the paper work apart from actual accounts for some time remained at a very low priority. It seemed enough that not only were the names of members known to everybody, but more important, the names of non members. It was simple enough to allocate share numbers on the spot at Budu. Confusion did occur, however, when the co-op. department, now anxious to help in the paper work, decided to go round each longhouse to obtain their be all and end all forms completed. This would have been a great help but being a little autocratic, they also allocated share numbers with no system at all of keeping numbers related to longhouses. Mac of course started tearing his hair a bit. Realising even then Mac's own ability to organise, I gave him full authority to carry on as he thought fit. After all, the store had to open, goods had to be brought up from Saratok, trainees had to be selected to run the shop. Prices had to be fixed, bearing in mind the cost of transport from Saratok, a system of accounting had to be devised to ensure that at the end of the year, Mac would know how much each member has bought. Times of opening had to be fixed. There could be no alteration in the timetable of opening since H.E. the Governor had been invited to open the project officially. Mind you, when he was invited, it was never expected that H.E. would accept, both because of the very arduous journey which he would have to undertake and because it was most unusual for a Governor to travel off the beaten track as it were. The Governor being the great man he was, decided to give the scheme the maximum support possible by being present himself at the opening ceremony. How well he played his part can be read elsewhere.

It is no wonder that with all the work which had to be done, neither Mac nor Arthur had time to wonder whether they were homesick or even whether they were hungry. I was equally busy organising the first adult education course and carrying on the Primary School, not to mention the administration of the project. It was all great fun though for, from the start, Mac and Arthur, gave the maximum help not only in their own specialty but wherever they were needed. We shared the teaching. We all helped to finish the buildings immediately needed. We cleared the hills and for an hour, morning and evening, we worked with the pupils and trainees, terracing the ground to be ready for more planting of such cash crops that were available, such as rubber, coffee, cocoa, tea, pineapple, fruit trees and oil palm. There was no time to be bored. We were alive, healthy and with a zest for living and we had plenty to do.

Somehow Mac got the shop organised. Goods started to appear on the shelves. Arthur's dispensary began to look like one. Order seemed to come from chaos and it began to look as if we could open on schedule. The Budu people were magnificent under their great leader, Tuai Rumah Gelau, helping in every aspect. Gelau died a few years ago but there was no man who was held in such high respect or who did so much to give the scheme a good start. He well deserved the honour bestowed on him in a memorable ceremony at Saratok, a few years before he died. I was always touched by the deep pride he held for his award and when important visitors came to see him, he would carefully unwrap it from reams and reams of tissue paper.

The opening ceremony is still a splendid memory of what can be achieved in a short time by a people determined to find a way of progress. Everything seemed to go as planned from the moment that H.E. the Governor, Sir Anthony Abel, quite informally and quite unexpectedly was seen wading across the river to the scheme site with his trouser legs rolled up and a big smile on his face. His journey to Budu had gone completely off schedule and the previous night he had had to spend in a tumbledown attic of a school that was in the process of being rebuilt at Ng. Budu some three hours walk down river. The very informality of his arrival put everyone at their ease and when he left two days later we all felt that an old friend had gone. His attitude, his spirit of confidence in the project made such an impact that to this day one only needs to recall his visit to obtain maximum effort.

Mac immediately got down to long term planning. As his decisions are vitally important they must be recorded briefly. He devised new forms and membership registers. The Co-operative Department now use them as standard. Members numbers were issued in blocks so that the proposed branch shops at Ng. Budu, Ng. Grenjang and Engkilili could very much more easily take over local control. Times of opening were fixed by A.G.M. since the trainees had to continue with their education, the shop was only opened one hour at mid-day and all day Saturday. This was opposed by the department but both Mac and I stood firm. It seemed inconceivable that from the meagre share capital, a full time employee should be paid and in any case there was no competent person available locally. To bring at this stage someone from a more educated area would defeat the whole object.

Staging posts were quickly organised and were just small huts where stores could be left until the water in the river justified a large canoe. More important than all, however, was that, even from the first few days of operation, it seemed that it would be necessary to obtain supplies from other than Saratok. The traders there at that time thought, and they were in a sense right, that the prices could be dictated by them. As we had to establish some independent supply route, so began the long association with Scottish General Products, the export department of Scottish Co-operatives. Nothing was too much trouble for those at Laidlaw Street, Glasgow, from bales of salt fish to bales of good cloth, cases of jam, and tins of sugar, sweets, biscuits and cheese, not to mention milk. Consignment after consignment arrived and to a smaller extent continues to this day. The traders soon realised that Mac was no fool and that they had the option of fair prices or complete by-pass. Now there is keen competition to get the trade to the remote parts and fair prices are arranged. Indeed Scottish General made a great contribution to the project, greater than they will ever realise and we consider we owe them much. Courtesy, long term credit, good marketable produce made their name a by-word at Budu and subsequently at all other nine centres which throughout the years were opened up.

Mac also by this time began training his own engine drivers, lads who could do more than just pull the starting cord. The trainees soon began to realise that engines were not just bits of this and that put together anyhow, but something that almost lived and which would last if they were given the care and attention they deserved. Both Mac and I hate to see engines roughly handled. Hitherto when we had received word that a canoe was stuck with something wrong with its engine, Mac had sent a rescue canoe down. This was both costly and unremunerative. He became firm, and rightly so that if an engine left Budu in good condition, then it had to come back that way. There would certainly be no more rescues. This worked remarkably well and trainees really got down to understanding engines and maintaining them. Mac's work is evident throughout many parts of Sarawak to this day. In the early days of Budu, it was quite usual to have one canoe a week sinking with a loss of as much as five hundred to a thousand dollars. Both Mac and I knew that this could not be allowed to go on and for a period, without thought to economy of loads, lads were trained to handle canoes over the many difficult parts of the rivers. Now we seldom even hear of a canoe sinking.

Soon, however, major problems arose. Once again the Co-operative Department was the cause. Naturally enough, when people brought in rubber sheets to sell we had bought them, giving the people a fair price. It was obvious both to Mac and myself that if rubber could be taken down in the canoes and goods brought back, a sound economy was assured. The Department wanted a completely separate co-operative. Only ten years later did the Department accept officially the multi-purpose stores which is now the main policy of the Department. Mac feeling justified and right in his approach had, with my consent, carried on buying the rubber sheeting.

After two years running, the Budu co-operative was well established and served as a training ground for the future expansion, cash sales had increased from a mere five hundred dollars per month to some five thousand dollars and were steadily rising. After five years and when the branch shops had been opened, sometimes we reached the dizzy heights of thirty thousand dollars each month. When one considers that all the goods had to be transported in canoes carrying around ten hundredweight, Mac was running each Friday some ten to twelve canoes. It all required careful organisation. Alun's launch would arrive at Engkilili on the Thursday. Large canoes were then despatched early Friday from Ng. Budu to Engkilili. Smaller canoes left Budu and Grenjang going as far as Ng. Budu which naturally became the supply centre for the upriver shops. There was an excitement and a challenge in all this and a tremendous satisfaction when on the Sunday morning we all left our branch shops and clinics to return to Budu where for a hectic hour or so, all cash was counted and entered in the main books. On the Sunday evenings we used to relax singing and dancing with the trainees.

A most important feature in the development of the co-operatives was in Mac's insistence that any expenditure was based on a percentage of revenue or turnover. Thus as it was essential to provide funds for training it was decided that 2 per cent of turnover was allocated to a training fund. In addition, as both Mac and I were determined that the trading and marketing side of the project would be only one branch of the project and not become the ruling authority, it was further decided that no co-operative stores within the scheme could own premises. Such premises as needed would be provided and built by the Progress Society and that 2 per cent of turnover would be allocated as rent, paid into the funds of the Committee of Progress. Both these vital decisions were opposed strongly by the Co-operative Department. We could never really understand the reason except perhaps that the Department did not relish working under the authority of the Committee of Progress. Such a policy as devised by Mac should have been hailed as a great step forward in the development of co-operatives, since, in effect, the Progress Society members were able to co-operate truly with the members of the trading and marketing society for the benefit of the whole area. For years the battle went on with members of the Department continually trying to change the estimates of income and expenditure. Each year when decisions had to be made regarding distribution of surpluses, the Department would try to allocate funds from surplus for building when time and time again the Department was reminded that by the bye-laws of the Progress Society it was impossible for any minor co-operatives to own buildings on any scheme ground. Fortunately the land had been gazetted as being owned by the Progress Society. We used to have considerable amusement at the expense of some of the members of the Department when, as necessity demanded, an extraordinary General Meeting had to be convened to ensure that members could and did decide by themselves as to how the surplus was divided or shared. Often of course we were criticised by the Department, who maintained that such decisions were our decisions. This was quite untrue. Throughout the adult education classes, Arthur, Mac and I gave to a considerable number of people basic knowledge. That we explained why the Progress Society should be the ruling power and not the actual Trading co-operative is true. This was our job. The people, however, made the final decisions. The people were well aware of the plans even then, to select and send for further training to Scotland, certain of the trainees. The people knew that money would be required for this part of the project. It seemed common sense to them as to Mac and me that funds had to be laid aside to help pay for this. It was common sense also to the people that 2 per cent of turnover was necessary to maintain buildings in good condition and provide for extensions under the Committee of Progress.

It seemed common sense also that there should be no expenditure based on a set figure, but only as a percentage of turnover. For example, the Co-operative Department continually asked that specific sums were estimated for the salary of the Secretary of the Co-operative at say $150 per month. This was opposed strongly on the grounds that to agree to do this might jeopardise the whole share capital. It is certain that this policy of limiting expenditure to a percentage of turnover is vital to the success of any co-operative. Indeed proof, if proof were needed, can be found on examination of the stability and present strength of the nine co-operatives opened up under the project. Those whose committees have adhered to this policy are still in a strong financial position. Those whose committees accepted the advice of the Department after the schemes were handed over to local control are fast eating into capital reserves accumulated over the years. Indeed three of them are likely to be forced to close.

By the fourth year, branches had been established down river, one at Ng. Budu some three hours walk from Budu, one at Ng. Grenjang also some three hours walk from Budu and one at Engkilili some two hours by canoe from Ng. Budu down river. It may be asked at this stage why it was thought necessary to establish Budu first, the difficult and the most remote. Surely, many people said, it would be much easier and more profitable to establish a base shop at Engkilili where the tide allowed a launch to bring fair loads daily from Saratok. There were several reasons for this policy of establishing the more remote first. First and foremost was that under the project it would be impossible to find money to buy the wood from saw mills near Saratok. As it was infinitely easier to take wood down river, sawn from trees in the jungle, it seemed sensible to establish the most remote place first. The question of supply routes had been solved temporarily by establishing more sheds at certain points. A second and probably more important reason lay in the fact that it was thought by both Mac and Arthur that if we could establish the more remote places like Budu as an example of what could be achieved, there would be little difficulty in setting up centres down river or in other places equally remote. Those who lived down river became jealous of what the people of Budu had and were determined to have as much in a shorter time. We are all convinced that, had the project started with a main base down river, the project would most likely never have been completed. Chiefly because the down river peoples, being closer to Saratok, did not feel the tremendous need for a dispensary or a shop or a school or even rubber gardens and other cash crops. Those people were only a few hours from Saratok and they would not, at the beginning, have been prepared to expend the energy necessary to set up local schemes, even though everything would be at their door step.

It must be admitted also that simple psychology, applied, proved to be right. It was known that the people of Budu were often sick, often hungry, that they had little in the form of cash crops to buy essential commodities such as milk and sugar. It was known that communications with Saratok were extremely difficult. Because of its very remoteness, the chances of obtaining good teachers for the school would be very small. So we thought that just as hungry man could find satisfaction in getting even a little, so the people of Budu would be probably more than willing to do things for themselves on the chance that that very little might be achieved.

As the years passed, even they expressed surprise at what had been achieved. They had a clinic and a dispensary at Ng. Budu run by Government and this itself repaid all the efforts since it was so much closer than Saratok. They could pay their taxes locally, their gun licences and buy ammunition. They could sell and buy mostly what they wanted at their shop across the river at prices which were at least controlled. They had at their doorstep a good school well equipped and staffed by trained teachers. They had about 4,000 high yielding rubber trees on scheme ground and each family had been given enough to plant some five acres and this belonged to themselves. They had in training abroad some twelve keen, well educated sons who were to return to help their own efforts. This gospel was carried far and wide. Areas without directed leadership and without funds began to do many things for themselves in the hopes that they would catch up with the people of Budu. Hardly a week passed but deputations from areas some distance away came to ask if we could help them as we had helped the people of Budu.

Whenever it was possible to set up other centres, the challenge was accepted even at the expense of the physical health of the team members. So by the fourth year and because we had senior trainees now to help, Arthur and I set off on a journey some twelve hours away to Entaih to begin the work of opening up the main Entebai river. Mac was left in charge of all centres on the Budu side. His work alone, with only occasional visits from Arthur and I is an epic of endurance, ability and conscientiousness.

Fortunately it was at this time that having approached about five thousand doctors to ask if any of them would come to help under almost the same conditions as Arthur and Mac, that I met Dr Ronald Lees and he agreed to join our team.

It is difficult, impossible really, to describe how splendidly Dr Lees, our Doc as he was soon called, worked as a member of the team. His own story can be read in the chapter dealing with medical coverage. In what time he had to spare, like Arthur, he interested himself in all aspects of the scheme, even to running a branch shop at Ng. Budu. Mac often adopted many of the ideas provided by Doc, the most important one being that the Ng. Budu branch could be developed to feed the two shops up river, one at Budu and one at Grenjang. Nothing was too much trouble for Doc. He became fluent in the language in just over two weeks by walking around with a notebook in his hand and studying at night. He thought nothing of walking some three hours to visit a sick patient even in the dark. He would carry out emergency operations under the most difficult conditions and go with his patient on the long uncomfortable journey to Kuching to ensure that his patient was properly hospitalised. All this and running a shop, not to mention his work outside setting up pig sties, terracing ground working alongside Dyaks and adding new buildings as they became needed. I have never ceased to marvel at my fortune in finding Dr Lees. He was with us for six years and I think would have stayed longer had plans been finalised and agreed on to extend the Budu type of Community Development.

Mac and Doc, as I have said, worked very closely together but Doc had often to leave the Budu site to help me at Entaih. Arthur, unfortunately, on one of his short holidays at home, was compelled to extend his leave to ensure that the tuberculosis symptoms were treated properly. Both Doc and Arthur knew that there was a considerable incidence of tuberculosis especially on the Entebai side and it seems certain that Arthur contracted the disease at Entaih. I personally am sure it was an old Dyak called Buja who gave it to him. Buja had a habit and still has to this day of talking into one's face. Arthur will never agree to this though.

We all tried to persuade Arthur to remain at home but this he would not do. Nevertheless we all learned a good lesson since after this episode and with Doc's insistence, we ate a lot better no matter the cost.

Just as on the Budu side, so on the Entebai side, the co-operative at Entaih, the most remote centre was established first. To this day it is probably the best and strongest. From Entaih, we went down the river and up another one, the Mujok, and there established a centre at Ng. Maong. When this was done we went up another river, the Kanowit and established a centre at Tappang Punggu. Then and then only did we establish our real base at Ng. Entebai. Like Ng. Budu it became the supply base for all four shops not only in goods but for all agricultural extension work, for materials to complete the full programme of development. The Entebai side had problems quite different to the Budu side, owing chiefly to the distance between each centre and the fact that travel between them was only possible by canoe. Paths there were, but only close to each centre serving locally placed longhouses.

Mac did as much on the Entebai side as he had done on the Budu side, although he visited only from time to time and especially when I myself was on short leave home. As time passed more and more trainees became proficient and could be left to do routine running. This hedge-hopping that came to pass from sheer necessity, was never planned but it had the great advantage of forcing us to leave centres under the control of a senior trainee, whether we liked it or not. There was just no other way. It was of course a tremendous strain on the small European team, consisting only of myself, Mac, Doc and Arthur. By this time also, Mac had opened up a centre at Kadup, reached by a three hour walk from Budu. Supplies however had to be brought up the main Julau river and could not come from Saratok. Kadup became Mac's special baby, probably because it was his from the very beginning. When he left it, it was not only in sound financial position but he had inculcated in the minds of the people a real desire for progress on a long term basis and not for immediate profit. That some of Mac's dreams about Kadup have not yet materialised is no fault of Mac's. There is still plenty of time and perhaps the people are right to go slower. That they have no option, this being the matter of the times in 1968, is not the fault of Mac, nor would I say the people who remember him with such affection.

Much more could be written and I hope very much that Mac, one day, might be persuaded to write up his own story with all the interesting details which only he could supply. Since this chapter, however, may help others doing similar work I am summarising the more important points and policies that almost one might say grew out of our own experiences.

I would list those points as follows:

1. Before any actual trading concern is set up, it would be necessary to establish an authority, such as the Progress Society, in sole control of the land and environment of the shop.

2. That care is taken to ensure that all concerned realise from the beginning that the trading and marketing co-operative is only one of the five main co-operative ventures under the project. The other four being, medical coverage, adult education, agricultural extension work, administration and of course schools for the young children.

3. That expenditure is calculated as a percentage of turnover and not a set amount. This ensures that even if the shop remains closed for one reason or another, there is no eating into share capital at all. When of course there are sufficient reserves the position is different.

4. That a source of supply of most commodities has to be arranged, further from the nearest supply to ensure fair prices.

5. That the co-operative shop which is nearest to main supplies becomes the supplier to the shops up river, but this only after the upriver shops have been established.

6. That a well planned trainee system is worked out to ensure that the managing secretary is both capable and trustworthy. This depending on the initial standard could well take some years. At Budu it was some seven years.

7. That such trainees should be indentured apprentices rather than haphazard selections.

8. That a sufficient surplus of trainees be trained to ensure that if there was a wastage, there would be no shortage. It also ensures that branch shops are more easily opened.

9. That, in the early days especially, times of opening be restricted to enable a good surplus to be built up. This avoids any question of full time salaries being paid out.

10. That agricultural extension work is emphasised in the immediate area of the co-operative shop. This ensures that cash crops are available as time passes and this in itself brings progress to the shop and through it, a higher standard of living so desired in the whole community.

There can be little doubt that so long as the co-operative trading and marketing side of Community Development is well controlled and properly supervised, the success of it can be assured. Reading through Mr McBride's statistical report, well over $80,000 were provided from surplus to help pay for the education of the selected trainees. At date of writing it is certain that at least the two main co-operative shops, one at Budu and one at Entaih, starting with only about $800 share capital, have assets totalling around $15,000. Considerable help is still given by those co-operative shops to help pay for higher education in Secondary Schools. Without such help it would not be possible for them to carry on with their education. Above all, such co-operatives ensure that trading and marketing is in the hands of the local people and by virtue of their own efforts, ensure that no monopolies are possible locally. When communications and roads are well established between the remote areas and the urban, the need of co-operatives will diminish except perhaps in some large scale cash crop venture in a particular area. I would expect also that as time passes, private enterprise will make the running of the co-operatives too competitive but having served the need, this is not regression but merely an expected result from education. I think that one should try to understand, not just deplore, that emerging peoples must also find out for themselves that to be avaricious does not necessarily bring either happiness nor the hoped for riches.

The Manang or Dyak Doctor examining the " Heart " of a pig

CHAPTER SIX

MEDICAL COVERAGE IN COMMUNITY DEVELOPMENT

Although Batu Lintang was just a few miles from Kuching and a hospital, I had not been Principal long before I recognised the need to have within our own compound, and run by ourselves, a kind of sick quarters. This consisted of just a large room with six beds and a glass cupboard to keep the various simple medicines and remedies that were from time to time needed.

It was basically run by the students themselves with a sick quarters committee, responsible for cleanliness, taking temperatures, giving medicine at the stated times and taking to the sick such food as was advised. While Father Galvin, my Assistant Principal, was usually available to help me the ultimate responsibility was mine. This being so I began to become interested in diagnosing and studying simple treatments for the easily recognised diseases. At the beginning I was often in doubt and when any of the students were sick I was often to be found in the evenings and during the night, taking the temperatures and trying to determine just what was wrong with the patients. Medical services at that time, even in Kuching, were inadequate to serve demand. The hard pressed doctors could do no more than look after the hospital and although I knew I could always telephone for an ambulance in an emergency, I was loath to do so, for just what might turn out to be a simple fever. Over the years my confidence increased as well as my knowledge. I came to accept that high temperatures of even 105 degrees did not mean that the student was about to die. I came to accept that the students could have a temperature of 105 degrees one day and be up and running about the next. It was quite amazing.

Naturally enough also, when I travelled in the remote regions to recruit Dyaks to be trained as teachers, I always took with me a small supply of medicine. It was not long, however, before I came to the conclusion that I knew very little indeed and that until I did know more, then I would be wiser to confine myself to aspirin and stomach powder only. It was not long before I decided that much more was needed than just a kind of first aid box. In almost every longhouse there was evidence of virulent malaria requiring probably hospitalisation, or certainly out-patient attendance, before there was any chance of cures being effected. While temporary relief could be given for dysentery using sulpha drugs, it was clear that most suffered from amoebic dysentry requiring a course of injections for cure. Almost every child and adult suffered from worm infestation to a greater or less degree. Even then, there seemed little point in treating for worms except in extreme cases. Their very way of life and sanitation was such that the giving of worm powders was almost a waste of time and would only delay the day for the problem to be tackled basically by sunk pit latrines and more hygienic approach to living in the longhouse which is so much part of Dyak life.

It was heartrending to be asked to help a mother giving birth to child. When the pains became severe, it was quite usual for the grandmother to assist by either jumping on the mother's stomach or by sitting on it to force the child out. When this had been accomplished, the mother was then tied in a sitting up position to a stake and behind her a large fire was started and for almost fifteen days, there would the mother be, drying her womb. More often than not, third degree burns were a result of their efforts to dry the womb quickly.

Old men would invariably be found lying incapacitated in odd corners and on being asked to help cure them I would find on examination advanced suppurating ulcers on their legs and feet. On questioning them, such virulent ulcers seemed just to have started from simple wounds which if properly treated at the time, would have healed up within a week or so. Only hospitalisation could help in those cases since one injection of penicillin would have done more harm than good in the end. They were strangely reluctant to take their sick to hospital, partly because there was no money but I also think because they had the deep rooted fear that once they were unable to walk they would die in any case, and this being apparently inevitable, they preferred to die in their own longhouse where at least they were sure of being properly buried. They didn't appear to fear death so much as being wrongly buried and buried without the intimate personal possessions needed for their journey after death.

I am sure that it was when I saw so many children sick, their lithe and lovely bodies wracked in pain and sweat pouring from them, that I was determined something more had to be done than merely to provide hospitals in urban areas and more especially since those hospitals were so far away in time and money that they were not providing even a minimum of medical coverage in Dyak territories. I am sure too that, although basically the reason for my going to Budu in the first place was to teach, I knew I would inevitably be involved with the sick people. This I did not fear, but I did fear that what knowledge I had would be quite unable to meet the many situations that would develop from time to time.

Nevertheless, having seen a great deal in my travels, at least I realised what I had to learn before going off into the interior on my own and I knew that I would require not just a kind of first aid box but a goodly supply of drugs, syringes and other simple medical equipment. Despite, therefore, the shortage of time and with the help of the Director of Medical Services I was allowed to work in the main dispensary in Kuching for several weeks, studying and becoming familiar with the more advanced treatments. Having done this to the satisfaction of my teacher, a very fine and painstaking Chinese nurse, I was given all the drugs that I asked for. I felt very grateful that I was to be trusted but I did smile when the Director made clear that probably out of a hundred patients I would cure about ninety and kill the other ten. He returned my smile when I replied that I thought that those ten would die in any case whether I gave them any medicine or not so the balance would still be in my favour by doing what I could. He was a very fine man and indeed it was not his fault that more was not being done for the remoter peoples.

So on the launch that took me to Saratok on the memorable morning of 1st January 1953 I had all that I needed and certainly all that I knew I could use with such knowledge as I then possessed. It was some weeks, however, after my arrival at Budu, that I allowed to be known that I had medicine with me and even then I said that it was for the school children only. My first concern was for the pupils, however much my services were needed for the adults in the longhouses. On this I was adamant since not only was I fully occupied teaching in school every day and most evenings, I was far from deciding just how much I should help. Knowing a little of the principles behind Community Development, I did realise even then, that no matter the need it would be quite wrong to start anything that could not carry on when the time came for me to leave them. It seemed wrong too not to give such help as I could when I was there. I was well aware that in having medicine and being reasonably confident that I could effect some cures and certainly be able to stitch up severe wounds and help in simple fractures, I had the means for creating the stimulus so essential in any work of Community Development. Through giving some medical help, I was reasonably sure that a human contact would be made, and a contact that would bring me very close to the people. A great deal, however, depended on just how this help was to be given.

After much soul searching and talking things over with Empeni, the one and only person I could discuss anything with since my knowledge of Dyak had not reached conversation level, I decided to make a beginning. Calling the people of the near-by longhouse to have a meeting with me one Saturday I then told them I wanted to help any who were sick. I hastily pointed out, however, that my first duty was to the school and that only on Saturdays and Sundays would I do this, except for treatment of severe wounds and broken bones. As I felt strongly that the people even then had to learn and realise that medicine just did not fall from the skies, but had to be bought and paid for, anyone wishing me to treat them would have to bring a cup of rice or its equivalent in paddi or vegetables. No one however was ever turned away if by any chance the cup of rice was not brought. To prevent such forgetfulness becoming a habit, Empeni always made a great show of listing not only those who paid but those who did not. This moral pressure was enough to ensure that almost all rice debts were paid in due course. That the cured patient would possibly travel some two hours just to pay the cup of rice gave me considerable confidence in my curative ability and an ever increasing faith in the simple honesty of the average Dyak. Empeni was not so easily impressed and he used to tell me with a wry smile that the average Dyak was a bit chary of paying for something before he was sure it was worth it. I felt he was probably right, especially as invariably the cured patient would bring two cups of rice, saying very naively that he thought I should give him another dose so that he could take it home with him and be ready to cure his sickness when it returned. It was very easy to oblige if on looking up the book in which I kept accounts of all medicine given and when, that the patient had been cured of a simple stomach trouble with stomach pills. It was quite a different story when I saw that to please him, I would have to give him one of my three syringes and a phial of penicillin. So long as I returned his extra cup of rice, all was well and he accepted philosophically my negative reply and with a gleam of amusement in his eyes he would just say that of course he understood but that he thought it best to ask, to save me future trouble. This kind of patient was welcome enough in the mornings when I was fresh but if he happened to be about the ninetieth that day, I must confess I was a bit brusque.

The very numbers, however, that were now beginning to appear each Saturday and Sunday presented problems of some magnitude. My stock of medicine, adequate enough for a reasonable number, was fast being used up and I had to think of a way of restocking. In this I didn't need to worry as I found out. I had, according to private arrangement, kept the Director of Medical Services supplied with reports and incidence of disease and he made sure that I received all that I wanted. My humanities nevertheless became involved when soon it was obvious that many people who had walked some three hours were also having to wait their turn. This resulted in their having no food at all during the day. This problem was solved temporarily by arranging for one of the school children to cook the very rice that the patient had brought to pay for medicine. I could not help smiling and it was some time before I could get the Dyaks to agree that those who came from afar had preference over those who came from nearby. Gradually, however, this became an accepted pattern and the feeding problem resolved itself.

It soon became obvious that to cope at all I would need help. This was almost fortunate in that this necessity sowed the seeds of the pattern that was to play such an important part when Arthur joined me a year later and even when Doc arrived to help. In ones and twos I selected some of the older pupils and slowly but systematically trained them to be able at least to give out the medicine and to explain to the patient just what he had to do with it. As time passed, some like Chundie and Rabing who later, much later, went to London to train as nurses, were taught to give injections.

This was a great step forward and the weekend dispensary used to be completed by mid-day Sunday, enabling us all to relax for a few hours by swimming in the river or fishing. Those were happy hours and through them a bond of friendship grew between myself, as teacher, and the pupils. I marvelled that young lads, so full of fun and with few inhibitions, could so quickly become serious if the need arose. On those river expeditions, not for them the easy route, but the difficult and often dangerous, scrambling up through the cascading waterfalls and leaping from one mighty boulder to another. Their ages at that time could only have been about thirteen at the most and yet they had proved they could take and accept responsibilities even in a dispensary. I think their greatest charm lay in their intuitive acceptance that there was a time that they could play with their teacher as one of themselves, yet in a moment become the disciplined pupil in formal schooling. I was never actually conscious of instilling this automatic obedience to authority and it seemed to me even then a self imposed discipline which could stand the test of time and so ensure that in due course their own leaders would emerge to take over from me.

That they all enjoyed working in the dispensary was obvious by the keenness displayed when I had need of volunteers. As I was careful only to select senior pupils, the very young and junior lads studied all the more. Perhaps too they all realised that learning to read and write was not an end in itself but a stepping stone to true knowledge. As time passed their confidence grew even as mine did.

In the early days it was quite common for the patient after he had stated his ills and aches to demand almost that he be cured by an injection and not as he said by useless pills. The pills, he said, were not strong enough and only an injection would be of any use. This attitude had arisen from the accounts of the few who had managed to be admitted to a hospital. They had returned with miraculous stories of being cured by the doctor just injecting what looked like water into their arms. They were quite unwilling to accept that their particular form of ailment was better treated with an ointment or pills. In vain I used to explain that some illnesses were better treated with such pills and it was often obvious that they were just not prepared to believe me. However I was equally determined that I would be no party to curing people by giving them injections, and to keep them happy give them an injection of distilled water, a practice that I knew was quite common in some urban dispensaries. Psychological cures were, I knew, an accepted method of medical treatment but I felt it was a form of cheating. In any case even after a short period I recognised that many of their ailments were caused by sheer unhygienic living and that the sooner I made a start on a preventative approach to disease the better.

Fortunately, my understanding of the Dyak language had vastly improved and although it took much longer I often managed to explain to them just why they had become sick and just how they themselves could prevent a return of the sickness. This way I felt that I was actually making a more lasting contribution to aid them to look after themselves better. I knew too that as time passed more and more people would learn the causes of disease and gradually take steps to improve their living conditions. By inviting those who asked for injections to choose for themselves any one out of the dozen different varieties laid out neatly on a table, they quickly learned to accept what treatment was given, be it pills, ointment, or injections, or quite often just advice on what to eat and how to cook what they had to eat.

Of this I am certain, that it was from my own experiences during those weekend dispensaries throughout the first year, working alone, I became convinced that if ever I actually became involved in a planned scheme of community development, adult education would have a very high priority. It must also be of a type that would make a real and permanent impact on the area as a whole and not just a veneer of literacy. It seemed much more essential that underdeveloped peoples required basic knowledge in how to prevent disease rather than how to cure disease. Teaching them to read and write was certainly going to be far down the list of priorities, until at least they had been taught the rudiments of clean living, proper sanitation, how to cook better, how to grow vegetables, how to plant the various fruit trees, the fruits of which would in themselves prevent much of the common diseases, some of the simple sciences, a little elementary geography, what food to give to the very young babies after weaning, pre-natal and anti-natal care, animal husbandry, rearing and looking after hens properly to ensure a greater supply of eggs and protein, the causes of beri beri and how to cure it by not eating too highly polished rice, first aid and home treatments and above all more enlightened and temperate drinking habits. It seemed certain that many who suffered from various kinds of stomach ulcers had brought the suffering on themselves by drinking a cheap and immature form of arak or other alcoholic drink.

How fortunate, as I look back over the years, that Mac and Arthur did not arrive at Budu with me. Had they done so it is certain that Arthur would have confined himself to spending all his time in a dispensary treating the sick and Mac, no doubt, would have built up a chain of co-operativee stores, while I would have remained in the classroom. Each would have become just an entity, totally and completely involved in his own little world and possibly quite oblivious to the real and fundamental needs in planned community development.

Instead, when the scheme eventually began the following May, we began as a team, with each of us involved as much as was practicable in the other's main work. I had myself proved that young lads could play a very useful part in the dispensary and because of this the whole concept of in-field training, parallel to academic learning, was born. More important still, it was possible through this in-field training to assess aptitude and avoid waste of trainees potential. I was certain that if young lads could assist capably in a dispensary they could prove equally useful in agricultural extension work, in co-operative trading and marketing, in routine administration, in teaching the younger classes, in the maintenance and handling of engines and in helping to teach adults. The only problem was going to be organisation but, with thought, I was sure that difficulties could be overcome.

Busy and all as I was during this first year, subconsciously I must have been planning the project and the whole pattern of training. It seemed only a question of obtaining the right kind of professional help with medical services, agriculture, co-operative trading and marketing, teaching and administration. If this help could be found, the aim would obviously be to have three parallel streams of learning at the main community development centre. The very young, who in time would feed the more advanced stream of pupils already engaged part time or apprenticed to medical work, agriculture, co-operative development, administration or maintenance of engines, and the adult education stream. That this adult stream was vitally important need hardly be mentioned. It must in effect be the spearhead of attack and development at the village or longhouse level, thus enabling parallel progress to begin within the area of the scheme. If the proper emphasis and impact could be obtained with the twenty-five to thirty-five age group, by the time products from normal schooling emerged those products should find the beginnings at least of an improved form of living standards. If these products during their schooling were given the right attitudes to work coupled with knowledge that would be useful and productive in agriculture, medicine and co-operative development, I felt that the conditions for true development would be laid. At this time of course it was all theoretical but at least I had formed broad plans and time alone could only tell whether such plans were to be just dreams or actualities.

Generally speaking, I think it could be said that over the fifteen years since the project began at Budu and subsequently at nine other centres, there has been a steady although gradual improvement in the standards of living in those areas. It is true that the average Dyak seems to feel he is no better off than he was but he will smile when he is asked to compare what he had fifteen years ago with what he has now. He will almost grudgingly admit that he does own an outboard engine and that in his little bilek he has a radio, a bed, a table, a few chairs and possibly a cupboard to keep all the clothes he didn't have fifteen years ago. If asked whether his food is better than he had he will agree that it is but add that it is not enough. The actual money in cash that he possesses today is possibly less than what he had fifteen years ago but he has not reached the stage in his own development to assess the difference between need and want. I believe that it is almost necessary for anyone, and more so the developing Dyak, to go through this phase of buying things that he wants but does not actually need before he finally reaches the stage when he will be able to plan for the future and model his way of life accordingly. Underdeveloped peoples must be allowed to pass through a stage of development even as our own youth are allowed. The young generation from an advanced civilisation almost without exception spend their first salaries on things that they want but do not really need. Maturity comes in due course and in this maturity they begin to plan, using their money to buy essentials and saving the balance for the kind of living that they decide on. That such maturity comes over a period of a few years with the young from a well developed civilisation does not mean that one should expect the young from an emerging civilisation to mature at the same speed. On the contrary I am of the opinion that a whole generation must be born before the second stage of development becomes apparent, if only for the one important reason that the environment of the more developed is quite different to the environmentt of the underdeveloped.

It is of course very difficult, if not impossible, to measure progress. What yardstick have we to use? The material, the spiritual, the incidence of crime, the extent of selfishness or unselfishness, the interest that is taken in local and countrywide government, the number of children at school in comparison to fifteen years ago, the increase of population, the incidence of disease, the difference in the buying potential, the cash economy, the extent that new customs have replaced the old ones or even the number of converts to Christianity. Basically, progress comes by and from the will of any people, be they in an advanced or backward stage. By helping the latter to set up schools, by creating a better if not perfect medical coverage, by initiating agricultural and cash crop improvements, by setting up co-operative marketing and trading facilities, and in ensuring a means by which those very people can play a part in their own government, allows at any rate that the will of the people can emerge, should they so feel inclined to make the effort. Community Development using help from outside must stop somewhere for at least a period of time, if only to assess their own self determination which is the sole ingredient to progress.

But I seem to be digressing.

To return to the purely medical aspects, it was not long before I was faced with the problem of the Dyak Doctor or "Manang" as he is called by the people. Fortunately I knew that the Dyak believed that all sickness was caused by the advent of a spirit which one might say resided in the sick person's body. The body in effect was just the medium through which the evil or bad spirit could make itself evident. Being such, obviously to the Dyak the only way to cure sickness was to engage the service of the Manang to exorcise this spirit. I had myself been present at several "gawai darah", the name for the ceremony of exorcision of the evil spirit. I had also witnessed several almost miraculous cures and it was not surprising that the Dyak had every faith in the Manang. The patient was always made as comfortable as possible and was usually surrounded by relations, who were always ready to help force the evil spirit from the sick body either by loud incantations to their Gods or by purely physical means from gentle stroking of the body to rhythmic beating of it by the hand of the relation. The Manang seemed only concerned in ensuring that the immediate environment of the patient was cleared of all possible spirits. Depending on how serious the illness was, so depended the nature of the ceremonies performed by the Manang. It varied from the very simple to the very complicated, spread over a whole long night till dawn when a pig was usually slaughtered to enable what the Dyaks refer to as the "heart" (but which is actually the liver) of the pig to be examined. If the patient had survived the night, all the wise men could from the manifestations seen in the "heart" tell whether the patient would now get well or if the Gods decreed that death was inevitable. It seemed to me that it was in effect a custom whereby the responsibility, or the task of informing the relations of the patient that death was imminent, was being shared. I was always fascinated as I sat and watched the plate on which the "heart" was carefully laid out, being passed from hand to hand. I tried to deduce from their faces just what their decision would be. When I too was handed the plate (and courtesy demanded this since I was considered a wise man) I felt all eyes upon me and took rather longer than they had done with my examination. Nothing was ever said and there appeared to be no discussion at all. When all who should examine the "heart" had examined it, there seemed to be no single decision but somehow everybody knew whether the heart was good or bad. If it were pronounced good the patient would live, if bad the patient would die. I was always strangely moved at this finality and although I had seen just a "heart" with no apparent manifestations displayed, I always felt in spiritual agreement with the decision. I could never explain this feeling, even to myself. Although I had mental reservations on medical grounds of the effect on the patient of the stifling atmosphere and inevitable lack of air, coupled with the beating of gongs to keep the evil spirits at bay, I never felt I had the right to advise the Dyaks to cease such customs. Nor did I, and I believe Arthur and Doc felt the same way. It is true, however, that I did feel peeved when I observed that choice morsels of food were carefully put together and hung up to appease the Gods, or when the patient was brought to me for treatment after all other hope had been given up. Nevertheless, I did what was possible but I do not recall a case that survived after the wise men had pronounced that the "heart" of the pig was bad. Possibly I was equally under the spell of inevitability and equally prepared to accept that the patient would die.

One good result from this attitude or philosophy was that no friction developed between myself and the Dyak Manang and I think this was fortunate. It was even justifiable that I made a point that good relations continued since at this stage, the Manang, having considerable power spiritually, could have advised the people to have nothing to do with any proposals towards progress. By the time Arthur arrived and Doc, the die had been cast and when both performed miraculous cures against all omens, this rather tended to increase their Dyak determination towards progress. Both Arthur and Doc treated the Manang with great respect and so far as I know no ill feeling ever developed.

While I could relate many interesting incidents, I am only concerned in this book to indicate that it was from my first year's work that the pattern of medical coverage and training was laid down. From Arthur's point of view and Doc's, medically it was in many ways wrong. A balance, however, had to be maintained between training, preventative and curative. Both Arthur and Doc realised as I did, that if their professional services were used full time on curative, there would be little long-term improvements from this approach. Both, I think, also realised that economically it would be a very long time before an everyday medical coverage would be possible. They knew my ultimate aim, in that I was striving with every means at my disposal to ensure that the medical services to be provided permanently could be paid by locally imposed taxes assisted with profits from the co-operative trading and marketing projects. It was for this reason that, generally, dispensaries functioned fully only when the shop was open. As it was usually possible to open the shops for a short period at mid-day, so it was possible for Arthur and Doc to treat urgent and emergency cases. The people themselves, since they had heard it so often from me, did understand that schooling and training had to go on. That other services, such as being able to pay gun licences and Local Government taxes, buy ammunition, register births and deaths, were available was an added incentive to come for treatment on the Friday afternoons, Saturday and Sunday mornings. As the sick had usually to be brought in canoes, this enabled them also to buy the heavier goods required as, for example, tins of paraffin.

I am not trying to justify this restricted medical coverage, available only when shops were opened. It just seemed essential to prepare for the day when we, the Europeans, had to leave. Had I known that Government would in the course of time take over and run the two main dispensaries at Ng. Budu and Entebai, my policy would have been different. This was unforeseeable and actually not expected. It was hard to imagine that funds would ever be available, however desirable, for government to consider providing dispensary services in such remote places. Possibly proven demand forced it as indeed it forced also the establishment of a maternity clinic at Ng. Budu and Entebai.

Nor must it be forgotten that the entire in-field training in all the various branches of development, agriculture, medicine, administration, teaching, trading and marketing and engine maintenance, depended on the important fact that the trainees were available during main opening times when normal school was suspended. It would have been literally impossible to raise the standard academically, of the trainees, had the rules of opening not been strictly enforced. Arthur and Doc being fully aware of what was at stake, accepted the pattern with certain reservations, even though medically they did not subscribe to it.

Not much more need be said by me except that immediately following this account is Arthur's own personal narrative of his years of service in the Budu, Entebai and Iban Team Projects. Following Arthur's is Doc's own account. I have altered nothing and each is, to me anyway, a fascinating story, in fact almost two completely separate stories with different emphasis. To read Arthur's without Doc's would be rather like having porridge without cream and to read Doc's without Arthur's would be the cream without the porridge. Neither, however, has as much as hinted, far less stated, the tremendous difficulties that they had to work under. As I look back, I realise that the physical strain, the effort asked from them and given without thought for themselves, marks both Arthur and Doc as two men whose example and unique contribution to mankind leaves behind a legend which will grow as time passes and in itself may be the stimulus for future progress.

Written by Dr Lees

The medical side of the Budu Development Scheme was, in many ways, the easiest to work in and, certainly, the most appreciated.

This was because we tended, in the beginning, to tailor the services to what the local people asked for and, almost, expected. The first medical aid in the area was provided by Mr Wilson, in response to the obvious needs of the people living near his school at Budu. Their wish to avail themselves of modern medical methods was stimulated by the clear-cut and dramatic curative properties of antibiotics, mainly Penicillin, in the treatment of the many examples of sepsis to be found in any longhouse, and was reinforced, at a later date, by a campaign for the injection of Penicillin, as a single large dose, to every person living in the area of the scheme. This was carried out primarily to eradicate the Yaws which was thought to be prevalent and (although I have considerable doubts as to the correctness of the theory of the prevalence, having found only minimal evidence of the disease in other Penicillin-less areas) it was certainly a popular measure.

It is difficult to provide a balanced opinion based on any significant statistics as to any improvement in health from before the start of the scheme, and due to the services being provided by the scheme, or as to whether any improvement found was due mainly to our scheme or to more general changes, e.g. economic, educational, in the country. It was equally difficult to change the pattern of services in the medical field being provided before I arrived.

The original work in the medical field was done from the dispensary at Budu which was opened at regular times through the week, but where also emergencies could be treated at any time and from which journeys to neighbouring longhouses were made on request. This, in addition, of course, to the full range of other duties of any Community Development worker including the teaching of adults and school children about health and hygiene. Later, other dispensaries were opened and these were visited in rotation by the medical team which began to spend more time travelling to and from these far flung dispensaries, usually on foot, sometimes, rather more easily, by canoe. Visits to longhouses to see a single patient had to be cut down as the distances increased—I well remember spending one very long night stumbling through the moonlit forests to a house many miles off, and, although one never found such calls to be frivolous, usually it was possible and more efficient to get the patient to come to the dispensary. This, later, became accepted practice and one remembers a tiny girl carried overland—a two day journey—with an accidental perforation of her abdomen and a woman carried a similar distance suffering from a cerebral haemorrhage. Of course, only those who had stout-hearted friends could arrange to get themselves transported thus for treatment and this considerably influenced the kinds of cases seen. Sometimes, the dispensaries seemed to be full of women from the next door longhouse, mainly with rather minor complaints, while one hour or so's journey away one could, probably, find considerable disease and disability. Another factor was that even in the area visited there were sometimes people who, not having helped in the establishing of the scheme, felt barred from getting help from the scheme, although help was, in fact, never refused for this reason.

Even as the scheme expanded its sphere of influence, however, the medical aid provided, no matter how inadequate, was still basically "general practice" orientated in that it was a very personal thing between the Community Development Personnel and a relatively small group of people, usually well known to him, and the problems were seen as problems of those individuals and not so much as problems concerning public health or statistics or any "wider view". This tendency of the staff to be so much involved in, and associated with, the local people's problems and aspirations was, of course, a characteristic of the scheme and, along with the fact that Budu was seen to be providing educational and vocational opportunities at least as good as those in nearby towns, produced within the scheme an independent, indeed almost insular, attitude and led to the possibility of training local boys and girls to work within the area, e.g. in the dispensaries, despite the temptations to leave the area; temptations which are more usually intensified by the arrival of outside influences in a primitive society.

In general, however, the attack by the scheme on disease patterns— previously completely unaltered by conventional Medical Department methods—while essential in the early stages, hugely appreciated by all and very effective as an inducement to those who were hesitating to join the scheme and thereby missing many other benefits, was undoubtedly localised, transient, and certainly not capable of being duplicated in other areas of Sarawak unless the Government was prepared to agree to the continuation of the training and use of trainees for these other areas, with the need for a larger medical establishment also. In this respect we were disappointed when the Government decided not to continue the Travelling Doctor Service in the 2nd Division and not to let us extend our training activities to other areas and other races in Sarawak.

We found that this training of local youngsters to become assistants in the dispensaries, in the adult teaching courses, in mass immunisation schemes, proved extremely successful. I was given some of the best of the trainees, indeed I sometimes wondered if our "Med. Dept." was not being rather too well provided for in this respect at the expense of some other equally important, but possibly less glamorous, departments, e.g. Agriculture. The result in any case was that a group was produced, hardened to the rigorous work involved in almost continual travel from longhouse to longhouse, capable of explaining the health visitor's advice in the form most easily understood by the local folk, able to cope with very simple treatments and simple drugs, to stitch wounds and give first-aid in the many situations where no other help was at hand. From this group, we had, by further training and after they had proved themselves in the field, one doctor (M.B., Ch.B.), two nurses (S.R.N.), one radiographer (M.S.R.), several midwives and many more who will I hope, be going on now to further training. Even those trainees who did not proceed to take any kind of formal career, on returning to their longhouses, took practical knowledge of a kind that can only be of the greatest benefit to themselves and their neighbours.

This seemed to us a much better system for producing medical assistants—ulu dressers—call them what you will—than the conventional one of training a man (usually town bred) in a hospital and then eventually sending him to up-country dispensaries where he might or might not be able to withstand the strains inherent in such a situation.

To illustrate the kind of medical work being done, I came across a figure of 344 patients in one week at three widely separated dispensaries in 1958 (the exact week was not recorded) and that total was reported as being made up of, roughly, children 25 per cent, "antenatal visits" 10 per cent, and tuberculosis 10 per cent, the rest "various".

The majority of cases presenting were from a great variety of conditions mostly of the kind seen in General Practice in any country. Epidemics of various types occurred affecting children especially. There were outbreaks of flu', sometimes associated with pneumonia, measles, chickenpox, diphtheria. Most of these responded well to the usual therapies—the diphtheria organism was very sensitive to Penicillin, but, although this epidemic occurred in a longhouse only about two hours journey from Budu, the disease had caused two deaths before we heard of the outbreak.

An epidemic of cholera which occurred in the urban areas of Sarawak, e.g. Kuching, did not spread to our area possibly for geographical reasons, but we carried out a prophylactic mass immunisation scheme when, with the help of our trainees, a large population was given protection within a short time.

Injuries of various kinds frequently presented problems. Most commonly these were slashes caused by the jungle knives (duku) used so universally. These cuts, usually involving the lower limb, healed well if sutured within the first 24 hours, whether by medical staff or trainee, but, if unattended, became, after that time, almost always septic. Other traumatic episodes produced crushing injuries from tree-felling operations, an extremely dangerous business; injuries incurred in the course of quarrels, usually at cock-fights; and twice gunshot wounds, which may or may not have been accidental. I was called to one case of murder and spent an uncomfortable night in that longhouse where the murderer was, and whose identity everyone except myself, knew. The police arrived the next day after I had departed, for once having no patient.

One boy fractured both femurs after a fall from a tree. His father stood patiently outside our buildings till school was over before coming forward to announce this. Fortunately the lad, though shocked, was able to be transferred to hospital, where he made a good recovery.

The bite of the cobra and its lethal effects were demonstrated to me very clearly when, as detailed in the Sarawak Museum Gazette, the death occurred of a patient who suffered such a bite. The patient was taken quickly the short distance to the dispensary, given all our stock of antitoxin, but proceeded none the less to die of paralysis and asphyxia without the progress of the poisoning being affected at all.

We found usually, at each dispensary session, several cases of conjunctivitis or iritis sometimes occurring in epidemic form. These conditions responded well to local short term antibiotic treatment, fortunately, because we saw many older people with badly damaged eyes due to an unimpeded attack of such an infection.

With regard to mental illness in the area there was some uncertainty expressed among ourselves about the comparative incidence of this, expecially of neurosis. My own impression was that when one was able to get to know these people well, one could uncover a fair number of cases of neurotic illness of one presentation or another and that the impression of the people living a primitive untrammelled life with resultant good mental health was a false one. Indeed the stresses of living in such a community with its immense problems, of, at times, poor rice harvest, poor cash crops, epidemic diseases, cannot be much less than the admittedly different stresses of an advanced community.

Of the more obvious psychotic illness we noted several severe cases of depression. One such episode, probably with schizophrenic aspects also, resulted in our losing one very promising schoolboy. Two cases of suicide were made known to us and one tuai rumah (head man) became quite a problem when he suffered delusions. It can be imagined the anxieties of his friend over the difficulties taking this man down river in a small canoe en route to Kuching, but they all got there safely, the head man under heavy sedation, and he made a good recovery.

It was not easy either, to determine much about the diseases of old age—not because there were no old people, but because they were unable to come or had no one willing to take them to the dispensaries. Indeed, they tended to be pushed to one side or even hidden away when the medical team visited the longhouse (the theory that in this primitive society old folks would invariably be well looked after within the extended family group got many a nasty jolt). These old folk, very often female, and sometimes, by appearance at any rate, very old, suffered mainly from anaemias, from chronic—usually tuberculosis—coughs and from osteo-arthritis of knee and especially of the spine, with resultant severe deformity, possibly due to the many jobs which involve prolonged bending or stooping, e.g. weeding the padi fields. One old man presented us with an unusual form of acute urinary obstruction due to his rectum being absolutely packed with the seeds of fruits which he had swallowed without the usual preliminary of spitting out the quite large seeds. Manual removal of the mass of seeds restored normal urinary flow.

In the earlier years of the scheme the W.H.O. spraying teams were beginning to work in the area to get rid of the malarial mosquitoes (and many other longhouse insect pests also—temporarily at any rate). This was shown in the dispensaries by a dramatic fall in the number of patients with malaria and a similar, but later, drop in the incidence of enlarged spleens among the children, so that it was rare, in the later years, to find any child with this sign, or to see malarial parasites in a blood film. This gratifying response was followed by a similar one in the Entebai scheme area. At all dispensaries surveillance for any recurrence of the disease was carried out and trainees proved very helpful in taking blood samples from any suspected case.

Children suffered also from worm infestations, anaemias, occasionally from protein lack, as well as from intestinal and respiratory infections. The mortality seemed high and one heard of several, and saw a few, who died of potentially curable conditions, e.g. one of intussusception and one of intestinal obstruction of uncertain origin—in both cases the parents resisted all offers of help to get the children to hospital or even of local attempt at operative treatment. On therapy for children, although sceptical even at first, we tended to give away anthelmintics, iron and vitamin preparations without anything in the way of laboratory or chemical control, or of much thought as to what would be the cure rate or the relapse rate. We did, however, hope to influence the dietary and hygienic habits of the people by example and exhortation and even bribery, e.g. "no sanitation—no anthelmintics". We found antibiotics extremely helpful in many of these children's infections, and the parents, too, realised their usefulness and preferred an intramuscular injection for their children despite the latter's objections and from our point of view it ensured that the Penicillin was in situ. We used, otherwise, mainly Sulphadimidine and for a while, Chloramphenical.

Antenatal care consisted of fairly regular antenatal checks at the ordinary dispensary sessions. The main condition we were able to detect and treat was again anaemia, which we thought was aggravated by certain prohibitions "pemeli" against certain articles of diet for pregnant women, for example, eggs. Eclampsia and pre eclampsia did not appear frequently. There were several infertile women but the rest tended to high multiparity with all the dangers of malpositions, etc. in the later pregnancies. These malpositions were often found and corrected at the dispensary but further close supervision was not possible and relapse of the abnormality often occurred. It was, because of distances involved, very rarely possible for us to be present at a confinement in a longhouse and similar difficulty was encountered by the rural midwives who later undertook this work. For example, we were called to, but arrived too late at a case of breech delivery with delay of the delivery of the head resulting in the death of the child. Attempts were made to get the expectant mothers to come to stay near the midwife when their expected date of confinement came near, but problems arose especially in trying to determine that date from ill remembered and unrecorded dates of the last period. That it is, even so, very important that local help should be available at delivery was highlighted by the deaths of no less than three women, all friends of ours in the scheme, in the course of about five years, from post-partum haemorrhage with no one in the longhouse able to do anything at all.

Among the other obstetrical complications dealt with was a woman who had a retained placenta for two days before we were summoned and were able to carry out a manual removal of the placenta. Another woman developed an obstructed labour in the second stage. The midwife present (the patient being the schoolmaster's wife) thought the foetal heart had stopped but they all piled into a canoe and took her down river to the dispensary where a live child was delivered by forceps.

Several girls educated within the scheme have now taken training and positions as midwives and are able to instruct and advise the local woman and assist in the process of delivery. It is hoped also that further progress will be made by these girls in teaching the care of new born children as considerable ignorance exists about this subject. We found one neonate with severe anaemia due to cutting with a sharp knife of the umbilical cord without ligation. Another custom was that of, literally, stuffing rice into an ailing child's mouth so that one found poor dehydrated children with great gobs of rice sticking to dried tongues and lips.

It was early suspected that pulmonary tuberculosis was present in the community, but with time it became obvious that the disease was widespread—causing both high morbidity and mortality and being the greatest health hazard even before malaria was eradicated. We diagnosed it at first on clinical grounds only, although it was later possible to have microscopical studies done in the laboratory. These clinical cases were easily diagnosed—presenting features of an acute disease in a susceptible population with haemoptysis and gross physical signs. One remembers a girl named Obay who presented with the classical "galloping consumption" and began to fade away before our eyes—she lived very close to Budu—before treatment was instituted.

In addition there were the great numbers of, usually, older folk with chronic cough, poor appetite ("enggai makai") and excessive thinness. The tubercle bacilli was responsible for most of these cases — which though did not help to reconcile us, in the least, to the horrible early morning chorus of hacking, coughing and spitting so well known to those who have spent a night in a longhouse. One European member of the staff developed Pulmonary tubercle in the course of his duties but responded well to treatment in the U.K. and was, happily, able to return to Budu.

We treated these cases with I.N.H. and P.A.S. on an outpatient basis, despite the knowledge that three drug treatment, i.e. the above two plus injections of Streptomycin is thought to produce better results, because regular daily or even less frequent injection could not be arranged. Our impressions were that cure or arrest of the disease could be produced in almost all who took these two drugs regularly. We found that full co-operation, with regular drug taking, seemed to be obtained from most patients—certainly they came for repeat supplies at the proper calculated intervals—but that although this small proportion of the population benefited greatly we were, for various reasons, missing a large number of cases and the total incidence of infection and infectivity was only minimally diminished.

This particular problem remains, therefore, largely unsolved and control of the disease will necessitate a widespread and costly campaign in which again, the contribution of locally trained medical and community development workers would be vitally important.

Another problem largely unsolved was that of longhouse hygiene. Longhouse dwellers defecate and urinate from the veranda (ruai) to the ground several feet below, which area becomes, thus, very fertile ground producing excellent crops of vegetables, etc. when the longhouse is eventually moved. Removal or at least dispersal of the excreta was done by pigs which roamed loose under and around the house. We introduced, and in many cases, succeeded in getting implemented a policy of the use of deep latrines, usually dug by several families in co-operation but sometimes made by one family group for its own use.

It was hoped that this would reduce the incidence of bowel infections carried by the multitudinous flies, allow the pigs to be fenced and so also permit the cultivation of vegetable gardens near the longhouse. The people soon noticed how much better the environment was without the pigs and mess, but found difficulties in feeding the penned pigs as this involved collecting and cooking large quantities of green matter. The work devolved on the women who had therefore less time for their more traditional tasks, e.g. pounding rice. On revisits to these houses it was found that, in many cases, the labour involved in digging sufficiently deep latrines, sufficiently often, into the rock spurs on which most longhouses are built, was too much for the menfolk and that such latrines as existed were shallow pits with ill fitting covers where the excreta were inaccessible to any scavenger pig and to the rays of the tropical sun which might dry out and partially sterilise them, but wide open to the ubiquitous flies. So with few exceptions, usually schools, hygiene remained inadequate. That we were not alone in failing to solve this dilemma is shown by correspondence at that time with Med. Department on this subject in which either deep bored (by auger) latrines and riparian latrines were suggested.

The first method was tried at the Entebai scheme but extremely poor progress was made with the auger sent for us to experiment with, in what was probably difficult ground, but, as indicated above, most longhouses are built in awkward places anyway. The Riparian system means that, simply, the faeces go straight into the local river and while feasible in the tidal lower reaches of the larger rivers, would be quite unsuitable for our small rivers (sometimes in the dry season very small indeed) with a largish population living nearby, bathing in and taking drinking water from the local stream.

What lessons did we learn from the scheme? We found it possible to observe and report many changes occurring in this remote area of Sarawak especially in disease patterns. We saw the considerable morbidity with loss of working time due to disease in the longhouses some of which diseases we were able to repel, temporarily anyway. We watched with delight the disappearance of malaria from the area and with sadness the ravages of the tubercle bacillus. We noted, too, the rapidly increasing interest among the Dyaks in European medical advances, the inefficiency of the dispensary services provided, both those of the Government and those of the scheme, the gradually increasing survival rate among children, the increasing population and, probably associated, the appearance of signs of lack of dietary iron and proteins. We were impressed by the usefulness of young trainees in the medical field, the improvement in health that could be effected by adult education courses at the centre, the absence of an effective answer to the problems of longhouse living, bringing up the old question as to whether the tendency to the break up of the longhouses into individual small family houses should be encouraged—on the whole I think it should. I began to have some doubts about our shop's contribution to health when I realised how much these shops were gaining from the sale of such popular items as sweets to school children, tinned fruits to adults and feeding bottles for babies and how the availability of items like these might be considered a retrograde step although, of course, on the other hand, the shops sold, often at reduced prices, foods of high protein value, for example dried fish from the coast and tinned meats.

If starting again, we would probably make some changes in our approach to health problems. It would be better to assess, at the outset and rather more accurately, the health of the community and then to become involved in schemes to eradicate from the area diseases amenable to such attack. For example, immunisation schemes for children mainly against Diptheria, Cholera, Polio, Tetanus, Smallpox, Measles and possibly Tuberculosis (by B.C.G. vaccination) would be a good start. For adults, the adult education courses would be used to teach a limited number of subjects of proven usefulness, e.g. to encourage co-operation with the various projects under way, like the malaria eradication one, or to encourage improved nutrition, or to encourage those in need of more sophisticated treatment or hospitalisation to seek this, or to instil a knowledge of elementary First-Aid which is completely lacking in most longhouses. Soon, undoubtedly family planning will need to be discussed with these peoples. One would not wish to become involved again in running several widely separated dispensaries, but would use just one central headquarters from which to run a sort of Schools Health Service to all the nearby schools and from which also to make forays with a few trainees to the longhouses to expound on two or three of the above subjects while suggesting that the sick folk in the house be taken to the dispensary unless they were really very ill in which case they would of course be started on some therapy there and then. This practice of *not* trying to cure every disease process, however minor or however liable to relapse, when visiting a longhouse was one which we could not have considered in the first enthusiasm of working in the scheme but which was, in fact, essential if one wished to educate as well as medicate, and was quite acceptable to the longhouse folks. It was when these strands of instruction and assistance and their willing acceptance by the people came together and intertwined that community development was seen at its best.

(WRITTEN BY ARTHUR THWAITES)

The Sea Dyak attitude to sickness and injury has been recorded elsewhere and it is interesting in itself. Certainly it is an important factor affecting the medical side of Community Development work amongst Sea Dyaks and the brief summary which follows is relevant.

Foreigners may attribute the incidence of ill-health to disease carrying organisms, unhygienic living conditions, unfortunate accidents etc., but Sea Dyaks know that evil spirits are the real cause.

Living three or four days away from the nearest hospital, in times when travel was so slow, the number of sick people who could afford the time and subsistence money to go down river to Government dispensaries was very small indeed. Thus unrelieved personal suffering and its effect on the hand-to-mouth farming methods of the family resulted in a dread of ill health.

A class of Dyak Medicine Men called Manang came into being who still give of their best to succour those people whom the evil spirits have made sick. As well as farming to support their own families the Manang may be called upon at any time of day or night to accompany the informant back to the sick man's longhouse. There, by dint of various magic divinations they endeavour to diagnose and treat the sickness.

The Manang palpates the part which is thought to be affected, sometimes using smooth divining stones, then he goes into a self imposed trance in order to move over into the spirit world and there contact the soul of the sick man which is wandering free of the diseased body. The aim is to reunite the soul with the body and, at best, the Manang may believe himself to have been vouchsafed the remedy which will cure the sickness.

On recovering from the trance the Manang soaks his medicine consisting of various unusual stones, pigs tusks, and other charms in water, anoints the affected area that night, and again the following morning.

With luck the patient proceeds to recover, but if this is not the case the Manang may well be called back at a later date to do the same thing again, and this time a pig will be sacrificed and its liver examined in order to ascertain the patient's prognosis. The lie of the lobes of the liver, amount of bile, and the length of the duct are all of importance in assessing the patient's life expectancy.

If the liver is pronounced to be a bad one then the patient may hold another similar ceremony at a later date in the hope of a better reading, but these undertakings are expensive.

The third and last hope is to call in the Lemambang, who has less knowledge of personal sickness than the Manang but a greater familiarity with the spirit world. The human skulls hanging from the rafters are brought into use and after a night of continuous chanting it is hoped that the Lemambang will be able to wrest a favourable prognosis from the Gods when another pig is ritually fed, washed, combed, slaughtered, and its liver examined the following morning.

This is only a very rough account of the Traditional Dyak Medical Services and there are many variations and facets of ritual and the treatment of specific illnesses which have not even been touched upon here. From what has been said, however, it will be appreciated that western medical practice is foreign indeed to the Dyak mind and the idea of creating positive health, attending to diet, sanitation, avoidance, isolation or destruction of infection, all these things are considered to have no bearing whatsoever on what the spirits have in store for a man.

Personally I consider western medicine and drugs to be extraordinarily effective in curing diseases amongst Sea Dyaks and I would rather treat bacillary dysentery with sulpha drugs than rely on the medicine of the Manang. However I have noticed that identical patients with identical diseases, on identical drugs, (give or take a hundred Statisticians' buts) don't always react identically to treatment, even in the best western hospitals. Some get better quickly and some of them go and die, so that I am quite prepared to believe that there is another factor in the successful treatment of sick people. In fact, having done everything I can to cure a man and yet still feeling that his condition could be improved by attention to this other factor I may refer him to the Manang as a specialist.

In return the Manang send their cases down to me and a little child who has been chanted over and had a bunch of leaves and lime hung on the bilek door to ward off the evil spirit might well be a case that I diagnose as pneumonia and give penicillin and sulpha drugs. Or a man with a fracture may come down to have it set when the Manang has done his bit (in the early days as Budu I had just to get on and set and immobilise fractures as well as I could myself, but since the roads came nearer and river transport faster, those cases who can afford it go on to the hospitals with their X-ray facilities and surgeons).

As a matter of fact I too am called Manang and many Sea Dyaks know me by that name and no other, even though Dyak methods and western treatment of diseases are so very different. It will be readily appreciated that a sick man who wanted to try new medicine but felt bound to the customary rituals could well become a battle ground if there was no understanding between the Dyak Manang and myself. Tolerance of each others methods is not difficult when everyone is doing their best and one never knows whose efforts will help the patient most.

At dawn one Sunday I was lying in bed planning to do a whole morning's work on my vegetable garden when I was called out to visit an elderly man who "had had a bad dream during the night, been made ill by a spirit, and had become half an animal". What diagnostic equipment, drugs and other paraphernalia does one take with one on a case like this? Nothing really heavy because it's a two and a half hours' walk to the longhouse and will be two and a half hours' walk back again!

Having got to the longhouse the diagnosis of a "stroke" was unmistakable and the immediate treatment was obvious too. The bilek was crammed full of folk, most of whom were beseeching the patient to speak to them and tell them what was wrong with him, and shouting the same questions louder, when he replied with the only kind of grunts he could manage. There seemed to be a rather critical lack of oxygen left in the room and the din was somewhat remarkable. Everyone was very worried about the poor chap, and indeed he looked so desperate and forlorn trying to get people to understand him. They must have been shouting to him for hours. The men had tied a thong round the shoulder and proceeded to flail the paralysed arm briskly in order to drive out the devil but that particular therapeutic measure had already been discontinued before I arrived. Glad of a good relationship with the local Manang attending the case, I agreed that it was an excellent thing that folk should be beating the gongs, but suggested that the instrumentalists might like to summon the Gods from the ruai outside instead of right at the patient's ear. Fair enough, the Manang agreed and he himself led out the band and encouraged a lot of other people to accompany him. This gave enough room to get some of the windows opened on the outside wall and to put the patient in a more comfortable position and allowed me to explain about nodding symbols and the different ways of framing questions until his speech should return.

After I had done a short physical examination I gave him a drink and explained to the family about spoon feeding, assisting with his toilet, frequent changing of position etc. etc. and came away feeling that the phenobarbitone I had left him and the demonstration of simple nursing procedures and quietness would make all the difference to the patient in the next few weeks.

Actual times I have forgotten but I think that it was a mere four weeks before the patient himself arrived at the dispensary having walked all the way from his longhouse, an amazing recovery. How did he feel? He was "feeling very much better but the illness had been severe. He had wandered away into a very fine country and was thoroughly enjoying the visit until he met his brother. His brother having died some time before he then realised that he must be in the land of the dead. The brother jumped on his back and prevented him from returning to the land of the living and though he struggled and shook himself this way and that he couldn't dislodge the brother. Fortunately his wife and friends had kept calling to him and finally he'd been able to throw off the brother and was now practically well again".

Indeed I am often amazed by the sick man's assessment of his cure, and frankly astounded at his ideas of what was wrong with him in the first place. If I were to write down the history, symptoms and probable cause of the disease just as it is given to me by each patient then I could add another tome to the medical textbooks on tropical diseases. The diseases would be the same as those already known, but no one would recognise them in the form that I hear them.

When I first started designing the ideal dispensaries to be built at the different centres, the inner sanctum, in which the patient was to tell me all, had impressively high walls, windows and a door that closed, and could only be reached by the patient squeezing himself down a narrow passageway. Strictly one patient at a time, no one else was to listen and I was very angry each time people climbed on forms to look in over the high walls.

Because I do believe that a patient should have privacy and professional secrecy I added yet another plank to the high walls and incidentally made the room hotter still. After that I could not see people's heads. I could, however, see the eyes of my patients and it soon became evident that they were looking at a row of eyes over my head. That in fact, the patients were describing their ailments to the people outside and not to me at all.

Nowadays, I have half walls or no walls at all in the surgeries and patients can tell all to all, unhampered by my European reticence. Those waiting to be seen and those waiting to hear what the next patient has got, encourage whoever is in front of me with the Dyak equivalents of "that's just what I've got" or "good heavens" or "I reckon that you've got so and so". Far from wanting privacy, I have had patients turn their backs on me altogether and tell their story to the crowds quite oblivious of the fact that I am wanting to ask specific questions.

When it comes to the bit it is difficult to get accurate information about the illness anyhow, because the patient is concentrating on an entirely different set of phenomena to me. Whereas I am looking for a history and clinical picture which suggests this or that disease process, the patient relates his suffering to the influence of evil spirits.

To this day, the idea of digging and using a sunk pit latrine in order to cut down on worm infestation and dirt disease is considered to be harassing folk to no advantage. Likewise, if the old lady is practically housebound with pulmonary tuberculosis, then she might as well look after the infants while the nursing mother takes her place in the farmwork. After all somebody has got to do the weeding or else they will all starve. The other occupants of the longhouse are certainly not going to get on to the old lady about spitting all over the place. She has quite enough to contend with as she toils wanly through her household duties. To think of isolating her, marking her infirmity by asking her to use separate crockery, or even remonstrating a little, would be too unkind.

However, a number of the young men have been away in the Sarawak Rangers and there they learnt something of the efficacy of pills and injections in curing diseases, thus remedial aspect of medical work is an acceptable starting point in each area. The gradual introduction of health principles and prophylactic measures, first to the young in school, and then to adults in the adult schools, follows with varying degrees of success.

Sea Dyaks are normally fit, strong and energetic. Small in height, they are nevertheless well muscled and indeed beautifully proportioned. The fact that most families move out of the communal longhouse to live in widely scattered farm huts for certain seasons of the year is probably the main reason why the Dyaks were not decimated by disease long ago. There being no latrines human excreta, refuse, food-waste etc. which drops through the floor of the longhouse, is consumed or churned into evil-smelling mud by the pigs and hens which roam underneath, and into the resultant morass they add their own excreta. The fly borne intestinal diseases and infestations of roundworm and hookworm flourish in such conditions and the sickening smells are unlikely to speed recovery in other diseases not specifically attributal to these conditions. Moving out of the longhouse for two or three months at a time, and living in a newly built hut made of freshly cut leaves and split bamboo, on a new piece of ground each year, dramatically cuts the accumulative contagion of the dirt diseases. Fresh air and sunlight stream into these huts which the men have not been able to make spirit-proof, and even though the doors and windows are still tightly shut each night, it is impossible to prevent oxyen from seeping through the leaf walls and right into the room.

It is not only the healthy farm workers who benefit from the move out of the longhouse as they are outside most days anyhow, but the benefit to the very young and the very old, the invalids and the chronically ill people is great because they also move to the farm hut.

Rice is the staple food and the hand pounded Dyak rice alone, eaten with a small amount of rock salt only, seems to give enough strength and energy to work hard over quite long periods. However, shifting cultivation and an entire lack of any machinery limits the amount of land which can be farmed each year and inclement weather, blight, pests or sickness among the farm workers may make a nonsense of the padi yield, and what was expected to last the family the whole year and a bit more may be enough for a mere six months or at worst two months. If the price obtained for rubber and pepper is also low, and the wild illipe nut trees have not fruited that year, then many Dyaks go hungry and wild sago and a few fern do little more than sustain a miserable existence.

People living up river in places where they are still farming virgin jungle and supplementing good rice harvests with game and fish, tend to have a good diet which gives them the strength to work harder to maintain their standard and these people are not so badly hit by fluctution in the market price of cash crops. There are many taboos associated with food. Some of them are inherited from preceding generations, others are prescribed for individuals by the Manang, some are self-adopted after listening to the old wives' tales.

Thus much good advice on the eating of nourishing foods is nullified by taboos or non-availability of supply. A very few people do grow vegetables all the year round but most people have seasonal gluts of the different vegetables which they planted at the same time as the padi and then long periods without. Wild fruits too are gorged during the three months season and there is such a variety of fruit that practically everyone is tempted to eat his particular favourite to satiety and many people eat all kinds to excess with predictable results. Many longhouses have small engines for dehusking the padi, and this saves the women many hours of hand pounding using seven foot poles in a specially shaped box. Fortunately, however, the padi engines are forever breaking down and then folk return to hand pounded rice with its appetising smell and high vitamin B content.

Vitamin deficiency is not a big problem up river, though there is more B one deficiency on the Budu side than at Entebai, and a few of the many skin diseases have responded favourably to Vitamin C.

In 1954, one third of the dispensary patients presented with malaria, therefore the subsequent work of W.H.O. Malaria eradication teams in the area brought dramatic relief from suffering and the resultant disruption of the pruning programme. Pulmonary tuberculosis deserves the same large scale effort at eradication, and though the dispensaries have done much to treat florid cases on an out-patient basis, it is good to hear that the Government has plans to extend its anti t.b. campaigns to the remote areas. It is hoped that the campaign will pick out the early cases with subclinical t.b. and treat them before there is much damage.

An Anti-Yaws campaign, in which 3,000 people in and around Budu were given a single massive injection of INICEFF oily penicillin, was also worth doing. Because penicillin had been so little used there it cleared up many other ailments as well as the Yaws.

In fact the Anti-Yaws campaign increased the tendency for all patients to ask for injections instead of pills, and explaining the dangers of penicillin resistance to patients who believed that injections were being given only to favoured patients, slowed down the speed of treatment considerably. Because it is common for patients to walk five hours to attend the scheme clinics and there are often 100 and occasionally 200 new patients in one day, speed is essential. Few of the centres have overnight accommodation for sick people and, though the patients would gladly have moved into the school dormitories along with the children, that convenient solution was expressly forbidden to them.

To do full time dispensary work would allow more time to be spent on prevention and treatment of sickness: instead of this dispensaries were confined to lunch times and weekends in order that other work could be undertaken. This other work of teaching young and old in schools, co-operative trading, and trying out new methods of agriculture, was related and vital to the promotion of good health.

Thus teaching academic subjects full time in the school helped to turn out students of a sufficient standard to undertake further studies leading to training in medical work. Jawie has since qualified as a Doctor at Aberdeen University, Rabing passed his S.R.N. at Dreadnought Seamen's Hospital, Greenwich, London, Morris passed his S.R.N. at Hairmyres Hospital, East Kilbride, and went on to do Mental Nursing at Gartnavel Hospital, Glasgow. Lambor passed out as a Radiologist also in Aberdeen. Nyipan passed her Midwifery exams in Kuching. Another boy, Chundie took his S.R.N. training at Dreadnought but failed to pass the finals. He was a good practical nurse out here but is one of those people who just cannot pass exams. Also there are such people as Inyang and Mapan, Juing and Bau who have done excellent work in the dispensaries. Even when they were young schoolboys they were left in charge of dispensaries when Doc and I were travelling. They went ahead treating common complaints and stitching up wounds thus providing an invaluable service to the community.

Also all the dispensary workers did their share on agricultural projects and worked in the co-operative shops because the relationship between a higher standard of living and better health was obvious from the start.

Adult schools gave the dispensary teams time to teach a lot of people at one time about First Aid, home care of the sick, hygiene and diet (although the last two came to little).

There is some improvement, but there never was much enthusiasm to attend to these matters, because folk continue to believe that failure to respect bird omens or bad dreams is the real cause of the evil spirits visiting sickness upon them.

A few families dug sunk pit latrines, penned their pigs, and grew magnificent vegetables in the rotten refuse surrounding the longhouse. Sooner or later the fence fell down, or more often than not somebody in the longhouse refused to do his share of the labour involved, so one family's pigs could set at naught the work of all the other families in that house.

Early on, the Local Authority was approached to pass a law requiring these one or two renegades to follow the majority in making the improvements to longhouse hygiene which can make such a difference to health and the pleasure of living in the longhouse. (There are many good things about longhouse living that are not found in smaller units.) However, the Local Authority was probably right in refusing to make a law which they could not enforce, but because there is no such law, any interest in doing all this unnecessary work just to please the Community Development Staff has waned, and most longhouses have relapsed into squalor and an impressive toll of dirt diseases. Nevertheless, though this part of the adult teaching came to little or nothing in the end, it did produce some amazing vegetables right next to the kitchen and the latrines were used long enough to allow the population to be dewormed as a whole.

Childbirth customs with their rigorous strictures and resultantly high death rates amongst mothers and babies is worth a chapter itself but is rather harrowing and some readers may like to miss the next few paragraphs. Suffice it to say that the old customs were at least logical and not intentionally designed to kill.

On first opening the dispensaries I made it quite plain that I personally knew nothing about midwifery and that I did not consider it to be a man's job anyhow. Fair enough, no one disagreed with that, but then one man cheated and brought me to visit his wife who had a pain in her tummy and she was in prolonged labour. The family had already removed the tops from jars and tins, dragged the canoe up out of the river and untied its rope, and loosed the cords binding the rolled up mats which were not in use, so it wasn't these things which were preventing egress of the baby from the womb. Because I had no sensible solution to offer there and then, the three ladies who were assisting resumed their positions, one lady providing counter traction by straining at the mother's outstretched arms, the other two kneeling at each side of the mother pushing down on the fundus for all they were worth. The baby was born, it practically shot across the room, and when I saw them resume their pushing without pause it showed another reason why so many mothers died in childbirth. The cord is traditionally cut with a jungle knife and a rather unpleasant dressing applied.

After the delivery the mother is not allowed to lie down for a few weeks but sits up more or less straight, leaning against a horizontal board at shoulder level with a smouldering fire at her back night and day to assist the drying-out process. Every mother following the traditional custom thus has permanent burn scars on her back, and because it is forbidden to drink anything save small sips of ginger broth for the first day or so, some mothers succumb to dehydration.

The infant has a hand woven blanket draped over it like a tent, preventing the evil spirit from seeing it (or much air getting in), and over mother and child is suspended a fishing net to trap that spirit in the shape of a bird which swoops down to carry off the baby's soul unless the mother stays awake to guard it for the whole of the first two nights.

Eggs, green vegetables, fish, meat, most of the pleasant and nutritive foods are still taboo in this period just as they were throughout pregnancy, "in case it makes them ill". Frankly appalled by all I had seen I returned to my hut with much to think about. It had taken courage to start doing a few dental extractions but it now appeared that I had to start doing midwifery too.

Fortunately Miss Masterton, the Sister Tutor at the Edinburgh Mental Hospital, had explained a normal delivery to me in very simple terms and, most important, had told me that nature normally presented a live baby to a live mother with only a little assistance from the midwife. I also thought of Miss Noble, the Matron of Dreadnought Seamen's Hospital in London where I had been given such a good training, and Miss Shearman, the Sister Tutor there, and I knew that I would be letting them down if I did not take courage to help in midwifery too.

Having read up the midwifery textbook which I had brought with me in case of emergencies I then went down to see the Mair Rees whose work in organising and running midwifery services in Sarawak is legendary. A great character was Mair; short and plump, she drove a small box of a car to her various destinations with speed, accuracy and determination. (I understand that she once came first in a car rally over the particularly tortuous roads from Kuching to Seriam, the only lady amongst men in cars of far finer reputations.)

Most nurses work hard and Mair worked harder than most. In fact she surged through her work with speed, accuracy and determination, and if the water supply had unavoidably been turned off just when she was expecting a clinic of 200 patients, then she would ring up the engineer and get it turned on again immediately because people not only respected Mair's work-load but liked her too. Kind and generous to a degree, she made time to speak nicely to people, took a personal interest in her staff and colleagues, and after thirty minutes of a sit down at the end of a day's work she would be up again preparing food for dinner guests or preparing to go out herself. She was very popular indeed.

In one week Mair taught me as much simple midwifery as I can manage and arranged for the lady Doctor working in Kuching Hospital in 1954 to show me other things. One week amongst the lovely ladies does not make any man into a midwife. What Mair did is to give me enough knowledge and practical advice to allow me to introduce new methods which Dyak women were quick to appreciate, and by the time Doc Lees arrived, and later the trained midwives, a number of ladies had had their babies in the new way.

It did not all happen in a month. When I first broached the subject to the women attending the adult schools I kept very much to the general principles and washing-the-baby type of talk, and I did not borrow a real baby either because I was far too scared of dropping it. As a matter of fact I used to demonstrate the trick of folding the towel round the struggling baby, round a struggling cat, and as this dreadful lecture used to come round once a fortnight for school after school, the cat developed second sight and it required the services of half the schoolboys to help me find it just before the lecture started.

Forseeably there came the evening when a man came to tell me that his wife was due to give birth and wished me to deliver the baby in the new way she had heard about at school. Desperate to stave off the inevitable I pointed out that I had been teaching all day and that in any case it had taken him three hours to walk in from his longhouse and would take me the same going back. "Your wife will have had the baby by now and all you need to do is to go back and look at it." He replied that his wife invariably had a long labour and that I had been shouting about the new methods being so much better than the old and I just had to go back with him. Nothing to do but go, so I packed my gear and the midwifery textbook and set off with grave misgivings to my first confinement.

In the longhouse the bilek was almost full of ladies and children who had gathered to watch this demonstration of how babies are delivered in Britain, but the centre of the bilek was left conspicuously empty except for a glass jar containing a pickled full-term foetus. This was the unfortunate result of a previous pregnancy and it was exhibited there to attract the attention of the evil spirits so that they would wreak their spite on the mishap instead of the baby now due. Indeed it was well exhibited. It riveted my attention in the long wait ahead. The audience came and went during the evening until it was finally time to see some action. But always there were one or two ladies who relieved each other sighing and pointing out to the mother that the baby, and possibly she herself, would likely die because she was not following the traditional methods. The mother had no wish for either of these fatalities to occur so here will be clearly seen the heroism of the lady who was the very first one in all that remote area to have a baby in the longhouse by the new method. She was the calmest one there and she merely said that she had experienced the old methods and now she trusted me to bring her through the new method because it sounded to be better.

Having brought a phenomenal supply of cigarettes with me I was able to follow Mair's advice and divert the attention of the onlookers each time they decided that they must needs minister to the poor mother whatever we said, and finally she was presented with a boy child with no difficulty and the thriving baby and contented mother proceeded through a pleasant post-natal period, to become the talk of the area.

On the strength of this brave lady's "phenomenal" progress without roasting herself, losing sleep or denying herself all palatable foods, I was asked to deliver more babies and did a few more demonstrations in different longhouses, as well as commencing a considerable amount of ante-natal work. Forseeably, this extra undertaking clashed with other work commitments and I had to point out that I could not really deliver babies at night and teach their children successfully the next day. It was now time for the ladies to take over, practising what they had learned in the school and from the few demonstration deliveries they had seen.

This little ploy did not provide the Budu area with an adequate midwifery service at little or no cost to Government. In fact the pressures to conform to traditional customs and be rewarded with a live baby could not but affect the school ladies too, and because they themselves had been brought up in the old traditions it is unlikely that their newly acquired advice on the management of delivery was heeded and quite likely that they themselves joined in the "pushing" when it came to the test. It was not until Doc came and set up a lying-in room that deliveries were conducted properly and at least people knew about the new methods then, and by the time Nyipen had trained as a midwife and returned there the majority of people came in to have their babies this way.

Ladies attending the Entaih, Mujok and Tappang Punggu clinics have been slower to accept the new method but even here the start has been made and ante-natal services are improving their condition.

Of mental illness I have found surprisingly little. There are some mentally defective people who cope as best they can and whose limitations are accepted by the community, but apart from these and one or two hypochondrical patients who have more than the usual worry about their aches and pains, I can remember only three people with overt signs of psychotic disorder. Two were manic depressives and one was schizophrenic and all three were admitted to the Sarawak Mental Hospital for treatment.

These patients were taken down to hospital, but many others needing surgery or laboratory and X-ray facilities for adequate diagnosis never do go down river. Most do not have the money and a number are afraid to go into hospital, so with such people one can only cope with palliative and conservative medical treatment.

The scope of remedial medical work on the schemes is considerable and when I first started I was very fortunate to have the support and encouragement of the Director of Medical Services in Kuching. Dr Glyn Evans encouraged me to write directly to him about medical problems and his advice was a boon. When Doctor Lees came then I really was in clover, because though we only met every two or three months and the eight-hour walk between us did not favour the sort of cases I most needed to send to him, we occasionally swopped over and it was a great relief to have someone so competent to take over my problem cases. Doc had the deeper knowledge I lack and the willingness to help me and the patients all he could. When he left, the dispensary teams were a credit to him and many Dyaks owe much to his skill.

H. 311 (Rev. 1/62)

RETURN OF DISEASES FOR THE MONTHS OF *July 1st 1967 to 30th June 1968*

DISPENSARY *Ng. Entaih, Ng. Maong, Tepusng Tunggu*

~~HOSPITAL~~

1. *Morbidity Return*

Disease or Condition	International Detailed List Numbers	No. of Cases
Tuberculosis of respiratory system	001–008	16
Tuberculosis—all other forms	010–019	
Syphilis	020–029	
Gonorrhoea	030–035	
Typhoid and paratyphoid fevers and other Salmonella infections ...	040–042	
Dysentery, all forms	045–048	254
Diphtheria	055	
Whooping Cough	056	
Leprosy	060	
Tetanus	061	
Yaws	073	43
Acute Poliomyelitis and its late effects	080–081	
Measles	085	10
Chickenpox	087	10
Mumps	089	
Trachoma	095	
Malaria	110–117	
Filariasis	127	
Worm Infestations	123–130	22
Scabies	135	
All other diseases classed as infective or parasitic including fevers of unknown origin	036–138	223
Neoplasms (Tumours)	140–239	2
Allergic Disorders (asthma, urticaria)	240–245	20
Diseases of Thyroid	250–254	
Diabetes mellitus	260	
Avitaminosis and other deficiency states	280–286	180
Anaemias	290–293	156
Mental Disorders	300–318	
Conjunctivitis	370	244
Other diseases of eye	371–388	38
Blindness	389	
Diseases of ear	390–398	85
All other diseases of C.N.S. and sense organs	341–398	4
Diseases of the Heart and Blood Vessels	400–468	
Common Cold	470	576

(*Continued overleaf*)

Disease or Condition	International Detailed List Numbers	No. of Cases
Tonsillitis, acute	473	19
Influenza	480–483	135
Pneumonia	490–493	3
Bronchitis	500–502	225
Other respiratory diseases	471–527	9
Diseases of the stomach	540–545	881
Hernia	560–561	
Diarrhoea and Enteritis	571–764	500
Other diseases of digestive system	530–578	46
Diseases of the Liver, Gall-bladder and Pancreas	580–587	
Diseases of urinary system (excluding Gonorrhoea see 030–035) ...	600–609	3
Diseases of genital organs	610–637	3
Complications of pregnancy	640–659 & 661–689	4
Boils, abscesses, cellulitis and other local skin infections	690–698	130
Other diseases of skin	700–716	279
Arthritis and Rheumatism	720–727	161
All other diseases of musculoskeletal system	730–744	198
Diseases, cause unknown	795	307
Road accidents	E810–E845	
Water transport accidents	E850–E858	
Accidents caused by fire	E916	7
Other accidents	E800–E999	100
Poisonings	E870–E895	1

	Male	Female	Child	Total
2. Number of New Cases	1246	1713	1937	4896
3. Total Number Referred to Hospitals				
4. Total Number Admitted to Rest Beds				

Remarks:* All diagnoses based on clinical signs and patients histories only; a mere 20 or 30 patients consented to go down to hospital for X rays, pathological investigations, and more accurate diagnoses by a physician. Many of the 881 pts. here classified as "Diseases of the stomach" were almost certainly suffering from worm infestation.
There were 85 new pregnancies.

DISTRIBUTION:

*N.B. Normal pregnancies not reported by a midwife should be reported in this section.

Signed: ....

Date: December 1968

Director of Medical Services,
Divisional Medical Officer,
District Officer.

CHAPTER SEVEN

ADMINISTRATION OF THE SCHEME

And you moved among these mysteries,
Absorbed and smiling and sure;
Stirring, testing and measuring,
With the precision of a ritual.

—J. S. U.

Even at the very beginning I knew there would be tremendous difficulties if only to co-ordinate the work of education with agriculture, with medical work with co-operatives and with local administration in Saratok, and still more to prevent each of the teams becoming area Directors of Education, Directors of Agriculture, Directors of Medical Services and Commissioners of Co-operatives. Above all I knew it would be extremely difficult not to be called upon at least by the local people, to act as the District Officer. In the early days a letter from Budu to Kuching could take as long as three weeks and a reply therefore could not be obtained under at the very best a month. It would therefore be impracticable to consider even for a moment that important decisions could be waited on from Kuching. Work had to go on and time was all important. It seemed impracticable, also, that authority to use monies, officially provided for the project, should be in the District Office, Saratok.

Above all, it seemed most undesirable that I myself became the on-the-spot "Director" since this would cut across probably the most important principle in Community Development. No matter how the problems were looked at and no matter whether corns were going to be trampled on, it seemed essential that the first step, the very first step, was to set up legally, with its own bye-laws, its own revenue, its own office, a Progress Society whose work would be administered by a small easily called upon Committee of Progress, elected as members at a General Meeting of the Society.

So with this important and far-reaching decision taken, we quickly got down to formulating the bye-laws. These were made as simple as possible. A General Meeting was held to adopt the bye-laws, a working committee was formed with considerable powers to take decisions, but such decisions had to be confirmed at the normal Annual General Meeting. Office Bearers were elected. Mac and I were elected joint secretaries and treasurers to enable one of us to travel and one to remain, as it were, at the helm. Arthur became the secretary of the sub-committee dealing with health. Tuai Rumah Gelau, that fine old man, was elected chairman. The Society was quickly registered in Kuching by making a special visit.

Since some of the bye-laws have become very important, especially now when there is no vestige of European control or supervision, it could help

Cpl. Moa Ari with his Radio Telephone, at H.Q. Border Scouts

those similarly engaged if mention is made of them. At the time they were incorporated in the original bye-laws nobody, least of all myself, thought they would be needed but with main roads being opened throughout Sarawak it was indeed fortunate that we were able to look far into the future, just on the off chance. First and foremost, all scheme land, that is land given to the project for building main centres and sub-centres, land for planting rubber trees, fruits and other cash crops planted within the boundaries of each centre, was titled in the name of the Progress Society. Such buildings and land could never be alienated and be sold. It could, however, or part of it, be excised to be owned by local authorities wishing to build proper schools and staff quarters. The importance of this bye-law will be apparent to anyone who knows Sarawak even a little. A second bye-law was that any revenue accruing from sales of produce such as rubber, coffee, pepper, could be used at the discretion of the Committee of Progress but only to further such things as educational advancement in the area, or assist in medical coverage, or assist in paying costs of advanced training for future local people. In other words, no revenue from any centre could be used to promote any personal profit to any single person nor could it be just divided up as a profit to members of the Society. The members could, however, take their calculated share of profits or surpluses in the co-operative and trading stores, according to the amount that each supported such. Thirdly, in order that areas around each longhouse could raise their own standard of living, parallel to the progress made on scheme centre land, any outside assistance, for example under the rubber planting scheme. should be made available to every member. So also, when available, piglets born from good stock at any centre must be given to local people at an agreed cost to improve their protein level. There were several other important bye-laws but such were only applicable to the Budu and Entaih areas.

So with the main plan of administration fixed it was possible to make immediate progress on the spot by reference only to the Committee of Progress. As secretary, decisions made by the Committee had to be carried out by me. Government Secretariat officials, District Officers and others, quite wrongly, came to the conclusion that the Community Development team had set themselves up as a small autocracy, when indeed it was true democracy. I argued, and still do to this day, that whether or not I was employed by Government the nature of this employment, to do it correctly, meant that as secretary of the Progress Society, my immediate superior was the chairman of this Society and it was my duty to implement the decisions of this Society. Fortunately, Mac, Arthur and I, all through the adult education classes over the first three years took every opportunity to explain ways of Government, how schools were paid for, how medical services were paid for and so on. Nevertheless there were times throughout the years when considerable friction arose between myself and members of the Community Development Committee, the authority in Kuching. This committee was important and I was perfectly aware of its importance. First, the chairman, usually the chief secretary, held considerable power in those days. The members consisted of the financial secretary, the development officer for

Sarawak, and the heads of all departments such as Education, Agriculture, Medical Services. I maintain to this day that when real Community Development in any country is to be tackled properly such a high-powered committee is essential. Even when it was suggested that I become a Director of Community Development in a separate department I opposed this strongly on the grounds that real Community Development was only possible with the full co-operation of each head of department who could be kept fully aware of the problems and so be able to sort things out round a table. Important decisions could be taken by this central committee of Community Development and such decisions were agreed to in principle by all heads of departments who were usually present at the annual meeting. It was through this committee that I managed to pacify those whose corns I had trampled on. It was through this committee that I was given a reasonably free hand and to this day I am most grateful for the confidence placed in me and members of my team. After a few years, it was generally recognised that our way was producing results. Most of the members of this committee did take the trouble to make the long journey to Budu, far from their usual home comforts, to see for themselves just what was being done in their name. One and all at least found a sincerity of approach in the members of the team and they certainly agreed that dedication was the keynote to its success. As the years passed, the Committee of Progress became the decision-making authority in the district and even Government subscribed to this by referring matters for discussion, instead of trying to lay down the law under circumstances and in areas which were not remotely similar in problem to the urban and semi urban areas.

While acknowledging that the setting up of local authorities in various districts is an essential part in preparing any developing country to become independent, it has always been my contention that such local authorities should not be set up from the top down but from the very village level up. Experience in Sarawak will prove that local authorities set up in the early days did considerable harm. This seemed to be an accepted result in the hopes that from the mistakes made the local authorities would learn their own lessons. This is true up to a point but just as a child does not become a man in his own rights just through making mistakes, so it seemed to me that such local authorities were just ahead of the times, especially as almost all members were inevitably illiterate. Being so, the members became pure "yes" men since they were unable to understand the various matters put before them for decision. To make matters worse there were few qualified secretaries in those days. Some used their position wisely and well but this could not be said of many.

I felt that the ideal in any developing country was to do what we were attempting to do at Budu. After a few years, most of the committee became literate and knowledgeable not only in Sarawak affairs but in important world matters. The meetings of the Progress Society became not only enjoyable but very interesting indeed. The hard work done on the adult education side was making a great difference and it was obvious from some of the decisions that the members were becoming thoughtful and wise.

By this time, also, other sub-centres had been opened up, one at Grenjang, one at Ng Budu and one at Engkilili. It seemed the time to set up stage two, namely a kind of Parish Council which could serve the whole Budu, Krian areas and so be an important link to co-ordinate the work of the main local authority at Saratok. It was quite simple to set this up. Three members were elected from each of the four centres and meetings were held every three months. Gradually official recognition was given to this Parish Council. It was not, I make haste to say, a law-making council. The Upper Krian Parish Council, as it is known to this day, only had powers to recommend and I was in agreement with this, since it seemed really democratic. I knew also that the Parish Council did voice the wishes of the majority and this was equally well known in Saratok. I cannot think of any major recommendation that was not accepted by the local authority in Saratok.

The importance of this Parish Council cannot be over emphasised. Slowly but surely misunderstandings were ironed out and after a year or so, the Upper Krian and Budu people really felt that they were having a good say in the routine running of their own area. Village shop licences, which had been a great bone of contention, had now to be approved or recommended by the Upper Krian Parish Council. Recommendations regarding staffing of the (by then) nine Primary Schools were accepted by the local authority and thence by the Director of Education in Kuching. The collection locally of rates, taxes, payment of gun licences, all became part of the work of the secretary of the Upper Krian Parish Council, thus making legal what we had been doing since the start. Plans for building new schools, new quarters, were passed to Saratok for implementation. Recommendations for further assistance from Agriculture Department were also passed on. Medical matters were discussed and recommendations made to the Director of Medical Services. The Committee of Community Development in Kuching at last breathed a sigh of relief since it was now fairly obvious that there was no autocracy at all and that none had ever been intended. It seemed to be a situation where democracy actually held full sway. Other areas in many parts of the country were advised to set up similar Parish Councils. Some were successful, some not, I think purely because insufficient ground work was done in real adult education in those districts.

So, with the experience of Budu behind us, it was easy to visualise the ultimate end on the Entaih and Entebai rivers in the third division. First the main centre at Entaih was established. Then two other centres at Ng Maong and Tappang Punggu, each on different rivers. Ng Entebai was the last centre to be established and it became an important centre serving Entaih Maong and Tappang Punggu. As on the Budu side a kind of Parish Council was set up. It was given, however, a different name, that of Committee enak Kanowit District Council. This just means that the committee at Entebai looked on the Kanowit District Council as the parent body. Also, as on the Budu side, three members from each centre were elected to act on this committee. To this day its importance vies with that of the Upper Krian Parish Council. It has done splendid work and continues to liaison with Kanowit and the remoter areas up river from Ng Entebei.

The administration of the whole project could well be summarised as follows. First and foremost a Progress Society at Budu had to be formed with its own bye-laws and be legally recognised. Routine administration was carried out by a Committee of Progress, members being elected from the members of the Society. As soon as practicable, various sub-centres were established, one at Grenjang, one at Engkilili and finally at Ng Budu. Each sub-centre had its own Committee of Progress but whose powers were limited under the parent at Budu which kept control over all main policies such as opening times, buildings, opening up of schools, and training. Then came the formation of the Upper Krian Parish Council, members consisting of three elected members from each centre, thus making a total of twelve members in the Upper Krian Parish Council. It should be said at this stage that no major recommendation was ever made at a first meeting of the Parish Council and that proposals were first asked to be discussed by the members at their own Progress Committee meetings. This ensured that almost to the last family all were aware of what was going on.

With the main bones of the administration in hand after a period of six years, it began to be obvious to even the most sceptical, that there had been a great purpose behind the selection and further training of local lads earmarked to take over from European leadership. Many kept saying that I would never leave Budu. It certainly looked as though I was not anxious to leave. This is true since I certainly had no intention of leaving Budu till Nairn trainees had returned and taken over. I was determined, even as Mac and Arthur were, that after all the work and thought which had been put into the scheme, the handing over was just not to be hurried and must wait till the lads at Nairn Academy in Scotland returned on completion of their education. It seemed elementary to me that only a lad who had reached a form five level could take over such duties as secretary of the Progress Society at Budu. Only a form five lad could take over the secretaryship of the Upper Krian Parish Council. Only fully qualified state registered nurses could replace Arthur to continue the medical coverage. Only trained teachers could take their place in the important Primary Schools. Only qualified agricultural assistants could continue the agricultural extension work that was still very much needed. Only able, dedicated lads could take over the running of the co-operative shops whose turnovers were at that time around thirty to forty thousand dollars per month in all.

So far so good but how was it possible to run and control all four centres and give to all equal coverage in medical matters. marketing and trading, administration, agriculture and education both adult and primary. I admit quite frankly that the early days were nightmares when the day was just not long enough and the three of us had to do the normal work during the day, and well into the night to catch up with the ever-increasing problems of administration. It was all possible, however, by the system of in-training started almost in the second year of the project. About twenty primary four boys of ages varying from fourteen to eighteen were provisionally selected as potential local lads who would take over in due course. No date for this could be given since it depended very much on the speed at which the trainees could absorb training and become academically able to run the scheme.

Mondays to Thursdays were devoted entirely to those twenty trainees. Outside work started at seven o'clock in the morning and continued for a full hour. So also in the evenings from four o'clock till five. This outside work was extremely important apart from the knowledge they were all gaining in planting, in giving fertilisers, in pruning and other agricultural matters. It was important in that, automatically, some lads stood out and showed potential leadership, others fell by the wayside. It was ruthless but necessary. Mac, Arthur and I always went out with the lads to work and so all of us were able to form opinions based on observation. From nine till four, all were in school with only short breaks for food and drink. Admittedly it was gruelling to both staff and trainees alike but there never appeared to be anything but a happy atmosphere. Possibly because we all felt that we were achieving something. On the hill could already be seen the fruits of our labours in new green shoots. In the classroom could be seen that a goodly number were making splendid progress. In odd moments there was singing and dancing, not only their own songs and dances but songs of other countries and folk dances. Concerts were organised to give experience to the trainees in stage craft and to bring out latent talents. A deeper purpose was to give training to all who wanted practice in speaking to audiences. In two years, although a few had gone, we were left with a splendid nucleus.

From Friday morning till late on Sunday night all of us were engaged in dispensary work, shop work, administration, engine handling, buying and selling goods at Saratok and all taking a chance at every job. No trainee in those two years was as yet allowed to specialise. Each had to know what was going on in the shop, on the river bringing up goods, in the dispensaries where approximately every Saturday and Sunday around a hundred patients were treated, some with serious illnesses, in the office where local taxes were received and receipted, on the hills where maintenance of high yielding rubber had to go on ruthlessly in the fight against disease, in the engine room where by now there were about ten engines to be kept in repair.

So it must be obvious now that any Community Development Officer while being essentially a specialist in at least two major jobs had also to know quite a bit in all the branches of development. By virtue of Arthur's work in the dispensary and since the dispensaries were always open when the shops were open or vice versa Arthur, while willing, could not spend much time in the shops. Each year we selected more trainees so as the years passed it was possible for the more senior trainees to travel at weekends to the other centres such as Grenjang or Ng Budu or Engkilili.

Grenjang was the least popular even with me, since the path took one through rather rough country but worst of all, about halfway, up a very steep hill. Luckily Mac, Arthur and I were always in fair training and even the trainees admitted that we, although Europeans unused to jungle travel, could hold our own. It was gruelling though and as I look back on those six years I begin to wonder just how we managed it. Could we do it again? I wonder! I think it was only possible because we three, and Doc when he joined us, knew it just had to be done. That it meant drawing on hidden reserves was certain but although we all became slightly thinner, our health remained good. Doc was a magnificent example in that even with his splendid qualifications and real ability in medical matters he was never behind in getting his hands dirty doing all kinds of jobs such as looking after the pigs we had at each centre and training the boys to do so. He became an adept trader and marketer and his knowledge of agriculture was to be envied. How he did all this and still ran the dispensaries is something we will never know. He gave, like Mac and Arthur, his very best in every aspect of the project.

As centre after centre was opened up (and in the fourth year of the project a start was made on a similar project in the third division, at Entaih, some ten hours' walk from Budu through virgin jungle with non-existent paths) so it was possible to give senior trainees the final tests of all before vital decisions were taken as to who should proceed for further training at Nairn, in Scotland, and who should not. Many people often ask me why I was so sure of our selections. My answer was that it was not difficult to know a lad if you worked with him, ate with him, travelled with him, taught him and listened to him on the many evenings spent in visiting other longhouses and passing on the gospel of development.

The full story of the Nairn trainees can be read in chapter eight. Suffice it to say here that after a great deal of soul searching and much thought we finally decided who should go abroad to finish training and education. Empeni and Paul first went to Scotland for a year, by arrangement with Scottish General Co-operatives, not so much to give them knowledge of how to run co-operatives but to give them, quite frankly, a prestige to smooth their work in taking over. Neither of them could be called academic, but they had given valiant service and this was their reward. Both benefited very much from going to Scotland and returned to do a good job of work in the centres that were just at the embryo stage at Kadup and Maong. They were just the type needed for this phase and they could be trusted to carry out plans with spirit and leadership.

Luke, Jawie, Bilun, Liman all had four years at Nairn Academy. During holidays and at weekends all were engaged in some form of work such as on a farm, in forestry, in travel, designed to give a full and comprehensive education. Chundie went to London to enter the Seaman's Dreadnought Hospital to try for his S.R.N. Although Chundie did not quite make it, his practical report was, as expected, very good. Unfortunately he contracted tuberculosis of the bone and his studies were interrupted considerably.

So in 1961 there returned from Britain Luke to take over the secretaryship of the Budu Progress Society and he did a splendid job. He remained secretary till June 1966 although he could have asked for his release in 1964. Liman became the number one in running the co-operatives and also became the secretary of the all-important Upper Krian Parish Council. Luke and Liman always worked very well together and affairs at Budu carried on frankly in many ways better than under European leadership. Bilun went for training as a teacher and returned to teach at Ng. Budu, a key school by 1963 and is to this day. Chundie, although not a fully qualified S.R.N., took over the dispensaries and carried on where Doc and Arthur left off.

By this time we, the Europeans, were all in the third division, consolidating affairs at Entaih, Maong, Tappang, Kadup and N. Entebai. The same general plan was followed for taking over. Jenuang, Kassin, Panggau and Henry were now at Nairn. Rabing was at Dreadnought to try also for his S.R.N. Jawie, luckily, was our spare and it was indeed fortunate that he was. Although having only a total schooling of some nine years, he was accepted into the Faculty of Medicine at Aberdeen University and in 1966 was capped with the degree of M.B., C.H.M.B. While knowing that the scheme would really miss his services it was quite impossible not to help him in every way to become if possible the first Sea Dyak doctor graduating in Scotland with an excellent degree. We were proud that he had even been admitted to university.

So in due course, to take over, returned Jenuang to Entaih, Kassin to Kadup, Panggau to Maong, Henry to Tappang. The gaps were filled in by using the most experienced trainees such as Enyang, Paul and Empeni. Rabing took over the dispensary at Ng. Entebai, having qualified as a state registered nurse. Morris and Eddie were sent to Nairn to be ready to fill such gaps as appeared by 1965, the final year of the project.

During 1964 and 1965, each centre was only visited by Europeans. Indeed after 1962, while we visited Budu, it was purely as ordinary visitors to see past friends but in no way did we hold any administration duties nor did we take part in any meetings.

There can be little doubt that the general policy of selecting young lads and sending them to Britain for further education was highly successful. While some have done better than others, the key trainees proved excellent in every way. It is interesting to note that of the fourteen in all sent, only two did not quite come up to expectations. Neither Mac nor I were surprised since even when those two were selected we knew that they had not had enough in-field training. Time was against us, however, and a chance had to be taken. It is certain also that selection cannot be hurried and must follow a pattern of in-field training and severe tests before final decisions be taken.

The administration of the Budu scheme and Entaih schemes can be summarised as follows.

Each centre required an organising secretary to carry out the decisions of the Progress Society. To assist the secretary, trainees are necessary and more in the form of apprentices than pure academic trainees. For each main watershed a qualified nurse is necessary to take over the medical coverage. Generally speaking this is still the formula to this day. Schools, however, have been taken over by the local authority working under recommendations from either the Upper Krian Parish Council or the Committee anak K.D.C. The two main dispensaries at Ng. Budu and Ng. Entebai have been taken over by the Medical services.

The work of the secretary is nevertheless still considerable, since he has to co-ordinate the five main branches of development.

PART TWO

"Military Aspects of Community Development"

By Brigadier H. R. S. Pain, D.S.O., M.C.

This is an opinion on the usefulness of Community Development work in helping to combat the Indonesian confrontation of Borneo. My own position was that of Commander Midwest Brigade during the last nine months of this conflict, that is from November 1965 to August 1966.

Midwest Brigade was responsible for preventing Indonesian incursions into the Second and Third Divisions (civil departments) of Sarawak, and in conjunction with the police for the internal security of the same area. The Brigade's share of the frontier with Indonesia was about 500 miles long and the area of responsibility was something of the size of Wales. The country was jungle from the hills where the border ran down to the swampy coast. There were many swift flowing rivers which drained the steep sided hills and such cultivation as was possible in the acid soil took place on the banks of the lower reaches of these waterways. The Second Division boasted one lateral road running parallel with the border; the Third Division had no road system at all between main centres of population. For years the waterways had been the highways of the country.

A Community Development Scheme was operated by Mr J. K. Wilson in the Entebai and Budu areas. To an outsider the aim appeared to be the total education of the population, not only of the native Dyak children but also of their parents. By total education I am also implying something that was not only an acquaintance with the three Rs but in addition a grounding in hygiene, agriculture and the simple economics of everyday life. The programme was striking because of the care taken not to isolate children from their parents through giving the young a superior education which was likely to be resented by their elders. Steps appeared to be taken to see that the older folk were kept continually in the forefront of the scheme and, if their standard of book learning was not high, their understanding of the reasons for their children's studies frequently discussed and rehearsed. By the time I arrived in the country Mr Wilson's scheme had been under way for many years. Not only were primary schools and clinics established but the first secondary school had been started as a private venture. A number of the more able boys had been sent (often at Mr Wilson's personal expense) to schools abroad in Scotland and in New Zealand. Several of these young men occupy posts in the growing civil service of Sarawak where their wider understanding of the world must be a healthy influence.

In order to appreciate what all this meant to a military commander arriving in the country during a state of emergency, it is necessary to digress a little to give some outline of the security problems.

The threat to Sarawak was broadly twofold. The incursions of Indonesian forces are probably better known about than the internal challenge to the Sarawak Government, posed in the main by dissident Communist Chinese. These dissidents, who numbered about a thousand, were a small proportion of the quarter million "Nanyang" Chinese domiciled in Sarawak and much of their discontent lay in the incorporation of their country of adoption into the Malaysian Federation. They had hoped for a Chinese-led independence for the state.

To complicate understanding of the overall threat there were also bodies of mainly ex-Sarawak Communist Chinese who had crossed the border into Indonesian Borneo. Towards the end of the emergency, these men had set themselves up as a guerilla force with a view to re-entering Sarawak when they judged the moment was ripe. In the Midwest Brigade sector the main Indonesian threat was opposite Second Division. That against Third Division was not as great, though we always had before us the knowledge that a successful Indonesian raid had been made on one up-country village earlier in the campaign. The internal threat in the Brigade sector again lay mainly in the Second Division, where a large proportion of the dissident Chinese elements lived in 1966 though earlier on there had been many Communist cells active in the western villages of the Third Division, not so very distant from Entebai and Budu.

As might be expected the deployment of Midwest Brigade to meet the combined threats led to a preponderance of soldiers being allocated to the Second Division. This left a single infantry battalion in the Third Division to look after the border situation and to provide assistance to the police in the maintenance of internal order. Of course it was only by the wide use of helicopters that such a large area could be adequately protected by a single unit.

The foregoing gives sufficient background to enable an appreciation to be made of the part played by the Entebai and Budu Community Development scheme during confrontation. It will be recalled that the villages were in the thinly garrisoned Third Division.

The main contribution came about simply by the existence of the scheme. This may seem rather a dull and negative statement and some explanation is called for. In an emergency of this type, it is important to retain the confidence of the home population in state administration and in the security forces, as it is to prevent incursions from across the border. By its educative process, the Entebai and Budu scheme had provided a degree of moderation and an understanding of the issues involved over quite a large area. Moreover it had most useful channels of communication through its teachers and students who travelled regularly to and from the schools, passing news and views by word of mouth as they went. I believe that the scheme also gave a feeling in these communities that something extra to what the state could provide was being done for them to provide opportunities for a fuller and more prosperous life.

Militarily there were two important benefits stemming from this. It is well known how steps to counter subversion depend largely on good intelligence and that a profitable source derives from ordinary people who are willing to watch and report on what they see from day to day. These ordinary people will only do this if they are assured of protection and confident that it will last. The Entebai and Budu peoples were in this frame of mind. In contrast, and to underline the point, it is just such lack of confidence by the populace that probably denies the best intelligence to the authorities in Vietnam at present.

Secondly, the existence of the scheme assisted military and police deployment. I have already pointed out how only one military unit could be spared for the Third Division and it was a relief not to have to station soldiers permanently in the Entebai and Budu areas. The security of the district against internal troubles could be left to the good sense of the stable community. This faith was justified. The mere existence of the Community Development scheme was then the foremost contribution but there was a secondary one. This concerns the participation by Mr Wilson and his students in the Border Scout Force. Once again I must digress a little to make understanding clearer.

The Border Scouts were raised in 1963 after the Brunei rebellion and at a time when British and Malaysian forces were starting to face the build up of Indonesian forces against the borders of Sarawak and Sabah. The force was created to assist the regular forces in surveillance of the long border. The essence of the movement hinged on the Border Scouts being deployed from their own villages and areas where their knowledge of the countryside and the people gave them excellent opportunity to detect the unusual. The story of the raising and training of the Border Scouts is a fascinating one but not part of this account. Suffice it to say that each division in Sarawak had its quota and the Third Division was no exception.

The Third Division Scouts were divided into three groups. The centre group worked alongside the infantry battalion whilst the northern and southern groups worked to a large extent independently. By that I mean that they conducted their surveillance under their own direction but in the knowledge that other military or police effort was on call to investigate further any "lead" they might obtain.

The opportunity of observing two independent groups of Border Scouts in the Third Division gave me the privilege of being able to compare them. The northern group operated over an area where several different ethnic tribes, mostly uneducated, simple of living, and in some cases only accessible after several days of foot and boat travel. This group, even though led by an excellent Dyak did not obtain as much information as I could have hoped for.

In contrast, the southern group based on Entebai was of a positive value and I can only attribute this to the fact that it drew its strength from being almost a part of the Community Development scheme. The group had, of course, immense advantage in being commanded by Mr Wilson who held an auxiliary police officer's appointment for the purpose. The channels of communication I spoke of earlier which spread Government policy outwards from the centre also worked in reverse to bring local information back to the Border Scout headquarters. The border area, looked after by the Entebai group, was an important one since it covered some of the communication tracks used by the dissident Chinese and their ex-Sarawak sympathisers on the Indonesian side of the border.

The strength of the Border Scouts came from their ability to work close to the ground in their natural environment in the same way as the successful subversionist operates. If I had a criticism of the Border Scouts, it was because of their keen and understandable desire to get dressed up in uniform and look like soldiers. Uniform was issued for use at base and it was a proud possession; but if worn on patrol, the trump card of anonymity was lost.

A conclusion to this essay is hardly necessary. All the facts point one way. Any stable community which is reliably on the side of lawful government is a pearl of great price in conflicts such as that in Borneo. The Community Development scheme at Entebai and Budu stood up to this definition and earned my regard as military commander of the area.

The entrance to a Dyak Longhouse

THE SEA DYAK BOYS IN SCOTLAND AND ENGLAND

I think I am going to enjoy writing this chapter. Of this I am sure, sending Dyak lads to Britain was probably the most interesting experiment that I have ever taken part in. That there were many difficult and anxious times I also certainly know. There was outspoken criticism of my actions and many friends even expressed grave doubts as to the wisdom of sending young teenage Dyak boys from a jungle environment to live in a country of sophistication and modernity. It is true I did not know whether the experiment would be a success but neither did I know whether the whole Budu Community Development Scheme would be successful either. I was convinced that it was vital to the success of the scheme to be able to hand over to not only well educated local lads, but to lads who had had more than just a normal school experience. They had to become men in as short a space of time as possible and there seemed to be no other way than to send the boys home.

In the *Nairnshire Telegraph* of 4th July 1967, the following column was printed.

NAIRN ACADEMY–SARAWAK COMMEMORATION

"A unique feature of the Academy prize-giving ceremony on Friday was the presentation to the school of a finely executed scroll to commemorate the association of the ten Sea Dyak boys with the Academy over the last ten years.

"The presentation was made to the Rector by Eddie Bryant, now due to return to his native Sarawak. He was previously given a specially designed Nairn Academy Certificate for himself, together with nine similar certificates for the other Dyak former pupils. Eddie is probably the last of the Dyaks to attend the Academy. The inscription reads.

1st June 1967. Sarawak. Dyak Festival Day.

To The Rector, Mr A. Robertson, Staff and Pupils of Nairn Academy, Scotland.

'From compromise and things half done,
Keep me, with stern and stubborn pride;
And when at last, the fight is won,
God keep me still unsatisfied'.

"These words by Louis Untermyer epitomise the spirit in which Nairn Academy undertook a challenging service to a country 9,000 miles from its doors.

"In a memorable August of 1957, just ten years ago, in an atmosphere of encouragement and kindness with no vestige of racial prejudice, you accepted into Nairn Academy two Sea Dyak Boys, Luke and Jawie from Budu, Sarawak. Both had been selected to play no small part in a scheme of Community Development among the Dyaks in the remote parts of Sarawak. Luke and Jawie were followed over the years by eight other Sea Dyak boys all with the same purpose. All were received with the same courtesy, encouragement and kindness.

"Each boy as he returned more than fulfilled all that had been expected from him. All without exception treasure an affection, which time will not erase for Nairn and its people. Even now some are well on their way to hold high positions of responsibility in Sarawak. All are held in high esteem and are known as men of integrity, dedicated to the service of their people.

"I send this as a simple expression of my sincere gratitude. Nairn, its people and in particular Mr and Mrs Mactaggart, formerly of Grianach, can feel a just pride in the boys who not only received a sound education but became men of purpose and character."

J. K. W.

In a personal letter from Mr Robertson, describing the ceremony, he writes: "Prize day event went off very well, and perhaps before the biggest audience we've ever had. Eddie did a magnificent job. After all the prizes had been distributed he came forward and handed over the scroll, mounted and framed. He delivered it with as graceful a speech and as manly a bearing as I ever saw.

"I tried to behave with the same dignity and read out the message of the scroll to all the people in Church. I found it intensely moving and when I got to the very last word I sat down before I broke down. More than one person in the audience was in tears and if you ever doubted the esteem in which the Dyaks were held in Nairn, your doubts would certainly have been dispelled for ever last Thursday. If, as I fear, Eddie is the last of our Dyaks, Nairn Academy is the loser."

Auntie Jean (Mrs Mactaggart) as the boys always called her also wrote to me by the same post and she writes:

"How often have I wished that the sponsors of my 'bairns' could see them on certain occasions. Thursday was one of these days! How I wished you could have seen Eddie and how proud you would have been of him! At the end of the proceedings, up he came to the platform and presented the Scroll to the Rector, thanking him, the staff and all his friends for all they had done for the Dyaks. He started off by saying that one half of him was sad as he would soon be leaving but the other half was happy because he had been asked to present the scroll. The cheers he got! You might have heard them in Sarawak. The Rector then thanked Eddie and proceeded to read what was on the scroll. He was overcome by the time he got to the finish. Everyone thought it was a most moving ceremony and so many spoke of Eddie's wee speech afterwards. The Chairman, Mr Taylor, summed it all up when he said that a link had been forged and influence spread both ways that no one could estimate. Funnily enough, for myself, except for the sadness of Eddie's departure, I didn't feel sad—rather an uplifting and a humility that I had been privileged to play a small part in your great adventure. I know that your Dyaks will go from strength to strength."

By the same post came news that Jawie had passed his degree of M.B. Ch.B. and was now a doctor. That Morris had passed his S.R.N. That Lambor had passed his diploma and was now a qualified radiologist.

That evening, all the tiredness, all the hardships, all the uncertainties over the past fourteen years, seemed to vanish. All that I had done now seemed justified and no one could now gainsay me. Nor did I feel ashamed when on telling the pupils of Jawie's success, the tears also came into my eyes.

Almost similar scrolls expressing our great appreciation were presented to Aunt Ella (my sister, Mrs Collins) of Clarkston, Glasgow, to Auntie Jean (Mrs Mactaggart) of Nairn, to Auntie Dora (Arthur's mother) of Warrington, England, to Indai Mac (Mac's mother) of Maybole, Ayrshire. There can be no doubt that without the help given by those people at home, it would have been quite impossible to provide the important essential, that a real home and a home environment was part and parcel of the boys' stay in Scotland. It was moreover essential that they had to be treated just as any Scots boy. They had to help in the homes washing dishes, sweeping floors, making their own beds. They had at week-ends to provide their own pocket money but they were sure of a seat in front of a fire on a cold winter's evening and were sure of a warm welcome in several homes when Nairn Academy closed for holidays. Almost all our mutual friends were roped into this, friends in Dunoon, Edinburgh, Campbeltown, Maybole, Warrington and London. All deserve our sincere thanks for all played a most important part in this story of the Sea Dyak boys at home.

I have the feeling that the chapter should now finish since what more should be said. Nevertheless, for others who might follow the same pattern let me, as briefly as possible, answer the questions which have been asked of me over the years and now answered.

I have often been asked why Nairn Academy was chosen and why send boys abroad when there were equally good schools in Kuching? As it happened, I did try to get our trainees admitted to the Batu Lintang Secondary School but the answer was that it was not possible since the Budu Primary School was not registered as an Upper Primary at that time. I was advised to try either of the two Mission Secondary Schools in Kuching. As I felt environment of the right type to be important I was not very keen on this suggestion. Both Mission Schools had, as a majority of pupils, Chinese lads who by virtue of their very racial characteristics would not just be too willing to give that essential help to any jungle boy from Budu. Some of course would but the very character of the Chinese is such that each survives by one's own efforts and devil take the hindmost. Academically I was quite sure that both Luke and Jawie could more than hold their own against the others but as I have said earlier, if our trainees were to be prepared to take over all the responsibilities of the scheme, they required much more than just a seat in a school to learn and pass examinations. However, as there was no money in sight, I did compromise and ask that they be admitted. The answer I regret to say was again, No!

My Scots sense of fairness was now in revolt and unwilling to be beaten at the start even, I there and then decided, no matter the personal cost, nor the trouble, I would find some good school for our trainees to enter. I wrote to my old headmaster, A. J. Ross and explained the position. We had kept very much in touch since he had always been my friend even in school at Dunoon. He replied by giving me every encouragement and intimated that he would find out in his own way, the best school in Scotland and prepare the way for the admission of both Jawie and Luke. No man could have helped me more. He went to tremendous trouble, even going to Edinburgh to examine school statistics and talking to many of H.M. Inspectors of Schools who certainly were able to finalise. There seemed no doubt that Nairn Academy had it by a good head. As luck would have it, and really now is the time to say that I think I have been very lucky all through this project, the Rector of Nairn Academy was a contemporary of both A. J. Ross and myself. Mr Ross himself made the initial contact and explained the position to Mr Robertson the Rector. A. R. as I have always called him was not only sympathetic but was determined to help in every way. From then on he did as much for Jawie and Luke and for all the others that followed over the years, as any father would do for their own sons. The debt we owe A. R. could never be repaid. I think, like myself, he did gain a great satisfaction from just helping in this most vital experiment. In one of his letters he writes:

"I am perpetually thankful to hear you say how pleased you are with what was done for the boys in Nairn. The truth is that you sent me the kind of boys who could not have been spoiled anywhere. It is possible the atmosphere in this school was more congenial to their development than it could have been in some others. The fact remains that anything Nairn did for your proteges was certainly no more than the boys did for Nairn. By their industry, loyalty, cheerfulness and meticulous grooming they were an example to some who started with far greater advantages. I just wish the whole experiment was starting all over again. Unfortunately there is not enough time for me to see it through."

His letter brings up the question as to how we groomed the boys to the stage that they could enter Nairn Academy and act as though they had been in a similar school from the start. I think it is worth while to detail the grooming of Jawie and Luke since they were the first. The others followed very much the same pattern. The only difference between Jawie and Luke and the others was that since I myself even did not know how my own people or my friends would receive our boys I adopted them legally since I was determined that both would have this chance and as my legally adopted sons, my people and friends at least would receive them with politeness and kindness, even though they might not come to give them the affection which I wanted them to have in a foreign land. As it turned out, Jawie and Luke quickly, by their own personalities, as did all the others, brought out the best in all who knew them. To this day there is still a warm bond of affection and friendship.

Well, Jawie's and Luke's story of grooming went as follows. Having almost firmly decided that they were the first two to go, we set about the job just as any parent would I expect. Mac, Arthur and I brought them into our tiny room for the evening meals which we had together. We made cutlery out of cardboard and although it was never possible to have a four course meal we went through the motions. As Dyaks are normally the most polite of any people I have ever met, we knew that we had nothing to teach them. The wearing of clothes was the next thing we tackled. I took them to Kuching and despite the looks from certain peoples, we installed ourselves in the rest house for a few days. Off we went to buy clothes, not expensive ones, but enough to give them the feeling of being dressed like others. Luckily I had many friends in Kuching at that time and all were roped in, and they responded, I may say, with eagerness. Most because they felt rather than believed, I was trying to do something to help a much under-privileged people which the Sea Dyaks were and those who had travelled certainly agreed that something should be done to help them. Some considered me a bit mad, especially as it was generally known that I had given up my job as Principal of the Batu Lintang Teachers' Training Centre to try and help the Sea Dyaks. Some, since snobbery played its part, were willing to help me because of the known support, both moral and personal, that Sir Anthony Abel, Governor of Sarawak, was giving me. Sir Anthony, wise beyond measure, gave me just the leg up I needed. In all the years, he never failed to pour oil on turbulent waters and to give me advice. To this day it is so and indeed I am in his debt, very much.

So my friends for one reason or another helped me a great deal in this grooming business. Luke and Jawie were invited out to social functions, cocktail parties, meetings. Soon it was obvious that much of the scepticism was disappearing. Jawie and Luke were delightful lads. They took to the grooming like ducks to water and I was thoroughly enjoying myself. Their bearing and manners even in those early days were impeccable. While I have still an affection towards all the boys of Budu, Entaih and Entebai, Jawie and Luke caught my heart. There was so much at stake and as I saw them in Kuching that first time, my heart warmed deeply to them both. It was inevitable that in my heart they became my favourites but I did try not to make it too obvious. As time passed they became as they are today very dear to me. It must not be thought that they were without the usual mischief. Jawie and Luke could vie with any Scots boy in that line.

In going to Kuching I had two motives. One to groom and the other equally important, I still had to find money to finance the project. If I had to be ruthless about it, so be it. As it turned out, the Director of Education, the Development Officer, the Financial Secretary all knew me well and believed in what I was trying to do. So at the meeting of the Community Development Committee which I had managed to organise, it was agreed that Government would provide passage money to and from Sarawak. I breathed a heart-felt sigh of sheer relief since, although I had by now slight reserves of money, to pay passages amounting to $4,000 would have been quite a strain on my resources. I think all knew that I would have paid the cost myself anyway.

So with half the financial battle won, we returned to Budu. There Mac and Arthur were of course delighted with the turn of events and we gave our thoughts to ways and means of finding the other half of the money needed, namely for upkeep, clothes and incidental expenses. A full meeting of the Progress Society was convened and it was then only that the people were informed of our hopes that some of their boys would go abroad to finish their education. I explained what Government were prepared to do and then asked what they could do. The people were delighted that there was this even chance and soon showed their enthusiasm for the project by agreeing that each family would provide $10 per year to help pay expenses of upkeep. Parents of any boys so selected would somehow find $500 in a lump sum to provide for the clothes needed for Scotland. Furthermore, profits from the Co-operative shop, plus the training fund, were to make up any deficit.

The stage seemed all set. We had two boys almost ready. Money was forthcoming and by this time provisional arrangements had been made with the Rector of Nairn Academy. A more important grooming still was ahead. That of transition from one way of life to a completely new one in Britain. How best it could be done was the subject of long discussions with Mac and Arthur. In the end we agreed that I should take some leave and travel home with Jawie and Luke. That we should all travel tourist, in order that Jawie and Luke would feel just a little bit more at home among ordinary people and not be startled with some of the stuffiness to be found in travelling first class. This does not mean that all people travelling first class are stuffy. Indeed this is not so, but those who have travelled widely will agree that our decision was right.

So off to Kuching once again for a more strict grooming and to buy the essential clothes for travel even as far as Singapore. Travelling documents, passports and health certificates all had to be got ready. Passages had to be booked. Once again, friends in Kuching were splendid and now knowing that it was no longer just a dream to take the two boys home, the job of clearances in health, passports was quickly done. Back we went to Budu once again, this time to give even sailing dates.

As it was essential under Dyak custom before any Dyak went abroad to guard against the evils of the outside world certain important ceremonies had still to be gone through. So, on a memorable night at Rh Gelau, opposite Budu, Luke and Jawie with their parents beside them propitiated their God and prepared for the great adventure.

On the 1st of May 1957 I sailed on the Rajah Brooke with Jawie and Luke to Singapore. Both turned out to be good sailors and it was a pleasant trip indeed. Arriving at Singapore both were a bit startled at the traffic but quickly took this in their stride. With only two days to go before embarking on the P. and O. Carthage for London, there was not much time for sightseeing. Clothes had to be bought and the boys initiated into hotel living. It was fun though and I was thoroughly enjoying myself. It was so exhilarating to be with such boys. They were full of life and interested in all that was to be seen. Just what their own reactions were can be read in their own personal accounts and I should imagine their own stories will be worth reading. That they were not cowed nor even greatly impressed with Singapore was evident. Both gave the impression of just tolerating Singapore as a necessary staging point. They were not city boys and I was actually greatly relieved and knew that Nairn in Scotland would just be the right place for them.

There was never a dull moment on board the Carthage. A fairly strict schedule was kept. Up early, some exercises, breakfast and two hours of study. This had to be done since both were low on French, Mathematics and Science. Many of the passengers were deeply intrigued by the two lads. In their off time they could be seen being absolutely normal youngsters, rushing and laughing around the ship. At study, they would change completely to serious charming pupils. It was not long before they themselves made friends. I remember two of them, David and John. I think Luke still writes to John. They were splendid lads also, and much of the same age. I have much to be grateful for to those two lads since they taught Jawie and Luke many things in this new environment of the ship.

At each port of call, every advantage was taken to let both Jawie and Luke see all that could be seen. They were impressed with the Suez Canal and I can still see Jawie just sitting and watching with his bright eyes dancing hither and thither. Luke, being the more serious, at times wanted to know the history of it all. I kept wishing I had read more. As we landed at Tilbury Docks, London, I wished I could see into the future and as the real test was about to begin, I would have given a lot just to be back at Budu. There were so many unanswered questions in my mind. How would the boys be received both at home and at school in Nairn? Would there be racial prejudice which would defeat the whole project? Only time could tell and in any case the die was cast. Jawie and Luke were in London with me en route for Scotland.

Curiously enough, and yet not really knowing the tremendous affection that Dyaks have for the Queen, the only place they were in a hurry to see was Buckingham Palace. With the smart sentries on duty, the magnificent background of Queen Victoria's monument and the wonderful approach, both were visibly impressed and would hardly leave to go and see anywhere else. Taking them to the circus in the evening was tremendous. They just could not believe what they saw. Next day the Houses of Parliament and Westminster Abbey. Indeed it was a pleasure taking them around. London certainly they could understand, despite the traffic, and Singapore took a very back place in their estimation. It showed a discernment that I had not thought possible at this stage of their development. Jawie summed it up by saying that Singapore was all shiny and glossy but London was old and homely.

The subway was beyond what they had dreamed of. It was just incredible. The moving stairways, the fast trains that just appeared out of the big hole as Luke said. The diagrams, meant to help, as they do, led to many questions as to how the trains passed over each other. Tunnels were not something they could easily understand knowing the difficulties that they had making even small holes in the ground to plant rubber. To make a big hole, big enough for two trains to pass each other and even more than that, to pass above and below each other was beyond their engineering experiences. It was fun taking them on the subway.

However I was anxious to reach home and taking the Flying Scotsman we left London for Glasgow on the last leg of our journey. They had heard of trains and seen pictures of them. This journey from London to Glasgow was just the last word in comfort and speed. I think at times they were just a little afraid but certainly never said so. Mac, Arthur and I had taught them a fair amount of geography of Britain and it was fairly easy for them both to follow the journey. They were particularly anxious to see Hadrian's Wall and it is a pity that nothing really can be seen from the train to mark this famous landmark between England and Scotland.

On time, the Flying Scotsman came to a smooth stop at Glasgow Central and as luck would have it my sister and nephew could be seen from the carriage window. The next few minutes were going to be interesting, I remember saying to myself.

Much was going to depend on Leonard, although being young he was quite unaware at that time of the tremendous responsibility he was going to have to shoulder. On Leonard, luckily much the same age, was the task of giving to both Luke and Jawie all that they needed to know to habilitate themselves in a Scottish environment. Leonard was superb. I had always liked Leonard and knew that he would try, but such things cannot be forced if real feelings are not involved. Without talking down to them and behaving so naturally Leonard somehow put them both at their ease. By the time we reached home, they were blethering away and I knew that this first hurdle of acclimatisation would present no serious problem if Leonard could spare the time and patience.

Arriving at home, Bill Collins, my sister's husband, had just returned from his ship. The boys immediately took to him. He was of course a very fine man, knowledgeable, kindly, and essentially a man of the world. He just knew how to put them at ease. Bill had in any case been very interested in the whole experiment from the beginning and he was determined to help in every way. No one could have given me more confidence in myself than Bill. Throughout the years, until Bill died, the boys knew that they could always go to him in trouble. From Aunt Ella (Mrs Collins), as the boys soon called her, they received more than just affection. She looked after all their wants and this began even the next day by Aunt Ella taking them down to the large shops in Glasgow to buy, or begin to buy, all the clothes necessary. Aunt Ella was perfect for this. She was determined that the boys would be dressed not just in anything, but in clothes that were right. As she said herself many times afterwards "It would have been a shame if those boys, so clean and with such fine bodies, were not dressed in clothes that really fitted them".

On the ship we had made do with what we could pick up and the difference was very soon obvious. One could almost see them becoming little men, with a real pride in their clothes and stature. To this day, ten years later, Luke still has many of the clothes that Aunt Ella bought for him.

As soon as Leonard had any free time, he would take them out to teach them to ride bicycles. I used to sit at the window watching them and really it was fun. All the neighbours became so interested and helpful, especially as Jawie was to be seen, careering down the crescent, quite out of control and ending up with handlebars in the air, blood all over him, but still with that wonderful smile on his face.

Their efforts to master this demon as Jawie said kept us all in fits of laughter. The weather was kind and everybody seemed to be gay. Leonard persuaded them eventually to take to a field and there, with the sweat pouring from his face, Jawie and Luke finally mastered the cycle. Then it was a question of making sure they both remembered that they were NOT in the jungle and that there were rules of the road. However they were very obedient and gradually my anxiety about traffic faded. They were apt pupils as Leonard said. Over the years we taught them to drive motor cycles and cars, giving them that essential something which could prove to themselves that they were just as capable as any other lad, given the chance.

So the month in Glasgow passed very pleasantly with Leonard taking them both to learn to play golf, walk on the hills near Clarkston, swimming in the baths, sightseeing and learning how to use the telephone. Often Aunt Ella would get them to telephone her from somewhere so that they would know, if ever they were lost, just what do do. Leonard showed them how to travel on buses, tram cars, subway. Intentionally he would lead them somewhere and he would tell them nothing as to how to get home, unless they were stuck. Soon they learned that all buses did not go the same way and that their numbers and destination were equally important. I think Leonard enjoyed all this since he never tired of taking them about and around. Throughout the years Leonard gave each of them the same treatment and to this day they remember his help and often say how difficult it would have been without his help.

Somehow the news of the Dyak boys from the "jungle" reached the newspapers. Fortunately when I talked to the reporters they realised also how essential it was that such boys were to be treated normally and not as something strange to be peered at and perhaps made fun of, so they all co-operated and were content with a picture or two. The Rector at Nairn had a much greater trouble to keep the boys from newspaper publicity of the wrong sort. A. H. became adept at keeping the boys protected as it were.

While in Glasgow also, I took the boys to the B.B.C. at Queen Margaret Avenue. There we met Bill Meikle and Mrs Menary who over the years became firm friends, giving me tremendous help. It was essential that the boys still had contact with Sarawak and it was essential that their own fathers and mothers, their own friends and relations could hear news of them. So few around Budu in those days could read that in any case it was not much good sending letters home except to school friends. So it was to Bill Meikle that I gave the problem. Not only was he helpful but immediately agreed on a series of broadcasts to be sent by tape to Radio Sarawak. I knew that Radio Sarawak would be delighted since I had told them what I hoped to arrange. Bill put us in the care of Mrs Menary, a charming, capable and delightful lady who put the boys immediately at their ease. To both Bill Meikle and Mrs Menary, although for some reason or another I always called her Mrs Drinkwater, we owe a lasting debt. Over the ten years they never failed to receive each pair of boys with the same courtesy and encouragement. What was probably the greatest contribution through the B.B.C. was the Christmas day broadcast from each boy. I know for a fact that their parents used to sit all day in front of their radios, or someone's radio in case they would miss hearing the voices of their own boys. Bill Meikle or Mrs Menary used to keep me well posted and both went to a lot of trouble, even going up to Nairn to record, so that studies in school were never interrupted. Christmas day broadcasts from overseas boys to their homes far away, through the courtesy of the B.B.C. has become a feature of Christmas day in Sarawak, to this day, even though we have no boys at Nairn now. We owe a great deal to Bill Meikle and Mrs Menary and of course to the overseas service of the B.B.C.

Time was passing all too fast and the day was not long enough. I felt it essential also that both Jawie and Luke should meet the parents of Mac and Arthur as well as all my own friends. I was determined that they would feel integrated in the normal life in Scotland of those whom they trusted in Sarawak. So off we went on a memorable visit to Mr and Mrs Thwaites at Warrington. Auntie Dora and Uncle Alfred they became to all the boys as soon as they met. Uncle Alfred was rather like Bill Collins in so many ways. He was confident that with such boys, all would be well. I think both Auntie Dora and Uncle Alfred, having at last seen a bit of Arthur's work in Sarawak, laid aside any misgiving that Arthur was wasting his time. Nothing was too much trouble to Auntie Dora and Uncle Alfred. Part of each holiday was from then on spent partly with Aunt Ella, partly with Auntie Dora and Uncle Alfred. It just seemed to me to be so kind of everybody and each and all really went to a great deal of trouble to ensure that all the boys had this certain home relationship.

So also with Mrs McBride at Maybole. She became called Indai Mac, meaning Mac's mother. We never knew but it just seemed to be right somehow. Maybole with its near perfect scenery and proximity to lovely sandy beaches was an excellent place for the boys. Indai Mac was really so very motherly and kind. She too quickly felt that Mac was doing something worthwhile and was content to help in any way. She did this so often at short notice.

Next came the question of work during the holidays from school. Fortunately, Arthur came home for a short break and of course we all met. Arthur had a friend in Paisley, Kenneth Caldwell, who knew about the project and was a keen Scout. He suggested that Lord Rowallan would probably help in this, especially as the boys were from abroad. He very kindly arranged a meeting with Lord Rowallan and once again as luck turned out, I had previously met Lord Rowallan. The whole project was explained to him and he became most interested and immediately offered his help by suggesting that Jawie and Luke should work on his home-farm and live with his manager who could look after all their needs. He would provide pocket money and food and make their stay at the home-farm both educational and instructive. So it was arranged that Jawie and Luke would be brought down by Aunt Ella and installed at Lord Rowallan's home-farm for two weeks. It turned out to be an excellent arrangement and as with all the others who helped we owe a great deal to Lord Rowallan and in particular to his manager and wife who treated the boys as their own. They could see how others worked and lived on farms and be part of it as they were. Both were willing workers and all the boys had their stay or several stays at the home-farm.

Back from the farm, I took Jawie and Luke to stay with my own close friends in Dunoon and Campbeltown where I had spent a great deal of my youth. Uncle Ian and Aunt Effie, Auntie Mabel, the Misses McAllister, all gave Jawie and Luke that warm welcome that at this stage meant so much. Dunoon being the kind of holiday resort that it is, made them also realise that Scotland was not all smoke and dirt. They said so. Ian and Effie went to a great deal of trouble to ensure that they felt at home. Luckily they had a daughter, young Effie as we always called her and she was like Leonard. She could not do enough for Jawie and Luke, even taking them out to fish in small boats and teaching them how to row. After this visit to Dunoon, even I could see that most of the hidden fears of the boys were evaporating and my impending departure back to Sarawak was not going to be as though the skies had fallen. Finally to complete this attitude I took them to Campbeltown to see Mr and Mrs McGougan, very old friends of mine. Archie and Mrs Mac and I had spent many memorable days on the hills of Kintyre. To Archie and Mrs Mac must go the credit of casting out those horrid dreams that so many pilots were so liable to get after the war. The hill climbs, the rock climbing, the picnics on the rough but grand shores of Kintyre had been just the right medicine for me in those dark days when no longer did I have to fly into the night and undoubtedly kill. Then and now I could never see any justification for war and all its inevitable evils despite that at the time one felt there was no other way than to kill to win.

So in company with Archie and Mrs Mac, Luke and Jawie came to love the hills and shores. Archie was a fountain of knowledge and there was nothing he did not know about Kintyre and every bird almost, there on the hills. Even Jawie felt that Archie knew everything, as he did. Mrs Mac and I just sat and blethered of old times and the cares of the world seemed to fade away. We were all sorry to leave Campbeltown. I think both Jawie and Luke knew that I wished almost to remain, especially as my dog was there with Mrs Mac and Archie. He was a lovely dog, but all dog lovers say this about their own dog. Dubh, as he was called, was a massive black Labrador. It was such fun taking him on the hills too.

However as there were only a few more days to go before Jawie and Luke had to be at Nairn for the opening of the school we had to leave and return to Glasgow. We had one more place to visit and I think I had intentionally left this to the last. Yes, it was Edinburgh to see the Shrine, the castle, the gardens and to walk along Princes Street. I had and still have a few close friends in Edinburgh and two aunts, sisters of my mother. I was fond of them both. During the day we visited my relations and all gave Jawie and Luke the same warm welcome they had got everywhere. In the evening they met my old friends, Alice, Kath, Pam, Michael. Alice had arranged a celebration dinner at a fashionable restaurant. I had asked her to do this so that she could (and I knew she would be very honest) tell me what still I had to do with Jawie and Luke before I left them. As the evening passed, there was little doubt as to her opinions. Jawie and Luke were superb. Their manners impeccable and their conversation incredible, considering that only two months had passed since they had left the remote parts of Sarawak. I knew that if Alice "passed them" I had little to fear and I knew too, since I had known Alice for many many years that she would tell me just what she thought. To have friends like Alice is a privilege. When she said that she had no qualms at all, I felt well content and any anxieties that were still with me, seemed to fade away and I was confident also of tomorrow.

Finally in Edinburgh I took Jawie and Luke to see Mr and Mrs Alec Dickson. Both had been to Budu and both were extremely interested in this experiment of sending young Dyaks to Scotland. Alec had always been interested in the education of underdeveloped peoples and his knowledge and experience had been a great help to me. He is of course well known as the originator of the Volunteer Services Overseas Scheme which has played such an important part in underdeveloped territories. A more detailed account of his work and its relation to Budu and Entebai in particular can be found in Chapter Nine. We had also known each other for many years and had met at various seminars and conferences. Moira too is well known by her books. I cannot improve on her own description of the meeting between us all that day in Edinburgh. Those who are interested can read this in Moira Dickson's own book, "Season in Sarawak".

Back in Glasgow we went just to pack and leave for Nairn. While I had by now no great anxieties as to how the boys would settle at Nairn, I did not know how the other lads in school would treat Jawie and Luke. Nor did I know just how they would be received by Mr and Mrs McTaggart of Grianach where it had been arranged the boys would stay. The people of Nairn too were an unknown quantity. A visit of a few days to anyone is very very different to a visit of certainly a few years. Of the Rector's full support I was confident but one wrong step at this stage could jeopardise the whole project. However there was no turning back at this stage whatever qualms I might have had inside me. Nor really did I consider for a moment turning back and taking the boys back to Sarawak with me.

On the road North, we spent a most pleasant evening with A. J. Ross, my old headmaster. He was delighted to meet Jawie and Luke and we talked far into the night. He assured me of his confidence in the project and now having met Jawie and Luke he was certain that all would be well. On parting the next morning he handed me a letter telling me to open it later on. When I did, I found a cheque for £100 which in most moving words he asked me to use in whatever way I thought right to further the work I had been doing. Of course the money in itself was a tremendous help since I had been fairly extravagant travelling around but he could not know just how much this meant to me as a gesture of full confidence.

I remember to this day saying to myself as I drove on from Perth to Nairn, that whatever difficulties lay ahead in Nairn, somehow those would have to be overcome.

A. R. had arranged that we stay at the Windsor Hotel and as in everything A. R. did it turned out to be just the best possible place to stay in.

Both Mr and Mrs Munroe, the proprietors, had been abroad and had spent many years in Malaya. Although A. R. never said so, I rather think this was the reason why he had suggested the Windsor. He too was not taking any chances and I blessed him for his thoughtfulness. Mrs Munroe immediately took the boys to her heart, and incidentally gave both Jawie and Luke two large blocks of Cadbury's chocolate. I wonder if she remembers this seemingly small incident. It had a profound effect on Jawie and Luke since in their own longhouse in the remote parts of Sarawak, although certainly chocolate would not have been given to the visitor, some refreshment of one kind or another would have been. It somehow made all the difference to Jawie and Luke. To this day Luke loves chocolate.

Those who have stayed at the Windsor Hotel in Nairn will know how comfortable and pleasant it is. It was just right in every way, even to a small bar where there was almost everything to suit even the most particular of palates. The food too was just splendid and having had a bath and dinner we went out in search of A. R. who was expecting us at his home.

Mrs Robertson or Betty as I called her from then on, opened the door with a really charming smile on her face and ushered us in. Both Jawie and Luke were immediately put at their ease by finding themselves sitting round a lovely coal fire. The evening had got chilly and it seemed to make all the difference. Betty, being probably quite unaware of her importance as the rector's wife possibly did not realise that on her alone almost, depended whether Jawie and Luke would be given a traditional Scottish welcome when they went to school. I am sure both A. R. and myself did realise the importance of this meeting and we both breathed a heartfelt sigh of relief when it was obvious that Betty too had taken them to her heart. She was splendid and with her son Ritchie they chattered away to both the boys. I owe a great deal to Betty since from this very start she gave both her moral and physical support. Throughout the years, she made a point of inviting all the Dyak boys to her home, and was always available for advice and help at any time. They remember her with a sincere affection.

Ritchie then took over, just as Leonard had done in Glasgow. They were much the same age and we knew they were getting on fine together by the chatter from Ritchie's own little den where he had all his treasures of stamps and books. Ritchie too was an important influence.

A. R., Betty and I took the opportunity of discussing more deeply the whole project. A. R. himself did not quite know the reaction of the Nairn people and suggested that I might address the Nairn Rotary Club the following day. Although not a Rotarian myself, I had occasionally been invited to address the Kuching Rotary Club, when I was Principal of the Teachers' Training College, in Kuching. I was well aware of the importance and the honour of this invitation. Both A. R. and I knew that if the Rotarians at Nairn accepted the boys then all would be well. This was not snobbishness. It is well known that Rotary Clubs the world over give a helping hand where needed and moral support from the Nairn Rotarians would be vital. I think my answer to A. R. rather shook him. I must ask him some day. I said that I was not trying to sell myself but the boys and since this was the object, could he invite the boys as well. I knew this was a lot to ask since they were after all minors. Nevertheless, with the unfailing courtesy and kindness A. R. gave throughout our ten years of association, he did not see why it should not be possible and said that he would arrange this. I had few qualms as to how the boys would speak but it was possible, like any other boys, they would dry up as they got up to make their speech. So it was agreed that I would give a brief outline and call upon Jawie and Luke to speak for themselves. At least I could give them the important points to stress and I crossed my fingers that even if their words were unintelligible, I was sure that their manners would be favourably commented on.

I think most of the Rotarians at that meeting remember this occasion. Jawie and Luke spoke as though they were seasoned after lunch speakers and my heart swelled inside as I listened to them both. It was not what they said but how they said it. There was little doubt that the Nairn Rotarians would give their full moral support. Throughout the years the Nairn Rotarians have even vied with each other to ensure that all the Dyaks were received with the real Scottish hospitality. The Nairn Rotary Club has contributed much financially to the boys' upkeep both at Nairn and in Sarawak. We here in Sarawak are indeed grateful. The Rotary Clubs both in Kuching and Sibu, Sarawak, knowing of this have made special efforts to help the project also. The world can be a small place.

A. R. was as delighted as I was, and there remained only the question of the attitude of the pupils with whom Jawie and Luke would spend most of their time. Once again A. R. made the suggestion which as it turned out was just the right one. He thought it would be a good idea if I addressed the senior forms and members of staff and told them as much of the story as I felt I could. He thought that if the pupils were told of the importance of the project they would go out of their way to ensure that Jawie and Luke were given all the help that they needed. How right A. R. proved to be. From the day that Jawie and Luke were admitted to Nairn Academy as pupils, they received every possible help from both the staff and pupils, much more really than anybody else. To boys straight from a one class school, deep in the heart of Sarawak, to Nairn Academy with its hundreds of pupils, corridors and classrooms, the change must have been frightening at first, and this willing help from the oldest to the youngest was of supreme importance. I wonder if the pupils at Nairn knew just how important it was!

With A. R. I discussed the possible curriculum but since it was obvious he was immensely capable, knew by instinct the real needs of Jawie and Luke, I frankly left all this to A. R. My confidence in him was absolute and I knew he would do and give what was best for the boys. As the years passed and especially when Jawie entered Aberdeen University, after only a total of nine years' schooling, I knew I had few worries, if any, as to what they were studying at Nairn. The academic side while important was only a part of the project. The boys had to return as men with just that something that would make them stand out, men that people would instinctively trust and who would automatically receive the respect due. The words on the scroll at the beginning of the chapter are indeed sincere. The Rector, Staff, and pupils of

Nairn Academy between them all did a splendid job. Although A. R. keeps on saying that I sent him excellent material, craftsmen are needed to shape the product.

The following day I took Jawie and Luke to be introduced to Mr and Mrs McTaggart with whom, as I have said, they would live. As soon as I saw Auntie Jean and Uncle Mac, I knew the last of my anxieties were over. Both had been abroad and Auntie Jean had been a teacher. She proved more than a teacher. She had that wonderful capacity of understanding boys, knowing just when to be firm, and when to be kind. When they were ill, which luckily was not often, she cared for them as she would her own. She wrote me frequently, I think because she knew I just wanted to have news of them. Above all she did not spoil them by doing everything for them. She knew just what I wanted. They had to help keep the house clean, help wash the dishes, keep their own rooms clean and tidy and above all make their own beds. Auntie Jean used to make me laugh as she described some of Jawie's efforts at making beds. At Budu they had none. We all slept on the floor and in the morning we rolled everything up in a kind of mat. Later in the day, all this would be put out in the sun. At the beginning, Jawie would do this with his mattress, blankets, etc., and of course the result was more a mountain of untidiness than a neatly arranged bed. He learned.

Uncle Mac provided the suggestion that as he knew Lord Cawdor, he thought that at the weekends the boys could find work weeding and pruning in the pine wood nurseries. Off to Cawdor we went, armed with the introduction from Uncle Mac. As Uncle Mac was an important councillor and was also a magistrate, I knew his letter would help. Once again, help was forthcoming and we met the head gardener, Mr Macdonald, and his wife. He was a real typical Scotsman but what a heart he had when he allowed the gruff exterior to thaw. This he did often enough to show that if good work was to be done he would be the first to say so. If bad, well whether they were Dyaks from Sarawak or Indians from India or boys even from Scotland, they would hear the hard end of his tongue. He was superb. Just what was needed as I knew both Jawie and Luke to be discerning enough anyway and I knew also they would not cheat in any work given to them. I wanted this strict surveillance however, since boys are boys the world over and I did not want them to get out of doing a good day's work when needed. Pocket money was not the important point about this weekend work. It was primarily to keep them busy and bring them into contact with older men, men who had to work for a living and who knew that if the work was bad there would be no living. That Cawder was six miles away, and although I knew that the boys would have to cycle there and back, did not daunt me or make me feel that it was going to be too hard for them. Living in Sarawak was hard and they were in Scotland to prepare to live in Sarawak again. As it turned out the boys loved this kind of work and the only friction that existed was a friendly one between the men and the boys. The boys could and did work faster. They were in their natural surroundings and were at home in the forests. I did feel however that I was asking Auntie Jean to do too much, since she insisted on getting up early on the Saturdays giving the boys a hearty breakfast and making up their lunch. Could the boys have had a better chance? Auntie Jean's own experiences abroad greatly, I think, influenced her attitude and her methods. She, too, had seen so-called educated products returning from Britain after finishing their courses or schooling and many seemed not to fit in on their return. She was determined that the Dyak boys would share in the everyday life of any Scots boy. The boys were encouraged to go to Church on Sundays. This actually was my idea. The boys had often heard me saying that when in Rome, one should do as the Romans did but that it did not mean that one became a Roman. So by going to Church they were only in effect participating in the life of the people of Scotland. I reminded them that I often went to their own ceremonies even though I was a Christian, and I did so to understand better the Dyak way of life and thought. In any case the boys without exception enjoyed thoroughly the normal Sunday by going to church in the morning with Auntie Jean. I am sure this had a very steadying influence on them and certainly brought them into contact with real Christian ideas unrelated to bribery.

The aesthetic side was not forgotten either. All the boys were near experts on some form of country dancing. They had been taught by either Mac, Arthur who was the expert, or by myself. In this form of dancing they were naturally graceful and they loved it. Even to this day country dancing is taught in many Dyak schools within the Budu and Entebai areas. On my second visit home I took with me a full set of Dyak gongs so that the boys too could not only keep their own form of dancing but could, as they did, give exhibitions of Dyak dancing at certain functions. The Nairn people loved it. They were encouraged to join either the Air Training Corps or the Boys' Brigade. They could have joined the Scouts, too, but costs of uniform made this prohibitive. Jenuang and Eddie both became sergeants in the A.T.C. and learned a great deal which has been very helpful back in Sarawak. They were encouraged to take part in school plays and loved this. Performances of Jawie, Henry and Eddie are remembered to this day. Through the courtesy and great kindness of Major Noy of the Commonwealth Youth Fellowship most of the boys were able to see many different countries in the company of boys of their own age and thought. Jawie and Luke went to Canada to see the Queen open the St. Lawrence waterway. Jawie, chosen to give a speech of welcome to the Queen, made history by speaking in excellent French. This seemed to me incredible from a boy who only two years previously had left his leaf walled school for Nairn. Liman and Bilun went to Gibraltar. Jenuang to Norway. Jenuang incidentally became the school champion for swimming and diving. He was superb at this. He also represented Nairn Academy at the West of Scotland Sports and was second in the high jump and pole vault. I was lucky to be at home at this time and I was indeed proud of our Dyaks.

The boys were encouraged to speak publicly at Toc H functions and at Woman's Guilds and apparently they did this well.

So as the years passed the boys became men and when they returned to Sarawak they fulfilled more than what had been hoped for or expected.

Jawie is now a doctor, Liman and Jenuang are Sarawak administrative officers, Bilun, Henry, Panggau, Kassin are teachers, Morris an S.R.N. Eddie is still continuing his education with hopes that he might become a pilot some day. Luke still helps me in any and every capacity. He is wonderfully loyal and capable. That he remains helping me is his own choice. Indeed the words on the scroll at the beginning of the chapter are not only sincere but deserving. The Rector of Nairn Academy, the staff and pupils, Mr and Mrs McTaggart and the people of Nairn did a splendid job.

So we pass on to Chundie and Rabing who left Budu and went to the Greenwich Dreadnought Hospital to try to obtain their S.R.N. certificates. The Seamen's Dreadnought Hospital, Greenwich, was chosen for a very simple reason. Arthur had been trained there and he thought that if Chundie and Rabing managed to be admitted for training, there was no better place. Arthur wrote to the Matron whom he knew and who fortunately remembered Arthur. Miss Noble proved as helpful as the Rector of Nairn Academy. Of course she was willing and would give them every help and encouragement possible. This she did in no small measure throughout their training, often going out of her way to be sure that all was well with them. She was I think the perfect matron, rather like old Mr Macdonald at Cawder. A heart of gold but firm and determined that any nurses who passed out of Dreadnought would indeed be a nurse. We remain grateful to Miss Noble. Auntie Dora, Arthur's mother at Warrington, from the very day of their arrival looked after all their wants, even as Aunt Ella did for the boys in Scotland. To this day both write to their Auntie Dora frequently and happily. Auntie Dora indeed deserved her special scroll even as Aunt Ella. Rabing took his S.R.N. in the minimum of time and returned to help as planned. He was splendid. He is now senior staff nurse at a large hospital. Chundie, as I have said before, developed most unfortunately a bone T.B. infection which interrupted his studies and training. Although unable to obtain his S.R.N. he too returned to help at Budu and remained there till circumstances compelled him to transfer. Chundie was ironically enough a natural nurse and were I sick today, it would be to Chundie I would go were it possible, this despite the fact that he did not get his S.R.N. I remember Chundie with great affection since it was he who helped me in the first year at Budu, as I treated the odd hundred patients who came each Sunday.

Last but certainly not least was Lambor, adopted by Doc. Doc took him home to Banff and at Banff, Lambor went to school. Doc's father was also a doctor and his mother a teacher. Lambor indeed had every care. Banff being close to Nairn made visits easy and there was quite a coming and going of the boys from Nairn to Banff. Mrs Lees was always charming and despite the fact that six to eight Dyaks would descend on her, she made them always so welcome. Lambor has returned to Sarawak, having qualified as a radiologist.

Reading this through it would appear that with the boys at home it was all work and no play. This was not so although I grant you the time spent on play was limited to about two weeks a year. Fortunately I had a caravan well equipped with tents, blankets and ground sheets, at Loch Lomond. So it was to Loch Lomond and the district around that all the boys went to relax and have fun, their kind of fun. They loved fishing, climbing and driving outboards. They needed no teaching to handle outboards or boats for that matter since all through their training at Budu they had had to maintain and drive outboards through very much more difficult waters than to be found at Loch Lomond. There were the normal crises, common to any family. It was inevitable that at least some of them were caught with mist and low clouds at the top of Ben Lomond or other mountains and there were anxious moments. When I was at home I revelled in this life with them at Loch Lomond. When I was not at home, luckily Aunt Ella also loved caravanning at Loch Lomond and she was always ready to take the boys there and if she could not wait with them, she saw to it that they had enough food. My other sister, Mrs Sinclair, or as known to the boys Auntie May, with her husband Uncle Norrie also loved the open air. Auntie May was a great favourite with all the boys and knows more about Scotland than most people. It was Auntie May that took the boys to all the famous places of historical interest, places that the boys had read about either at school in Budu or Nairn. She taught them much in that spirit of fun and laughter. Uncle Norrie being the more serious minded came into his own when the boys grew older. It was he who developed their thinking on world affairs and gave them the chance to talk on more serious matters. They always enjoyed visiting Auntie May and Uncle Norrie, Eddie, Luke, Jawie particularly.

I remember too, spending a holiday at Tarbert with Aunt Ella, Alice, Jawie and Luke and Leonard. One morning the boys took a boat and set off to fish, leaving us on one of the islands opposite the delightful harbour. By mid morning however a near gale had sprung up quite unexpectedly and it was blowing out to sea. I was in a panic especially as I spied away out the three boys in the boat. Admittedly they were rowing towards safety and harbour but even I could see they were not going to make it without help. But there we were stuck on the island with no way of getting back to find the help needed. The waves started to get big and I can remember Aunt Ella, worried also about Leonard, running back and forwards trying to attract attention by waving her coloured blouse. By the greatest of good luck, the crew of a beautiful yacht anchored in the harbour saw her and weighed anchor to find out what the trouble was. They could not come close to the rocks on which we were standing, but by signs and shouts they somehow got the score and knew what had happened. Up went the sail and the yacht skimmed its way out to the open sea. Even the yacht was getting thrown around but the helmsman waved to us as much as to say, "Don't worry. We'll bring them back". Jawie, Leonard and Luke were by this time just a small dot on the horizon. Luckily Alice kept her head and cooled both Aunt Ella and I down. We were all for swimming after them so anxious were we. An hour went by and we could see the yacht getting closer and closer to where we had last seen the boys. Another anxious hour passed before we breathed a heartfelt sigh of sheer relief as we saw the yacht making its way back to harbour. Soon we were able to see the boys laughing and waving in the bow. To them it just had been great fun.

One other lad should be mentioned although he did not go to Britain. This was Jangga who curiously enough went to New Zealand under the auspices of the Sibu Rotary Club and Auckland Rotary Club. Although the offer was very tempting I did not agree however until I had got in touch with my own navigator, Keith Hodgson, whom I knew lived in Auckland. Keith and I had gone through much together, he expertly guiding me through flak zones. He was indeed an expert in air navigation. I maintain that it was Keith's skill that always brought us back often under very very difficult conditions of weather and enemy action. I knew he and his wife Gladys would if they could, look after Jangga for me. I had adopted Jangga and Eddie by this time since Sarawak was no longer a colony but a part of the Federation of Malaysia. Jangga is still at the technical college in Auckland studying for his City and Guilds Certificate. Keith and Gladys give him that real home so essential as I have said before to any boy going abroad to study.

There is little doubt in my mind that the project of sending the boys abroad was successful, only because we made sure that each and all would have that home influence and feel really welcome in a foreign land. Shortly before Malaysia came into being, I was paid what I consider the finest compliment. The then Chief Secretary before he left said that he just wished that he could lay hands on ten Luke Tungku's. I replied meekly by saying that it was hardly my fault that he hadn't. It had taken all my persuasive powers for Government to agree to help send ten boys. It was a pity we could not turn the clock back since there could have gone, Bagat, Salang, Enyang, Kunchie and quite a few others.

There was no magic used in this production of an "elite" as the Budu boys came to be called. We all drew on our experiences of working with lads. Being a trained teacher with fair experience it was easy for me professionally to select the academically fit. My experiences in Flying Training Command where for almost a year I had to test fly about forty potential pilots each week and as those who were graded as unfit for further flying training had to be assessed to become navigators, bomb aimers, air gunners, I had to evolve my own system of tests. Mainly however the selection of the boys from Budu to proceed abroad was a team effort with Mac, Arthur and Doc providing useful data to enable finalisation to take place. Every boy was tested fully in the field under almost every possible and conceivable situation. Character had to be taken into consideration and rightly so. We all agreed on this. It must be stressed however that there was no haphazard selection. The work in the co-operative shops, the dispensaries, the office, and in bringing up the tons and tons of stores through difficult waters of the river meant that Budu became almost an "Outward Bound School", but with no artificial hazards to overcome. Those who could not keep up with the pace, just had to go home. I was often criticised for this severity. The high standard expected was set however with a fully determined purpose. In an area just developing it was just as essential that within the longhouse, boys with a fair education and especially with a bias towards agriculture returned there to bring progress within the village structure and it was calculated that those, as it were "who fell by the wayside" would fill this gap. It is certainly true that in this day and age, there are more form two boys living normal farming lives in the Budu area than anywhere else in Sarawak. I would agree that it was a ruthless policy but necessary. The boys who could not go on knew this, however, and so they went back to their longhouse if not content, certainly with a realisation that higher education was beyond them. This seemed to make all the difference in their attitude. I certainly never heard any complaints, possibly because we were fair and just in all our assessments and examinations. We never sent anyone home. We just waited till they asked and agreed that they should go home.

It must not be thought the Dyaks who went to Nairn Academy were the only Dyaks to complete their training and become fully qualified Community Development Assistants. Generally speaking, about thirty per cent of any intake at Budu couldn't last the pace either physically or academically, and incidentally fell short in any case in character standards expected. Over the years of the scheme there was only money enough for the ten who went to Nairn, although had more money been available we could have trebled this. Those who could not go to Nairn only through lack of funds completed their training with us in Sarawak either at Budu, Entaih or at another centre. The seventy per cent who survived their training locally have given valuable and loyal service. Many are headmasters, mostly in remote areas and where they can, they give service to both the pupils in school and to the people of the district. Nevertheless, had we not sent our ten best trainees to Nairn, every centre would have been without that essential leader, so vital to the success of phase three of the planned scheme. It was basically impossible to give that intangible "something" which all the boys obtained at Nairn, here locally in Sarawak. The people almost without exception were prepared and willing to follow the advice given to them by those who had been to Nairn or abroad. In other words, knowing the Dyak, we knew that if their own boys went to the same kind of schools as we the Europeans had there would not only be no difficulty about handing over centres but rather an eagerness that their own kith and kin should take over at the earliest possible moment.

Had Nairn Academy been other than it was, had the Rector taken only a cursory interest, had the people of Nairn not given a warm welcome and had the boys not had the home which they had with Mr and Mrs McTaggart, then indeed much could have gone wrong. The ten who went, while it is certain almost that they would have returned to Sarawak, could well have returned to take up more remunerative work in urban districts. Indeed we owe a great deal to Nairn and the environment which it provided.

It is fitting that this chapter should end with Mr A. R. Robertson's own appraisal of the experiment which he calls "Scottish Interlude". Himself, the author of at least four of the finest English teaching books available, he manages in any case to say in five pages which I have taken almost twenty. He begins. . . .

SCOTTISH INTERLUDE

(Written by Mr A. R. Robertson, M.A., Rector of Nairn Academy)

The reason for the coming of the Sea Dyaks to Nairn, a little town on the Moray Firth, in the remote north-east of Scotland, is almost a story in itself. Before the Second World War, J. K. Wilson, the "original begetter" of the Budu Development Scheme, had been a science teacher in Campbeltown, a post to which he returned after distinguished service as a pilot with the R.A.F. during the course of hostilities.

After the excitement and challenge of the war years, "J. K." found teaching drab and monotonous. The vistas from the Mull of Kintyre were too restricted, and his energy, drive and vision required a new outlet. Soon he was on his way to Sarawak to become Principal in the only Teachers' Training College there. But, warmly as he admired the work done in college, he had his own ideas of how Dyaks should be educated to be of greatest service to their own people. Accordingly, was born the Budu Development Scheme, for whose survival and extension it speedily became apparent that Dyak trained assistance was essential. It was then that Wilson decided to send boys to Scotland to be educated there in state schools under a system he knew well and respected highly.

Himself educated at Dunoon Grammar School, "J. K." sought the help of his own old headmaster, Mr A. J. Ross, long retired. His request was passed on to Neil B. McCorkindale, now Rector of Ayr Academy, but once Principal Teacher of Mathematics in Nairn Academy, a school for which he had, and still has, the highest regard. He knew, too, that Nairn Academy had a small proportion of children, mostly with parents staying in India and the Far East, who lived in a boarding house run by Mr and Mrs McTaggart. Mr McTaggart was himself a retired tea planter and Mrs McTaggart a former teacher in Dr Graham's School, Kalampong. Their home, "Grianach", was indeed "a sunny corner" as the Gaelic name implies. The children in "Grianach" were one big and very happy family, enjoying all the benefits of a settled domestic background to offset the disadvantages of separation from home and parents. To McCorkindale there was only one answer to the call for help from Sarawak—Nairn Academy and "Grianach".

Thus, in August 1957, Jawie Masing, Liman Numpang, Bilun Nunoi and Luke Tungku, the first of Nairn's Sea Dyaks, enrolled in Nairn Academy. All entered the second year of the secondary course and were absorbed into classes following the normal curriculum. There was never any question of adjustment. The boys from Sarawak simply fitted in and, by their friendliness, their industry, their impeccable grooming, and unfailing courtesy and loyalty, were soon immensely popular, not merely with their school-fellows but with the townspeople. Of the four, Jawie was clearly the student and it was no surprise to those who taught him that he was able to go to Aberdeen University after four years in Nairn and to graduate M.B., Ch.B. in 1967. Liman and Bilun played regularly in the first football XI, Bilun sometimes disconcerting teammates and opponents alike by playing in his stockinged feet. He was an outside-left of no mean ability with a penchant for scoring goals from non-existent chances. Luke, perhaps the most mature of the four, was always very conscious of his responsibilities to his own people. He profited immensely from his stay in Nairn but was not a good examination candidate. Both he and Jawie, nevertheless, were able to go to the U.S.A. and Canada on Commonwealth Scholarships during one summer vacation. In the same year Liman and Bilun travelled extensively on the continent of Europe.

The boys were encouraged to keep alive their native tradition of working to pay for their education, a concept many would applaud in our own country. Earl Cawdor generously provided them with an opportunity to work on his estate and the only adverse comment I ever heard was that they worked too hard.

To reach Cawdor, the boys had to learn to ride cycles and their first attempts were productive of great mirth and not a few bruises. The miles' ride out to Cawdor in the bitter cold of winter must have been an ordeal for these lads. But they treated it as fun and I shall never forget their unrestrained glee when they revelled in the first snow they had ever seen.

In August 1959 Jenuang Sudok and Henry Brayon joined the original four. Henry and Jenuang were totally dissimilar. Henry had not a care in the world, was not particularly industrious in the academic field but was everyone's friend, and almost Rip Van Winkle like in the assiduity with which he pursued unprofitable labour. Musically, he was the best of the Dyaks who came to Nairn and we were genuinely sorry when, six months after Bilun, Luke and Liman had gone home, he, too, returned to Sarawak, where I believe he is now a headmaster.

Jenuang conformed more to the traditional view held in the West of those who come from the East. In respect of ability, he was probably second only to Jawie. But, unlike Jawie, Jenuang was a natural athlete of the highest grade. He lacked one quality only—the killer instinct. To Jenuang, the game and not the result was what mattered. He was a very intelligent and highly entertaining footballer, but his real forte was in high jumping and pole vaulting. In both, he outclassed his rivals with such effortless ease and grace that one wondered what he might have done had he really tried. When he did win he seemed almost apologetic. Nevertheless, without any special preparation, Jenuang took first place in the high jump at the North of Scotland Schools Sports in Inverness and second in the pole vault at the Scottish Inter-Schools Championships held at Westerlands, Glasgow. Yet, even after Jenuang had been four years in Nairn Academy, I never felt I knew him really well. He was detached, always a faultless pupil, but a soul that dwelt apart. He was friendly with all, intimate with none.

In the summer of 1959 Peter Graves, who had just completed his sixth year at the Academy, volunteered to spend his "Year Between" in Budu and

128

help the Development Scheme in any way he could. Peter was engaged mostly in education but his versatility was a great asset and he turned his hand to many tasks. The boys who came to Nairn subsequent to 1960 spoke of Peter with real affection, and I know that he retains the happiest memories of his stay in Budu—now the name of the family Labrador dog.

With the coming of Panggau Kusau and Kassin Rengkang in August 1960 our colony of Sea Dyaks had risen to eight, the highest number ever in the Academy at the one time. Panggau was small and chubby. On the playing fields he bounced like a rubber ball and was never once hurt. Kassin was more in the Jenuang mould. Perhaps because they were the last two of eight, Panggau and Kassin left less vivid recollections than some of the others. Where all are excellent, it is difficult to stand out.

When Panggau and Jenuang left Nairn in July 1963 to return home the Academy found itself, for the first time in six years, without a Sea Dyak on the roll. The school was the poorer for their going, but within two months the loss was partially restored by the advent of Morris Tom at the end of August that year. Morris was in the mould of Luke, an extremely hard worker, with a highly developed sense of responsibility, and a burning desire

to justify his selection for a year's residence in Scotland. He attended the Academy for only one session and trained thereafter, mostly in Glasgow, as male nurse. He qualified in the summer of 1967 and is now undergoing a further year's training for mental nursing. At the end of that period it is expected he will return to his own country.

There is another hiatus in the Nairn-Sarawak story between July 1964, when Morris left school, and August 1966 when Eddie Bryant joined us. Eddie was the last of our Dyaks but he is remembered especially, not for that but because of his own lovable personality. If Jenuang was detached, Eddie was the opposite. He gave and awakened affection. On Prize Day 1967 he presented the Academy with a scroll, hand-drawn by Andrew, younger brother of Jenuang, on which was inscribed a record of the Sea Dyaks' ten-year-old connection with Nairn Academy and with Mr and Mrs McTaggart. Before the assembled school, and in the presence of a large and representative gathering of parents and friends from the town and county of Nairn, Eddie, with one year's formal schooling in this country, in handing over the scroll, made a speech so well constructed, so sincere, and so beautifully phrased and spoken, that few indeed in that large audience were not visibly moved.

With Eddie's departure the connection between Nairn and Sarawak came to an end. I am utterly convinced that Nairn Academy learned much and owes a lot to the ten boys who spent some of their formative years here. I should be happy to think Nairn Academy and "Grianach" did as much for them. That they should ever have been placed in my care is the most treasured compliment ever paid me. That, alone, makes forty years spent as a schoolmaster worthwhile.

Appended are the names of the boys who were pupils at Nairn Academy, together with the dates of their attendance.

Jawie Masing	20.8.57—30. 6.61
Liman Numpang	20.8.57—30. 6.61
Bilun Numoi	20.8.57—30. 6.61
Luke Tungku	20.8.57—13. 6.61
Jenuang Sudok	25.8.59— 5. 7.63
Henry Brayon	25.8.59—15.12.61
Panggau Kusau	23.8.60— 5. 7.63
Kasin Hangkang	23.8.60—12. 7.62
Morris Tom	23.8.66—30. 6.67
Eddie Bryant	23.8.66—30. 6.67

COMMUNITY DEVELOPMENT AND THE VOLUNTEER SCHEME OF SERVICE OVERSEAS
PART ONE

May 1961 . . .   *Written by Graham Riches*

Late in the afternoon the rain had begun to fall steadily, monotonously and without ceasing. The paths through the jungle became at first slippery channels and then gushing streams. To the jungle insects as well as to the twenty-year-old English volunteer making his first major journey on foot through the forests of Sarawak, it seemed as if he was wading up and through angry, storm-swollen rivers. Juing, my young Dyak companion, suggested that we might stay the night at the next longhouse only twenty minutes walk away, as we could not hope to reach our destination that evening. I gladly agreed, and found myself at once greedily looking forward to the customary Dyak hospitality which I knew would be offered us. The tuak, the chicken, the unhusked rice, bamboo shoots and other vegetable delicacies as well as pleasant conversation, a mosquito net and a mattress to sleep on. Simple comforts, but what luxury after struggling through the densely-wooded valleys since dawn.

As the sun rose on the following morning we were both anxious to be on our way. Never had we spent a more uncomfortable night. There had been no welcome for us, no food or drink prepared or offered, no cosy fireside chats, no nets, no mattresses, and no one concerned for our slightest comfort. We had, in fact, spent the night fighting sandflies and mosquitoes, the pigs rummaging about beneath the bamboo floorboards on which our mats were spread, as well as our own tiredness. As Juing explained sometime during the course of the tormented night, this longhouse had done us proud by merely allowing us to stay on its verandah. They had nothing else to offer us.

For the first time in my life I had experienced poverty.

With the sheltered background of an English Public School behind me, I found myself in September 1960 stepping from the stuffy cabin of an upriver Chinese launch into the depths of the Sarawak jungle, or "ulu" as it is known locally. I was on my way to take part in the Budu Development Scheme under the supervision of John Wilson. The journey to these remote parts had been long and arduous, but ever eye-opening. By British Rail from Liverpool Street to Harwich; ferry to the Hook of Holland; oil tanker from Rotterdam to Kuwait and on to Singapore; a quick flight across the China Sea to Kuching; and finally a series of Chinese launches heavy with goods, people, fowls and their pungent Oriental smells delivered me to my immediate destination of Engkilili.

Underwater fishing with a harpoon gun

As I stepped ashore, I felt as if I had abandoned one world which had succoured me for a new world which I was curious to explore and immerse myself in. I was at once aware that I would have to make inexorable efforts in this direction, as the welcome I received on my arrival was by no means spontaneous. Indeed, the young Dyak people I had come to work with and teach, in their Community Development Scheme, were passively sizing me up from behind the trees and bushes which reached down to and overhung the river. Contact was eventually made when one of the boys made himself known to me as Gemat and suggested that I might like to view my quarters, take a bath in the river and then have some supper.

Bathing that evening in the river, I wondered what had prompted me and volunteers like me to come to this jungle-encircled outpost of civilisation. Why prolong entering universities or extend apprenticeships by one year? On reflection, it was more for reasons of adventure and seeing the world than for any positive desire to contribute to the development of a country's people in however small a way. The choice to depart into the unknown was mine alone, but there is no doubt that my decision was influenced by men of insight such as Gordon van Praagh, my school's career master, Alec Dickson who founded Voluntary Service Overseas in 1958, and John Wilson himself whom I had met in England in the summer. He had initiated and was now the community development officer responsible for the Budu Development Scheme to which I had been assigned. And now here I was, taking a bath in a river!

Let me say a little about V.S.O. The aim was not only that young volunteers because of their youth would be able to identify and work with the young of other countries, but also that in so doing they would themselves develop and mature. In fact the problems of the developing countries—ignorance, illiteracy, disease and age old customs and traditions— would provide settings for the young of Britain and the developing world to develop attitudes and skills which would fit them for their future roles as leaders in their own communities. Learning situations abounded; they only required exploitation. In the early stages V.S.O. achieved this task. It is only sad to recall that on the one hand in the years ahead it was to be President John F. Kennedy and not Harold Macmillan who developed the dream and effectively captured the imagination of the young with the establishment of the Peace Corps; on the other hand, the developing countries themselves have failed to respond to the idea of reciprocity inherent in the scheme, in that they have been unable to understand that they too have something intangible to give—an education for the young. The use of such volunteers untrained and untrammelled by degrees, diplomas and certificates can only be assessed in the context of each individual project to which they were assigned. Within the Budu Development Scheme the volunteers had a variety of functions. While the scheme's future young Dyak leaders were completing their education in Scotland, the volunteers were able to take their places in positions of authority within the projects. At the same time, the volunteers' knowledge of and ability to teach English as well as most other school subjects added greatly to the education of the Dyak children. Added to this was the mere presence of the volunteers in the schemes which allowed the

Community Development Officers (Tuan Tuai, Mac, Manang and Doc), to travel to other areas and assist in the creation of new projects. How the members of the different Committees of Progress viewed the young volunteers is hard to say, but I have no doubt that they soon came to understand the fallibility of most of us.

After spending six interminable weeks at Engkilili I moved upriver to Grenjang where I took over the running of the centre. I was glad to be moved. Whilst I did not shirk hard work, Engkilili was proving about as much as I could take. Apart from teaching all day to a class of twelve education-hungry primary six children, I was also having to supervise (and participate in) the clearing from the terraces of rubber trees seemingly millions of cubic feet of a weed called lalang grass. Not only did it grow as fast as it was slashed with our dukus but it was possessed of extremely sharp blades which left their incisions on me. What with these cuts, mosquito bites and a peculiar skin fungus which I developed through not drying myself properly, I was well pleased to be rid of the monotony and aches and pains I was fast coming to associate with both community development and Engkilili.

Nanga Grenjang was an altogether much more delightful place. It was situated about a day's further travel up the Krian river. The banks of the river in which it was situated were generally a mass of hibiscus flowers, and whilst Engkilili could boast only a schoolhouse, dormitory, storehouse and the eternal rubber trees, Grenjang had in addition a flourishing co-operative shop, a medical dispensary, football pitch (of sorts), pig sty, boat shed and, by the end of my stay, a landing stage and a newly cemented floor to the schoolroom. Here there was a much greater variety of work and, what was more, the local Dyaks were always in and out of the centre.

My responsibilities at Grenjang and at the other centres at which I worked were manifold. In addition to teaching in school all day and working on the terraces, I had to ensure the smooth running of both the medical dispensary and the co-operative store. The latter I found to be a heavy responsibility as it meant seeing that the members of the scheme who sold their rubber to us received a fair price and that we in our turn sold it at a profit on our trading trips to the bazaar down river at Saratok. Such trips usually took place at the weekends unless the river was in flood, as this meant faster and easier trips, as the rapids—no mean hazards—became that much more negotiable in the longboats. Weeks of work were punctuated by Sundays when we cleaned the buildings and always the pig sty and then departed into the jungle to fish a stream or visit a nearby longhouse, to be treated, not royally, but as members of the family.

The demands of such a life were great. I had to learn the language and adapt to walking barefoot in the jungle (much less tiring and far safer especially on the mud-deep paths). Teaching involved everything from English to algebra and singing. Tuan Tuai once explained to me that we taught algebra primarily to get the boys to think in English. Many were the hours that the boys and I spent trying to puzzle out satisfactory answers to the X sheep minus Y goats equals what type of equation. Singing also did not gladden my heart as I had been told at school and at home that I was unable to pitch a note. However, with help from Jangga, Eddie, Luna, Juing, Gemat and Entebang, we pitched so successfully that our Dyak verses sung to Scottish folk song tunes were recorded by the Sarawak information services and came floating over the air to us one evening through the media of Radio Sarawak.

Arranging sports days, writing and directing concerts, erecting landing stages, dragging sand from the river bed, attending to the occasional snake bite, were all part of the job.

Vivid memories remain of the day the river rose so high that it washed the longboat shed away. I had just returned from a visit to Kuching and Ian, a schoolfriend and then a volunteer teacher at Kanowit, had returned with me to Grenjang. We both watched the shed float away and resolved there and then to erect a new one the following day. Dyak opposition to the idea grew: "Wait a fortnight," said Salang, "until the river really has subsided and then rebuild." But English common sense prevailed and Ian and I, helped by some rather sceptical but movingly polite schoolboys, proudly erected the new shed on the very next day. That evening the rains descended once again, the waters rose and rose and the following morning not a shed in sight. So much for native English wit!

Perhaps it was the lack of sufficient variety in the diet which led us occasionally into such follies. Breakfast generally consisted of cheese, jam, biscuits and coffee, with eggs as and when we could afford them. Lunch I found the most unsavoury of meals as we could only afford boiled rice and tinned (People's Republic of China) fish. In the evening we usually had some form of stew supplemented with bamboo shoots, or some other local vegetable. Not exactly the healthy diet for growing lads. However, on some days the boys or local people brought in fresh fish, chickens, and on one occasion venison. This in such quantities that we ate it at every meal for about three days as we had no refrigeration. My sister was so concerned for my welfare that she used to send me jars of Marmite and packets of Bemax so that I would get my regular doses of vitamins!

From a distance it is only too easy to romanticise about one's stay in the "ulu" of Sarawak: the trips to longhouses, shooting the rapids, the bare-breasted women, blowpipes and parangs, the early morning mists and the swiftness of tropical nightfall, not to forget the brilliantly coloured hornbills which were seen every now and then. However we were not colonial rajahs nor even lowly District Officers and because of this we were faced with the less romantic facts of Dyak life: illiteracy, disease, inefficient agricultural techniques, young mothers with the majority of their pregnancies resulting in stillborn babies—a list which easily becomes a vicious circle. Being so close to such problems and in fact being in control of some of the forces which were aiming to erase them, I found intensely satisfying. For the impressionable twenty-year-old hungry for new experiences these were the places to be; ideals were seen to be tangibly at work.

Of course there were times of utter boredom, physical discomfort and loneliness. I had expected all except loneliness, and the feelings of being by myself in a foreign country were not helped by the fact that this literally was my situation. If one of the boys felt that you had offended him in any way he was quite likely to go "malu", i.e. cut himself off from you completely. He would walk around with a long face for a week, be as unco-operative as possible and, if he was a boy with some standing with his peers, affect your relationships with the others as well. Fortunately such occurrences were rare but they made me very miserable as the boys were generally so spontaneous, full of life and, I thought, delightfully conceited.

Leaving Sarawak by plane was not the ordeal that my departure from Grenjang was. Not that there were floods of tears, but I know, as I watched my friends, who had gathered to bid me farewell, from the longboat as it turned the bend in the river, that I would probably never see any of them again. I was leaving well loved friends behind, and at that stage it seemed as if only Western materialism could lie ahead. What had been the most eventful and memorable year in my life was slipping away as the boat sped down river.

Inevitably the question arises as to the value of volunteers such as myself to the scheme and the reciprocal value of being associated with the scheme. I only feel myself qualified to answer the latter question. I had been a first-hand observer of seeing an ideal turned into reality. I had witnessed the dedication not just of one man, Tuan Tuai, to the solution of the deep-seated problems, but of the majority of those Dyaks who cared about their people's fate, and I myself had been engaged in this slow but gradual process of social and economic revolution. Little wonder that now in adult life I have practised and now teach Community Development in the Far East. And that is just another of the far-reaching effects of the Budu Development Scheme.

(Tuan Tuai, I think you should comment at the end of this chapter as to the value of the volunteers to the scheme as a whole.)

136

CHAPTER NINE

PART TWO

There are two reasons why I remember the inaugural meeting of the Overseas Volunteer Service held in Caxton Hall. The first, not important in itself, being that not since war years had I taken a car through London and having gone round and round Trafalgar Square some five times, I ended up by following any stream out of London and I could not have cared less whether it was south, east, north or west. Having got out, I garaged my car and took the subway to Caxton Hall much relieved. As I travelled to Caxton Hall I could not help thinking that progress can bring its own confusion if no sound preparation is made to participate in that progress.

I was by this time almost half an hour late but fortunately the meeting had only come to order. I was relieved to see Alec Dickson, one of the platform party, already there. I spied Mora Dickson, his wife, whom I knew very well and having made an inaudible apology I sat down beside Mora. With me was one of our own trainees, Chundie, who was studying for his S.R.N. at the Seaman's Dreadnought Hospital. I had brought Chundie with a very good reason in that I hoped that at a convenient opportunity he could rise and speak from the receiving end with confidence. Mora gave me an encouraging smile and a still more charming smile to Chundie whom she had got to know both at Budu when she and Alec had spent a few days there and in London during his off hours from hospital. It was actually Mora Dickson who mothered both Chundie and Rabing during their stay in London and gave to them a home when they could spare the time.

It was Mora Dickson who, as the years passed and as more and more Budu boys arrived in Britain, met them in London and put them on the plane for Glasgow. Often she had to spend many waiting cold hours when the aeroplane was late and it often was. When the boys started to return they returned via London. Again Mora was called upon to help. Never once did she fail although both the cost in money and time must have been considerable. This was her way of helping and being the fine person she is, felt a happiness in this giving. I do not know what we would have done had Mora Dickson not helped us. When the V.S.O. scheme is even mentioned, I think not only of Alec Dickson, her husband, as the man who started it all but of Mora, an equal if not greater partner in it. Just as Mora helped us to meet and shepherd the boys, so it was Mora who always seemed to have to see to the last-minute wants of the V.S.O. recruits, to comfort apprehensive parents when their boys left for foreign lands, to see them off on their journeys and to meet them when they returned. Mora was as much V.S.O. as Alec and needed.

Alec and Mora, while not coming to Sarawak especially to pay a visit to Budu, each was determined to see just how Mac and Arthur, being young, were standing up to the hardships of remote life and to assess, in view of Alec's long-planned dream of starting up a voluntary scheme of young helpers, just how both Mac and Arthur contributed to the work of the Community Development Scheme. Both Alec and Mora wanted to have some concrete evidence that young lads of the Mac and Arthur type, could fit in to life in a remote part and make a real contribution to the people. What both saw at Budu convinced them that in real community development work there would be ample scope for the young volunteer, fresh from school and who in any case had usually to wait a year before a place could be found in a university. What better way to spend a year while waiting than to give a year's service to some community such as Budu.

Alec Dickson was, as many people knew, no stranger to voluntary service himself. During the war, as a volunteer under unbelievable hardships and dangers, he had assisted many hundreds across frontiers into waiting ambulances in neutral territory. After the war, believing fundamentally in the need to strengthen the very character of the average African. about to emerge into complete independence, he set about doing what he could by starting up his own scheme, well known as "The Man of War Scheme" in Nigeria. His main aim was to create, if necessary, conditions under which the average African civil servant could find himself and prove to himself that he was no different to a white man in courage, ability and in giving service to the needy, while still retaining the Christian ethics taught during his schooling. From my own personal observations, having spent several months in Africa, although mostly in Southern Rhodesia, I was certainly convinced there was a need for some change but just could not put my finger on it nor explain it. Only when I knew of Alec's work did I realise just what he was trying to do. The moral and physical growth of the African had been stinted when at school. He was meek and mild and obedient, with lip service to various Christian faiths since he felt that in this way he could some day get above the sordidness and poverty of his way of living. He was envious of those who possessed things which he had not, but lacked, frankly, the moral guts to do anything about it. There were few chances when in school to foster physical well being in courage and give him a faith in himself and his own kind. There is no need, however, for me to labour on this work of Alec Dickson's except to say I was determined if I had the chance, that, in any work with developing peoples, it was vital to encourage such peoples to develop not only academically but to foster and initiate, if need be, circumstances or environment which would strengthen characteristics of inherent courage, endurance and honesty.

So, on this memorable afternoon in Caxton Hall, we three had gathered, with the same mind and purpose, not just to start a scheme whereby young lads from Britain could travel to foreign lands to give service but to give those lads an opportunity to develop their own resources, their own endurance, their own faith in themselves and in so doing, give help to those in need. It was meant from the beginning that those young men from Britain be given opportunities under trying and hard conditions and in so doing, achieve a likeness in their counterparts in underdeveloped countries such as Sarawak. It was firmly intended that the volunteers, if there were any, while being looked after basically as to their destination and other physical needs, should be given an opportunity to live almost as the people for whom they had come so far to help. There was not the slightest intention that such volunteers should become mere teachers, housed, and with an automatic respect given to them by virtue of school authority. This they could well have in due course after they had completed their own academic professional training. To have proposed that such volunteers became the stop gap in staffing an ever increasing number of schools would in any case have been wrong in two main ways. One, the volunteer would have found himself in the very worst environment to foster such qualities of character that it was hoped to foster. His ego, instead of being flattered as it should be after almost "idol" worship while captain of his old school team, would be given plenty of opportunities to swell further and create an almost insufferable character of "superior" knowledge. Two, but equally important, schools in developing countries, should not in any case be opened at a speed greater than their own output of trained teachers can staff them adequately. Good teaching demands a continuity that a volunteer for a year just cannot give, no matter how much he would like to. That he could be a supernumerary was accepted providing that such talents as he had were used in creating Boy Scout groups, organising expeditions, taking over the sports organisation or any other form of indoor or outdoor extra curricula activities. If such work was offered to young volunteers, their own qualities of leadership would emerge if such were there.

Many people offered their views at this meeting. My own short speech contained the substance of the above but I do remember stressing also that the great need in developing countries was for young men who were not specialists in any one thing but were able to turn their hands to doing anything that had to be done. Chundie gave a fair description of the possible life of a volunteer at Budu and also expressed the need not just for an ordinary teacher but for the type of person who could work with the trainees and by so doing advantages would be on both sides.

When the meeting drew to a close, it was sufficiently clear just what was needed and it was accepted that while a volunteer must be prepared to give in all things, that he himself was to be given opportunities to prove himself to himself under conditions of hardship and alone far from his own kind.

Alec lost no time and by September of that year, six specially selected volunteers arrived in Sarawak. Two went to the Padawan Community Development Scheme, two to the Budu Community Development Scheme, two to the Long Lama Community Development Scheme.

David and Richard were our first two. After a few weeks together at Budu, both to acclimatise them and brief them on the kind of work that we would expect them to do, Richard went off overland to Entaih to work with Arthur and David remained at Budu with Mac. Both fitted in excellently. So much so that Mac was able to take a short leave home leaving David in full charge. This was excellent experience for David and quite within the terms of reference. The volunteers had to be given opportunities to see if they could do things by themselves. While Mac was away, David ran Budu in such a way that when Mac returned steady progress had been made and more important still, David was a wiser man in every way. Richard, likewise at Entaih, stood in for Arthur for weeks on end, leaving Arthur free to travel.

So until Alec and Mora were eased out of all V.S.O. work, selected lads kept arriving each September, to Budu. There was John, Stan, Ken, Christopher, Graham and a second Richard. There was Peter Gordon, from Nairn Academy. He had volunteered direct to go to Budu and administratively we were able to arrange this. It seemed right that since Nairn Academy was so ably looking after our lads, so we were delighted to accept Peter. Peter was splendid all through and because of him, I was able to have a short holiday at home too. This gave Peter his opportunity and I think I agreed with his mother that he was just a boy when he went, but returned a man. Peter was a great fisherman and almost because of this he was revered by the trainees, many of whom learned to fish the right way. Jangga to this day keeps saying that it was Peter who taught him how to fish, even in small streams.

For the right type of boy, the boy who wanted to be of use and to gain something from his usefulness to others, there is little doubt that in the various Community Development schemes, he found the right kind of work and environment. On his side he gave in full measure, the service which he had promised. When Alec and Mora left the V.S.O., too many petty restrictions were imposed, such as that they had to work in pairs, all contrary to the original concepts. They had to be near medical supervision, they had to be housed more in keeping with Europeans. We, the members of the team, were busy men and certainly had no time to coddle the new type of V.S.O. although I expect he would have preferred not to have been coddled, so we declined to continue to accept the help from the V.S.O.

It was hinted that we were biting off our noses to spite ourselves. This was quite untrue. The V.S.O. carefully selected under the Alec Dickson committee knew what was expected from him. He knew that although conditions might be hard, he would in return gain something precious from giving his service to a less developed community. This was why he had volunteered to help. The real V.S.O. wanted, I am certain, to feel he was needed and needed he would certainly feel, alone as the only European for almost a day's journey distant. The real V.S.O. lad was essentially a lad who had always liked the open air, who had been used to camping and looking after himself. When the old type V.S.O. found himself giving his year of service in just an urban school the resulting effect was rather as though he, having looked forward to camping conditions, found himself having to make "camp" in the back yard rather than on the wide open spaces. There was just no place in Community Development work for the new type whose first question seemed to be, "Where is my refrigerator and what about my lamp to read at night? Who is going to cook for me?" and so on. No, there was no biting off our noses to spite ourselves. We sincerely missed having V.S.O. help but rather none than the type who felt that he was giving service leaning up against a refrigerator half the day and playing his transistor radio half the night.

The shades of David, Richard, John, Peter, Christopher, Graham, Stan, Ken, would have risen in revolt. David I know is remembered for his absolute devotion to the scheme, to the exclusion of all personal comfort. He was first to share the hardships of bringing goods up from Saratok with all its dangerous hazards. He was always ahead leading the boys to make terraces and in all the other kinds of work. When there was any "free" time, he set about making cement steps from the school to the river's edge. They remain to this day in his memory. Richard, although quite different from David, gave equally in his own way. He is remembered with affection because of his love of biology. The routine work Richard never shirked, but when he could get away, he was off like a shot with half a dozen lads to look for specimens which he brought back to dissect and preserve. The boys learned a great deal about the anatomy of reptiles, insects and the wonders of a microscope. So did I, although both Arthur and I used to look at the bottles of hard-to-get spirit with mixed feelings. The large stones around forty to fifty pounds weight, which John used to lift as though they were just pebbles, still lie embedded in the concrete mixture and look as though they will remain forever. John had only one major problem with the trainees. It happened that John liked porridge in the morning, as well he might since it is a wholesome dish, and insisted on this as the breakfast food. John did get a little angry one morning when one of the trainees, although not really meaning to insult, took his plate of porridge and gave it to the pigs. Graham, different also to John and David, made, however, a unique contribution to the change of thought process among the Dyaks. Of a seeking mind, Graham set about trying to understand the Dyak trainee and so enable him to lead them better, both in the classroom and in the outside work activities. That he succeeded has been evident in past years. Graham's trainees have that something which the Nairn trainees got by going abroad. Graham, with his searching mind and thirst for knowledge, was a most pleasant and worth while assistant. Christopher and Peter were alike in that not only did they give of their best, but managed more than the others to get close to the Dyak trainees without losing that essential quality of being automatically recognised as being in charge. Stan and Ken just wanted to help and being engineers made life for Mac very much easier. The why and the wherefore of the reasons to come to Sarawak to help, just didn't worry either Stan or Ken. Of all the volunteers, however, they were adamant that they got more out of helping than the scheme did. They are both remembered with good natured affection although one of them lost the only key to the large safe containing all the money. A journey of over a week was necessary overland to get the only duplicate. Poetic justice that the one who lost it had to go and get the other one.

In recent years, some lucky V.S.O. helpers found themselves attached to the Agricultural Department as opposed to mere schools. Unless, however, opportunity to give service in remote and unusual ways is provided for the V.S.O., the response from the true V.S.O. to volunteer will gradually die out, and while there will still be many who want to trip round the world and enjoy the comforts which can be provided by urban schools even in under-developed territories, this as I have said was not the original purpose of the scheme proposed and started by Alec Dickson. There is still great need for his type of volunteer, not only in Community Development but if he has to be a teacher, let him teach in remote areas where he will have to be resourceful to survive with any comfort at all, but in doing so he will return much improved spiritually and physically.

CHAPTER TEN

"MILESTONES"

As I write here in a small house beside the river, with Brown Feet, my dog, beside me, I begin really to wonder if the heading "Milestones" for this chapter is correct. Milestones suggest that the journey through the years was something paced out and that at each stage a little stone was passed marking out the end of each phase. This concept would be far from the truth since in actual fact we, the team, were like the blind leading the blind. We did not know that what was decided was for the best and whether by doing what was decided, we would from the result look back on the incidents as important milestones. So the word "Milestones" must be treated figuratively in the sense that after certain incidents or experiences we, the team members, knew at least how far we had travelled and that given the same approximate conditions we would know what road or path to follow.

I recall to mind three distinct episodes dealing with the much hated and feared cobra which to this day keeps appearing but not, I am glad to say, with the nerve-shattering results and confusion unbounded, as they did in the early days. In the early days when anyone saw a snake the cry "Ular" could be heard and by common consent to survive a future peril, anyone who was near grabbed a stick and came running. I grant you that it was very laudable on everyone's part to come and help but often the poor person near the snake was in greater danger. This meant, inevitably, that as people came from all directions the snake was surrounded as it were and would give fight. If the person on whose direction the snake eventually went was sure of hand and eye all was well. The cobra or snake was battered to death till it was just a pulsating mass of blood. Snakes are so hated that such displays were at least understandable but they were nevertheless gruesome bloody killings. It seemed to me that a better way would be to alert those near, form some plan of attack, and pursue the snake till it was battered to death. On one memorable morning while I was working in the office at Budu, to remain alive, harsh commands using my method had to be given. On the shelf just behind the desk at which I was sitting, someone spied a cobra all neatly coiled up, fortunately. He disappeared out of the door, shouting in a frenzied voice "Ular". The snake was sufficiently alerted to make it impossible for me to get out of the office and within seconds the office was surrounded with screaming shouting Dyaks. My only weapon was a Dyak "duku" or hunting knife with a blade of around two feet in length. It was not the weapon I would normally have chosen

since a fairly heavy stick is much better, but the only one to hand and I felt reasonably confident as I clutched it in my hand. Luckily Mac came on the scene and in tense voice I told him to clear the front of the office especially near the door. Everyone was to get behind and by making a noise I hoped that the snake would go out of the office without bothering me. This, strangely enough, it commenced to do and positively ignored me to my great relief. Sheer reflex action, not considered thought, made me swipe at the vicious ugly head and to my utter amazement the head was severed off to fall at my feet. I made no mistake in completing the job. The incident gave quite the wrong impression that I was cool and calculating. Nevertheless the incident was used in future teaching and to me was a milestone passed. The other two episodes were similar although I was not the main character involved, only on the fringe, but once again, had the same tactics not been used, certain death would have followed. My reputation for being cool and calculating was short lived since just a few weeks after the office incident I found myself having a late bath in the river for some unknown reason and to give light I had taken down to the water's edge my little reflecting paraffin lamp. Its beam was shining clear and bright on the water leaving me in total darkness. It was such a perfect evening that I stripped naked to soap myself down and was on the point of plunging in when straight towards me at Olympic speed came a "Kangkang Mau", a large green and yellow snake, some four feet in length. Completely and utterly demoralised I bounded and splashed to the bank and ran up the small incline, shouting my head off. Naturally enough I had completely forgotten that I was stark naked until Mac, drawn by the noise, laughingly pointed this out. I learned later that a Kangkang Mau will always "attack" a strong light, and so evolved new tactics for any future night bathing.

Under Adult Education another vital milestone was passed after what is generally called "The Midnight Walk to Rh. Bruang". The adult education classes had been going well and we thought that all was under control till one Monday evening, having prepared food for some fifty adults who had promised to arrive from Rh. Bruang for their course, no one arrived to eat the rice. Not one single person. That they knew to come was certain and I was not only angry but just did not know what action to take. For over an hour I kept arguing with myself that they must have some good reason but when I saw the large pot of rice going to waste I was at least determined to tell them what I thought.

As I said to Mac, "Even if a death had occurred a message could have been sent to tell us, so I am off to Rh. Bruang just to give them a piece of my mind". Pausing only to get my torch since it was now dusk, I grabbed my faithful stick and off I stormed. By ten o'clock I was at Ng. Budu and while waiting for faithful Birai who was at Ng. Budu, to lead me from Ng. Budu to R. Bruang, I made myself a cup of coffee in the small hut we used at Ng. Budu. I had to wait on Birai since although I knew the way in daylight I certainly didn't think I would make it in the dark. Birai and I had just finished our coffee when in came Mac and Arthur and some senior trainees. "We just wanted a walk so we are coming with you." Actually when I saw them walk in a warm feeling of gratitude sprang up inside me since I knew I had been foolish to come alone. By the time they and the boys also had a coffee it was nearly eleven o'clock. We were just about to move when along came Empeni with another batch of trainees also with the same idea as Mac. So although I started alone from Budu, we were thirty strong leaving Ng. Budu. Apparently Empeni had discussed things with Luke and some of the older Dyaks and all thought it would be wise if quite a crowd followed me. Rh. Bruang had the reputation of being a longhouse with at least some easily angered Dyaks and I think they were afraid of what might happen to me. Luke was left behind much against his will to look after things at Budu. Someone had to.

Unfortunately the rain came on as we left Ng. Budu. It was pitch dark and travel was both dangerous and eerie. Most of the way we had to slush our way through mud or small rivers. I was leading and coming to one of the few open pieces of ground I looked back to see how everybody was faring. It was like a torchlight procession since we all had managed to beg, or borrow torches. As we passed other longhouses on the way, there was consternation as the people thought we were all Dyaks on a foray. Arriving at Rh. Bruang a longhouse of some forty doors, I was glad to see lights still burning on the ruai or verandah. Climbing up the long log at the entrance, with Mac and the other warriors behind me in a long line, I thundered my way along the rickety flooring, not even pausing to say "Tabi" or give the customary handshake. The Head of the longhouse had his "Bilek" right at the other end and of course by the time I had reached it everybody had awakened to find the cause of this "invasion". Mac and all behind him followed my lead, saying nothing, but I doubt anyway if anyone could have been heard over the sound of almost marching feet along the ruai. It was ominous.

I stopped in front of the "Tuai Rumah" who was sitting with quite a number of Dyaks, smoking. They all jumped up when they saw me and hastily prepared a place for me to sit down. At this precise moment there seemed a deadly hush, since Mac and all the boys had also stopped when I stopped, all still in a long line. In a loud and angry voice I said:

"No, I am not going to sit down, nor will I shake hands with you or with anyone who breaks promises and I certainly will not drink with you. At six o'clock this night at Budu, rice was cooked for the fifty who promised to come to school from this longhouse."

The Tuai Rumah made to answer and I shouted before he could say anything.

"No I don't want to hear the reason now. I will listen to your explanation at Budu tomorrow!"

With that I made a quick turn round and thundered my way back with Mac, Arthur and the boys following, as though they were practising counter marching. No one else spoke and we all sensed rather than saw, sheer amazement on everybody's face as we stormed out of Rh. Bruang.

By five o'clock the following morning, we were back at Budu, tired, exhausted, wet, but not miserable. Over a hastily made cup of tea which Luke prepared (he had not expected us back) we all started to laugh and joke, as each attempted to relate what he had seen in Rh. Bruang. Seminai, I think summed it up when he said that he had never walked so far to hear three sentences spoken but it was worth it.

As events turned out, it had been worth the effort. Saying little had more effect than an evening talk. Never again would anyone lightly break a promise. By mid-day a contrite and apologetic Tuai Rumah from Rh. Bruang arrived with the fifty who had promised to come to school. Through the length and breadth of the area and beyond, the story of the midnight walk to Rh. Bruang to say three sentences, keeps being added to and is almost handed down from father to son. The trainees gained an insight into the realm of determination, an insight that in later days was to stand them in good stead. I cannot recall another case of a broken promise.

In many parts of Sarawak and certainly in the Entaih and Entebai areas, the Dyaks often hunt an animal called the "Kejang". It is a shy, excitable young doe, with large frightened eyes. It is good eating and as it also destroys your rubber, or eats the paddi in the farm, at least I can understand why the Dyak hunts it. Somehow, though, I hate to see one killed. They are easily caught and more often than not, as they swim across a river to escape from the hunting dogs. At Entaih one day, in came a Dyak with the most beautiful kejang that I had seen. It was terrified with nostrils quivering and large brown eyes giving a mute appeal for help.

"Do you want to buy it?" asked the Dyak.

"Yes," I replied. "I will give you five dollars for it."

"Right" said the Dyak and handed it over to me in a small wicker kind of basket. I gave him the money and he seemed quite content. When he saw me however cut the small thongs of the basket and let the kejang go running off free you would have thought I had given him a kick in the stomach.

He dived after it and caught it again. I said, "Who belongs to that kejang?"

"You," he said.

"Well, if I want to set it free that is my business, not yours!"

Away went the kejang free once more. I paused once to look round and although it might have been wishful thinking, I am sure I saw it smile in thanks.

Not so the Dyak. He was still angry. It was a story that was passed from mouth to mouth but from it came the tacit understanding that just as we, the Europeans, never even attempted to change the customs of the people so it came to be understood that the Dyaks on their side must not try to change ours. Writing of the kejang reminds me that

Arthur bought a small honey bear, a beautiful tame young beast with black furry coat and large black eyes. Arthur bought it for the same reason that I bought the young doe. He just didn't want it to be killed and eaten. So for a month or so Arthur nursed it and petted it, feeding it a tin of condensed milk every day. It was a great favourite but the time came when it became not just a baby playful bear but rather a big bear with sharp teeth. After it had spilt a tin of whitewash over the dispensary floor, broken some two dozen plates, climbed up into a dormitory and tried to bite one of the small children, even Arthur agreed it had to go. So it was put into a canoe with some of the trainees and taken quite some distance up the river. There it was let loose. Some three days later, bedraggled, hungry and wet, the same bear arrived back to sit at Arthur's feet. It was then caged but obviously unhappy and Arthur said it must go free, although there was no lack of Dyaks who wanted to kill and eat it. Arthur couldn't think of this, so into a canoe once again it went, but this time down river, almost to Ng. Entebai. There it was set loose in a cemetery where it was rumoured that there were other bears. As Dyaks never hunt in this kind of land, it has probably lived to a ripe old age. We often think of Arthur's bear and this incident did help to ensure that our customs were respected, even as we respected theirs.

The time came when, to enable planned work to follow a timetable, I had to evolve completely new customs applicable only, however, on any school or centre ground. It happened this way. Quite often pupils did not return to school on the correct day. Their excuse was always that they or their parents had had a bad dream warning them not to leave their longhouses on the day following or that they had set off to school right enough but on the way they had seen a bird of evil omen and to carry on meant certain death or some form of punishment. As time passed it became increasingly difficult to plan the erection of new buildings with the labour of the people, given free. I honestly do not think that they were trying to get out of doing their share of work and nobody but myself, Mac or Arthur need to raise even their eyebrows when certain people didn't turn up and just sent a message saying that they had had a bad dream or seen a bird of evil omen. It came to a climax, however, one morning at three o'clock. I awoke to the sound of the beating of a large drum called the "Tawak". This drum has a very penetrating sound and can be heard some miles away. It is only about three feet long and narrow; about six to seven inches in diameter. One end is covered very tightly with the skin of a deer.

From the direction of the sound I knew that something must have happened at Rh. Kau some four miles away. This drum is only sounded to bring help and dates from the days when longhouses were attacked by enemies. Nowadays it is usually only sounded when a longhouse goes on fire or occasionally, when, although not often, a Dyak goes berserk and there are not people around to restrain him. As I lay wondering whether I should respond, there was a terrific scuttering from both the pupils' dormitories and the dormitories where the adults on the adult education course were housed. I rose frantically, hoping at least to stop the young children but either they did not hear me or did not want to hear me, and in a few moments I was alone. "No", I said to myself, "this cannot go on". Mac by this time also had awakened and came over to see what was wrong. We both decided that some new custom would be formed on that very day, since, technically anyway, we as teachers were responsible for the children sent from longhouses far away and we just could not have them running off in the middle of the night, however justifiable the reasons. About two hours later they all began to return, rather sheepishly I thought, and with just a muttered "false alarm" they all made to go back to their dormitories. For two hours I had walked up and down becoming more and more intolerant of their customs. Such being human nature (and after all I was only human with a job to do) I had I think worked myself up and was determined to let off steam. I shouted on them to stop!

"Listen!" I said, "A school is not a longhouse and the quicker you learn that the better. Progress certainly does not mean following all your old customs and I am telling you, one and all, that if at the sound of a Tawak at some future date, you decide on your own authority just to scamper away, then be sure that I will not be here when you return. Get back to your beds and should anyone, adult or youth not agree with this rule, then pack your bags and go home!"

I went back to bed, but not to sleep. Instinctively I knew I had set in motion all that was needed for a crisis to develop. Sure enough, Mac came across just before seven in the morning to tell me that one or two had come to say goodbye and that almost all of them were indeed packing up to leave. Mac had tried to explain that it was true that a school was not just a longhouse where everyone pleased themselves, that a certain discipline had to be in force. To all his explanations they replied:

"Tuan Tuai (meaning old man, the name that they had given me as opposed to Mac being called Tuan Biak, meaning young man) and as opposed to Arthur being called Tuan Manang, meaning doctor) has insulted our customs. We cannot follow this new rule because we must obey the sound of the Tawak. So we must go home.

It had just turned seven o'clock, the time for normal morning assembly to allocate work in the working period till eight o'clock.

"Mac," I said, "quickly blow the whistle as though nothing had happened. By hook or by crook get them to form up on the small grass patch outside."

Mac, ever willing, ran to get his whistle and kept on blowing and sure enough, one or two began to respond and in a few minutes all had assembled in their normal places. By this time of course my anger had evaporated and I knew that I had tackled the problem in the wrong way. It was now going to be not a battle of wills so much as a battle for future prosperity and, one might say, disciplined living in a new environment.

Mac, meantime, bless him, had carried on normally by giving them the usual five minutes of physical training, consisting of jumping up and down and a kind of leap frog to finish off. Everybody enjoyed this five minutes.

This five minutes just gave me time to think, and of course psychologically, in body anyway, all were under discipline.

This was the moment for me. I took Mac's whistle in my hand and blew again and again on it. Then in a calm unhurried voice I said:

"When, you live in a longhouse, the sound of the Tawak is a signal that you must act on. I certainly agree. The sound of a whistle or a school gong is also a signal that you must act on. Supposing that you were all in a canoe and one half decided to paddle one way and the other half decided to paddle the other way, just what would happen?" I asked. There were nods of heads and even a few managed a half smile as they pictured what would happen.

I continued: "Supposing also that if a fire broke out at Rh. Kau, some few miles away, and also a fire somehow broke out at the same precise time here in your school that you helped to build, which would you follow, the sound of the Tawak or the sound of the whistle?"

I felt that they were with me and I quietly went on to explain that when parents sent pupils to school, be they old or young, those parents did expect that they were reasonably looked after.

Rubbing it in a bit, I turned to face the adults and added: "What would you think of me or Mr Mac, if at some future date when one of your own children was here in school and we allowed that child to rush off into danger and possibly get burned to death?"

Seeing that they were more and more with me, I ended by saying that I knew nevertheless that their custom of responding to the Tawak was important and necessary but only if they heard it in a longhouse and I would immediately, even that day, ask the chairman of the Progress Society to hold a meeting to discuss just how a school could follow a new pattern of rules, in that a pupil or anyone engaged in, or going to work in, the school could ignore bad dreams, ignore birds of evil omen, could ignore the sound of the Tawak. All my angry words of early morning were forgotten and holding to the advantage I said:

"Right, if you believe my way is best, then together we will sing our working song and off we go to work."

Our working song began with the words:

"Mansang ngagai bukit kin,
laban kitai ka ngator,
fingkat ringkat tansh nyain,
bulih untong dudi".

It was sung to the tune of "Step we gaily" and means simply that we went forward to the hills nearby to dig and make terraces to make the land more fertile. It was a song they all loved and although I led them rather shakily, it was taken up lustily and sung again and again. Nobody left and within a few days, a meeting was actually held. Gods were propitiated according to their customs and to this day all schools, certainly all schools throughout our areas, are free from longhouse customs of bad dreams, birds of evil omen and the sounds of the Tawak. The school whistle or gong is the authority.

A milestone representing mutual understanding and trust had been passed, although only just. The incident taught me not to lose my temper and to be more tolerant. The pupils had in fact acted according to their beliefs. The incident taught me also that Dyaks, for all the gold on the earth, for all the education under the sun, will not tolerate bad manners nor wrongful criticisms. To this day I am careful, very careful, to admonish only those who have clearly acted wrongly. The system, so often used in schools at home, of collective punishment does not work with Dyaks and, I think myself, rightly so. Each individual who is clearly in the wrong will always accept verbal or other punishment stoically and without rancour.

When I sit in the evenings in retrospect I am seldom lonely since I just ponder a little and think of the past. If the water is high in the river below and sometimes the level rises as much as forty-two feet above normal, the scene takes me back to the day when, travelling in a canoe with Empeni as driver, with quite a lot of miscellaneous goods, we came to "Wong Muas" just a little way up river from Kaki Wong. The river was in flood and the Muas rapids were ugly looking. When I saw them I was certainly apprehensive but having absolute faith in Empeni I merely clutched the sides of the canoe tighter, hoping I would not be seen. We got half way up when even with engine full and everybody pulling we just could not make it. Slowly but surely the water flowed into the canoe and in a few minutes we capsized and we were all in swirling angry water. Tins of biscuits, boxes of cornbeef, of milk and all sorts of things cascaded down the rapids. The canoe and engine slowly overturned and followed the boxes with Empeni grasping the sides. I never could remember just how I found myself to be on the only outcrop of rock, not that it was of more than temporary help, but there I found myself and I crouched watching everybody and everything just disappearing round the first bend. Then I did feel very lonely, so lonely that after a few minutes I could stand it no longer and let myself slide in, forgetting in my haste that I would be drawn into the fierce whirlpool at the foot of the rapids. I was, and I admit it, getting into a panic, trying my utmost to kick myself free and up. Indeed I heard a voice shouting: "Don't fight! Get your legs up!" Instinctively I reacted and sure enough I felt myself being whirled to the outer edge. One mighty thrust and I was out, floating smoothly down the river. No one knows who shouted. Round the next bend, there was Empeni clutching still the canoe with one hand since on it was still the engine and madly trying to get some sort of hold on the bank. The others had been carried much further down. I swam towards Empeni and between us we managed to tie up and heave the engine out to dry. Soon, as always happens, canoes from down river began to appear, all laden with things they had salvaged. Almost every Dyak is honest when something like this happens. He well help and only expect a very small share of anything that is saved.

The experience taught us a lot, not that it was the first time that we had sunk but it was the first time that I could piece together the reasons and from them new rules were made and followed even to this day. So when a canoe finds difficulty in mastering a rapid the driver must not fight but aim for a strategic withdrawal backwards. This is not too difficult providing the paddle is ready and it usually is. Having got safely down again, the canoe is lightened and another try is made. So it goes on till the canoe can actually get over. This experience also made the rule, used to this day, that no one should struggle in a whirlpool but lock the knees well up to the chest and go as limp as possible. Taking a deep breath helps. Invariably, the body is carried out to the edge and is not sucked under. So we learned, not to conquer rapids but just how to tackle them and return safely and with no loss.

When I hear the sound of a large aeroplane above, and especially when it circles as many seem to do, I recall the air drop of fertiliser at Budu. The Director of Agriculture, probably anxious to make amends for his policy of pepper planting, decided to make Budu the first place to try out air drops of fertiliser to be used experimentally on pepper gardens. When the idea was first mooted, I wasn't exactly keen although I did think getting free fertiliser, brought to the very door, was excellent. Budu nestled in between hills of around four to five hundred feet high and running through was the broad river. Apparently, however, the R.A.F. wanted some practice even though they were informed that it was a difficult dropping zone and the air drop was arranged. We did the best we could with strips of wood painted white to show the best approach and we had a large white triangle to mark the target of drop. The longhouse people had been warned but I should have known better. The morning of the drop dawned bright and clear making the problem of finding Budu quite simple. Dead on time, at 11.00 hours, the first aircraft came sweeping over low, making a dangerous steep turn to avoid a hill. My heart was in my mouth. I glanced round and to my horror Dyaks were coming from every direction and making straight for the aiming point. I began to visualise just what would happen if a hundredweight bag of fertiliser fell on anyone's head. By almost screaming at them and pointing madly first to the mark and then to the aeroplane, which was now on its run in, I frantically shepherded them below the nearest trees and stood panting. In came the two-engined Dakota, making the sound of thunder. We could see the crew madly shoving huge sacks out and in a matter of moments the sky seemed full of parachutes, all striped yellow and red. I saw one narrowly missing the roof of the school, another carrying on to drop just beside the longhouse on the other side of the river, another floating down on to the top of a tree. My eyes darting here and there I didn't actually see the three bags that dropped on the triangle but I heard the thumps. The aircraft then looked as though it was making for Kuching and the Dyaks began to run towards the aiming point to examine the bags. This was easy since in any case they had all burst open. Consternation developed once more as the Dakota came on its second run. This time there was no need for me to shout at the Dyaks. Never have I seen an area so quickly cleared and so many trees with Dyaks almost hugging them. The second drop was much more successful and all but two fell near the triangle. The other two went splash right into the river. The Dakota made a steep turn, just above the longhouse, and wooden slates just went flying in all directions. With a waggle of the wings, which I knew to be "cheerio", the Dakota flew off. "No more, no more!" I heard myself shouting as though the pilot could hear. I knew he couldn't but it was a relief to me to shout. Perhaps he heard through telepathy or more likely his load was finished because the Dakota did not come back. In due course I was informed that the first pilot had warned the others not to attempt the drop. I couldn't have agreed more. For weeks we were gathering bits of parachutes from odd trees and scooping up the by now sticky fertiliser. Perhaps the Director was getting his own back and not making amends. He did, for never again would I agree to an air drop with an aiming point almost at the bottom of a large cup.

In later days a small Taylor craft was used to drop money, medicine or urgent mail. This was exciting and delightful to watch and participate in. In still later days, when the helicopter came to Sarawak, it was even more delightful, except as I have written when there was an emergency night landing to cope with. Even that we managed to organise in the end by making the landing patch right on top of a hill with absolute clearance all round. Indeed, when confrontation was at its height, our landing pads at the top of the hill made it possible to bring in large Belvederes as well as Whirlwinds. The sight of Gurkha troops jumping out of helicopters, almost before they landed, to take up strategic positions with arms and machine guns at the "ready" was almost a poem of obedience and wonderful discipline for which, of course, those grand troops the Gurkhas are deservedly famed. The Dyaks and the Gurkhas got along famously together, possibly because of the rum that the Gurkhas always had, but actually I am sure because of the mutual respect each had for the other. They are alike in many ways.

Floods were always causing havoc. Our pig sties in the early days were built at what I thought to be a reasonable height from the river, around twenty feet above normal level. If they had been built too high the expense in extra concrete for drains was considerable. It was not long before I wished I had listened more carefully to the Dyaks. Admittedly they had told me that when the rivers were in flood they rose very high but as they all seemed to have different opinions on the actual highest level mark I took twenty feet to be reasonable. I certainly never expected rivers to rise forty-two feet and once a year this usually happens if not twice. So, in floods, apart from saving this and that, the pigs were our first concern. Let loose, they normally ran to high ground and there among the vegetables they made up for their incarceration. One particular Berkshire boar, instead of being grateful for being saved from drowning, took exception to one of the Agricultural Assistants, Harry Mujan, and with head down, tusks at the ready, it went in to the attack. Harry luckily just managed to reach a tree and only the heel of his sandals was bitten. But there was Harry, stuck there until Mac was summoned and, running to get his gun, made short shrift of the Berkshire boar. Determined even in death for revenge, after I had roasted it inside an empty petrol drum and was carrying it to the mess room with my teeth watering, I forgot that there was a huge hole in front of the "oven" and in I went among the empty tins and other rubbish with the roasted pig. Mac, Arthur and most of the trainees were watching me and by instinct, certainly not by conscious thought, as I fell, I threw the pig ahead of me where it landed at Mac's feet. Everyone being hungry, no one paid the slightest attention to my predicament and there I was with my nose literally just above the side of the hole and my hands up in the air. It was some minutes before anyone would or could help me for laughing. So we learned to build our model pig sties of better and better design, not twenty feet above normal river level but fifty feet.

The milestone that both Mac and I remember most is the one which took place strangely enough in the Rose Room of the Aurora Hotel in Kuching. When we heard that the first four boys were returning from Scotland—Luke, Jawie, Bilun and Liman—both Mac and I decided that they should be welcomed in Kuching. Arthur also agreed and after some weeks of thought we decided to invite the chairman and secretary from each of the nine centres to join in the welcome. The Information Officer in Kuching thought this an excellent idea and offered every help in making the visit to Kuching both one for meeting the boys and as an educational tour for the eighteen Dyaks from remote places. First we managed to persuade the Shipping Master, Captain Mathieson, an old friend of mine, to give us his largest launch. He had always been helpful and so, all rendezvousing at Budu, the journey to Kaki Wond and thence to Saratok took a normal course. Few of the Dyaks had been to Saratok far less Kuching. When we arrived at Saratok, the Menual was there all gleaming and white as most Government launches are. Mac and I had a hilarious time trying to explain this and that to the Dyaks and more important just what not to do and how to do it. I need not go into details. They were better imagined especially when one remembers that none of them had seen, far less used, a water closet. In good spirits we arrived at Kuching. There were no impending tussles with Government over this and that and both Mac and I were determined to make it a real occasion to remember. We had specifically arranged with the Information Officer that the party had to be accommodated in a reasonably decent hotel. For too long, Dyaks on going to towns or bazaars had been content to stay in attics above Chinese shops, cooking their own food wherever there was a fire and sleeping wherever they could find a corner. Some, I grant you, were forced to do this because of lack of money but even reasonably well off Dyaks who could certainly afford a few dollars for a room and bed were too shy, too diffident, too ashamed of their kind of dress to go anywhere near an hotel far less stay in one. Mac and I knew that most Dyaks could quickly harmonise themselves in whatever environment they found themselves in. I grant you that when Mac and I sorted them out in their various rooms and showed them their beds they gingerly touched the white sheets as though they were needles. But we were proved right. During the next day, having brought some clothes and clean white shirts, they looked and acted as though they had been doing this all their lives. Mac and I were impressed with their natural behaviour in such strange and unusual surroundings.

The boys were due to arrive the following day at the airport and we all gathered there to greet them. The news had of course got out and there were reporters with cameras from all over the place. The upriver Dyaks behaved magnificently and as the boys came out from Customs clearance, it was indeed as though royalty was being welcomed. Luke led them through with Liman and Bilun close behind. Poise, natural good manners were very evident and it was a really joyous meeting. It was then we learned that Jawie had not come since he was being interviewed to enter Aberdeen University. Of course we were sorry not to see Jawie, but the news of the possibility of his going on to Aberdeen University rather than come home was an added reason for being glad on that day. Indeed, even the most sceptical agreed that though they had left as boys, they had returned as young men with a gracious and natural manner and no affectation at all. They had not even succumbed to wearing a tie which always seemed to many, but quite wrongly, the hallmark of education or substance. Among the old Dyaks, they quickly showed that they had not forgotten their native tongue and they prattled about this and that.

It was not surprising that we received many telephone calls asking if it were possible for Mac or I to bring the boys along to meet certain people. As we had only two days more in Kuching and most of the time had been earmarked to take the boys to visit old friends we had not planned any official visits. Mac and I sat down to ponder over this, since we did realise that Government had helped considerably by paying the passage of the boys to and fro. I just didn't like the idea of either Mac or I taking them round officially by the hand to this office or that office. It was more than likely that, while not intentional, there would be some attitudes of condescension and Dyaks with their pride can sense this before all others. We both thought for a long time and suddenly I said:

"Mac! Let's give a kind of cocktail party and invite all those who should be met officially and, of course, our own friends to whom we would in any case be returning some wonderful hospitality given in the past when we took the boys first to Kuching some five years previously."

Mac looked at me in amazement and with the look that seemed to indicate that I was really daft.

"What do we use for money and in any case where would you have this cocktail party?" he drily asked and without the least bit of enthusiasm.

I said, "As far as money is concerned it will be on me since by the boys returning as they have done, just as I had wanted them to return, it will be my way of saying 'thank you' ".

He looked at me with just a little more interest and the beginnings of a gleam in his eye.

"Yes," I said, "if you are not proud of the boys, I am. To take them round is just too much like taking round peacocks for people to stare at and smile blankly with no meaning to it. If the various representatives of the nine Progress Committees acted as hosts with the boys at some social function, then they would be the ones at the receiving end, and those who came could in such circumstances size them up much better, with all the advantages on the side of the boys."

"By God, you've got something there!" Mac said, as he sat up interested at last. "But where?"

I doubt if I have ever seen anyone more astonished than Mac when I said quite calmly, "The Aurora Hotel".

"The what!" almost shouted Mac. "Can you see our Dyaks from the remote parts acting as hosts in the Rose Room?"

Mac seemed to enjoy the scene that came into his mind, since he went into fits of laughter. It was a bit infectious for I too began to think of some possibilities and to laugh also. When we had both recovered, Mac turned to me with a gleam in his eye to say:

"Just supposing that we could arrange the Rose Room, would anybody come?"

I said, "Well, honestly Mac, I just don't know, but if they didn't, apart from Luke, Liman, Bilun and the various chairmen and secretaries getting a kind of slap in the face if nobody turned up, we could save the situation and drink everything ourselves".

By this time I was becoming quite determined to have a cocktail party somewhere. I think it was my remark to Mac that I thought in any case it was high time that people began speaking to Dyaks as equals, standing up, rather than the traditional way of the Dyak sitting on the floor listening to words of wisdom from someone sitting high above them. From then on, Mac was with me and we hastily went down to the Aurora to see the Manager and to find out if we had enough money. Curiously enough, even for about a total of three hundred it was going to work out at something like four hundred dollars, very much less than we had expected. There was only a small charge for the hire of the Rose Room for three hours, a service charge and payment of the drinks. This clinched it for both Mac and I since we could at any rate limit the cost by controlling the consumption although we hoped everybody would have enough to drink.

We then raced round the shops and, with the help of the boys who had also thought it was a marvellous idea but a bit brave, we bought beautifully printed invitation cards. For the next three hours we were all busy, with Mac and I making out the lists and the boys writing them out and addressing the envelopes.

When all had been written and posted and having started the invitations off with no less than the Chief Secretary and his wife and thence right down the hierarchy scale to our own personal friends I did really begin to think that I had bitten off more than could be chewed.

By half past six the following day, Mac, I, Luke, Liman, Bilun and the Dyaks from the various centres had gathered in the Rose Room, the room where top society met, the Dorchester of Sarawak. It was hardly a room since it more or less took up the whole roof of the Aurora Hotel. When a function was being held, the casement windows were opened and the "room" therefore extended naturally on to the roof garden. Everything did look exceedingly fine and although Mac and I had had a little difficulty in persuading the older Dyaks to use the lift, which they had never seen before, everyone looked expectant, shiny almost, dressed in their best. Apart from having to put a few shirts inside trousers, we had no problems at all with dress. I could hardly believe that just a few days before most of those gathered had been wearing a kind of loin cloth usually called a "chawat" in Dyak.

"At least," I said to myself, "there are no reasons to be concerned as to their dress or manners."

Nevertheless, as it came nearer to seven o'clock, although outwardly calm, inside me I had all the misgivings possible. By five past seven, with still nobody appearing, I could have run away. Mac began to look glum and concerned. I would that we could have had a few drinks just to help our nerves, but both Mac and I felt that we couldn't start until somebody arrived. By a quarter past seven I had given up all hope and was about to tell everybody to help themselves when the lift door opened and in came Murray Dickson, the Director of Education. There could not have been a better first arrival. He always felt at home with the Dyaks and he came in with a broad smile on his face which put everyone at their ease. Dunggat was the senior Chairman and he went forward to welcome Mr Dickson No sooner had Murray Dickson met the boys and was being introduced to the others than the lift door again opened and the Chief Secretary and his wife, charmingly dressed, entered. I could have run to her and hugged her. Seeing them both I knew that all would be well. By half past seven, the Rose Room was a hum of conversation and movement here and there. Luke, Liman and Bilun were charming and kept introducing the older Dyaks to the guests. Everyone seemed absolutely at ease and many were talking away in Dyak to old friends whom they recognised from distant days when they themselves had been District Officers near Budu or Entebai. With traditional Dyak hospitality, most of the Dyaks were taking up plates of nuts, sandwiches and other delicacies to the guests. I was about to have my first drink when I spied Chairman Belayong. who even in his longhouse looked very like Emperor Haile Selassie and even now more so groomed and dressed for a cocktail party, taking a plate towards the wife of the Chief Secretary. She was actually talking to Luke and was quite deep in conversation with him and so did not notice Belayong who came to stand in front of her, rather like a soldier. He waited for a few moments but still neither noticed him. Belayong, however, not to be outdone, raised his right hand to the level of her stomach and as nice as you like gave her a gentle poke with his forefinger. It was even unexpected to me and I was watching the performance through half an eye and of course I choked on my drink and began spluttering. Somehow I could not restrain my laughter. Naturally enough the Chief Secretary's wife was quite startled and her glass went up in the air but luckily the contents just missed her dress. She more than demonstrated her graciousness and understanding by ignoring the incident and calmly accepted a few nuts from Belayong. Luke of course had jumped to the rescue and picked up the broken glass. I turned round wondering if many had seen what had happened. Many had, including Mac, who also could not restrain himself from laughing but the incident helped to put everybody at their ease and more and more talking and laughing continued till just on eight thirty, the time for all to depart. Everybody seemed to be enjoying themselves so much that it was not till nearly nine o'clock that the Chief Secretary and his wife said goodbye with some charming and encouraging words to Luke, Liman and Bilun who were waiting near the lift door. When everyone had left Mac and I indulged, to celebrate what had turned out to be one of the most successful social functions of the year. I remember neither of us had any dinner that night but went into a deep and contented sleep. Any doubts that some still had that sending our trainees to Nairn Academy had been wrong, were dispelled most definitely and completely. More important, by doing what we had done we had given ample proof that Dyaks could properly play their parts in a more civilised environment. It is, I think, worth mentioning that, when Malaysia came into being, elected from among those who had been at the Aurora Hotel that memorable evening, were one Member of Parliament, and three Councillors all able to play their parts socially and administratively with good effect. This incident proved to me at any rate that the work of a Community Development Officer is not finished until at least some of his "people" feel that they can conduct themselves socially with confidence in an environment not their own.

CHAPTER ELEVEN

THE HELPING HAND

Although few will believe me, had I been offered a million dollars to begin the project at Budu, I would have declined to accept such a sum of money. In doing Community Development work, while it is essential to have a basic minimum for salaries of essential personnel and for subsidies to be used for this and that, it is just as essential not to have too much. Too much would make things too easy and one would as like as not use money either to buy progress or to get things done quickly. It seemed then as it does now, that one of the most important principles of Community Development is that the people concerned had to provide almost more than they reasonably could. All through the ages, real progress has been achieved only by a people making tremendous efforts by themselves, beyond almost what they originally thought themselves capable of. At least it ensures that they have that sense of owning things rather than them having been given things. My own personal opinion is that much of the aid given so generously by donor countries to help the underdeveloped brings not progress but a begging attitude—an attitude which cannot bring progress at all.

History itself will bear me out and those who have travelled and observed can see the results of both ways. Help certainly is needed but this help must be given not only wisely but for a purpose and to an extent amounting to less than half of what can and must be provided by the people being helped. Even in the ordinary family circle this principle has been evident from time immemorial. Children only value those things which they have either earned or worked for. Any giving also must be in the spirit of trust and one might say affection to ensure that seeds of help can take root, grow into trees and have branches. The guarding of pride is as important as life itself if a people wish to emerge to take their rightful place in a fast developing world. Pity has to be given sparingly and preferably not at all. Over the years, there have been many incidents which bear this out. I can say with certainty that almost any Dyak who is a Dyak, prefers to work for his food rather than be given it. If this attitude is not present by virtue of the character of the people then it has to be inculcated. If this is found to be impossible and I grant you with some races it could be, I, personally anyway, would neither wish to help nor go out of my way to do so. So it is vitally important that any Community Development Officer must know the character of the people whom he hopes to help.

One of my main reasons in going to Budu in the first place purely as an ordinary local authority teacher was because I was fairly sure that, whether or not I could help the people, I was in an ideal position to make a study of them. Children generally are the images of their parents, not physically perhaps, but in nature and character. A few are not in this category but if

Jalai ngadu ka enti tulang bisi kena patah.

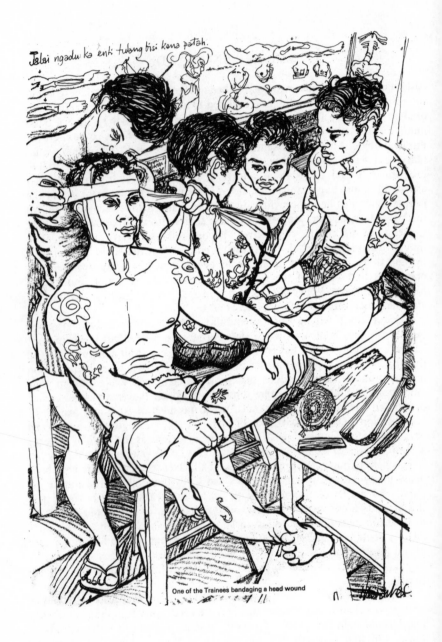

One of the Trainees bandaging a head wound

160

such were studied carefully, good reasons could almost certainly be found. So during those first six months at Budu I was quite frankly studying the character of the Dyak. I have no intention of writing my findings, at least not in this story. The understanding, however, of the Dyak character was a vital factor in planning the project. Had I not studied them how could I have understood why there was not even the words "thank you" in their whole vocabulary. Let me make haste to say that if they do not say "thank you" it certainly does not mean that they are ungrateful. It all hinges on this inherent pride. I learned quickly that to get the best out of the Dyak was really to ask him to do more than he thought he could. Frankly it was like a game of draughts and I often had to spend long hours thinking on my next move. Usually, luckily, I could think while walking and many of my immediate problems have been solved over the route from Budu to Entaih, Budu to Grenjang and Budu to Ng Badu. I may confess also that one of the pleasures of my life has been, when it was possible, to drink just at sun down one bottle of beer and as I drank, to smoke a cigarette or two. I have been almost ruthless in ensuring that I had this hour of the day for reflection, for planning the next day but most of all just to relax and assess what had been done that day. I must confess also that the Dyaks took a long time to learn that I liked just to be by myself at this time. By being on occasion brutally impolite they learned this in time. After all, as I often said to them, "I have never tried to change your customs. We Europeans have also got customs. One of mine is that I just want the one hour in the day for thought. So don't come at this time expecting me to listen to your troubles or about your wants". I daresay that if I had had plenty of beer and was less selfish this hour of relaxation would possibly have never started. It was the hour also when I listened to records on the gramophone. What a boon this has been! Not just to me but to Arthur, Mac and Doc. All of us liked music. Only Arthur, however, a fair hand at playing the violin, was able to say what record was being played. I just knew what I liked though from constant playing I have now learned that Beethoven's Emperor Concerto or Symphony number six is vitally essential if I have a difficult problem to work out. I then, I think, go down the scale according to the difficulties that lie ahead, to Grieg's Piano Concerto, something from Chopin, to records like "In a Monastery Garden". Arthur will never believe that I can think listening to music, but then he listens to the theme but for me it acts as the environment of thought. We had, of course, many other kinds of records and often we took the gramophone to school, not only to accompany the trainees in their efforts to sing but to use it for Country Dancing. Indeed we could relax and have fun, even in the remote parts of Sarawak. I can remember a former Chief Secretary, now a Governor in one of the few last remaining colonies, having the time of his life dancing the "Dashing White Sergeant" with the trainees.

However to get on with the helping hand.

So for those who may have misunderstood me so far, I say again, that help must be given carefully and with thought. Just also as it is important to be one of the people whom you are helping, so it is equally important, for different reasons to involve other people outside the area. It was no accident that I enlisted the help of friends in Kuching to help, not only groom, the lads earmarked for Nairn Academy or further training in Britain. It was also vital to involve them to ensure that there was an awareness of need. It was vital that the people of Budu knew that there were many other people thinking about helping them and that the extent of this help would very greatly depend on what efforts had been made by them, themselves. It is true that we chose those who could help best. Coming to Budu, to help in adult education, we enlisted the help of people like Miss Helen Wallis, Miss Mair Rees, both brave and valiant ladies who forsook not just once but several times the comforts of Kuching to sleep on hard floors, eat what tasteless food there was, just to help. I think they first helped because they thought they should and didn't like to say "No"! When they came a second and third time I knew they came because they really felt that they were needed as needed they were. It is not a man's job to teach sewing although both Mac and I learned enough to carry on. It was not a man's job to teach how pancakes should be made nor how babies should be cared for. Both left their mark and would be surprised that some of the Dyak ladies whom they taught have little mannerisms of Helen and Mair. Indeed they are remembered with affection and with gratitude.

From time to time over the years, more money than had been asked or approved was considered necessary. One such need was for some quicker means of communication, not only between the various centres but from Budu or Entaih to the nearest District Office. Much valuable time was lost by either trainees or ourselves having to carry important messages from place to place. As our supply routes became established it was possible for agents down river to despatch goods on receipt of letters or telegrams. Without some form of telephone communication it was still necessary for some person to have to walk or use a canoe before messages could be delivered. So the idea of a radio telephone link between main centres and a district office, which could send ordinary telegrams, was born. It was born out of necessity and the need to conserve energy and time. The Post-Master General on being approached was most sympathetic and was keen to experiment but it took more than a year before some four hand turning radio telephone sets arrived. Knowing of the probability that radio telephone communication would be more than a dream, I had during the year approached the Committee of Community Development in Kuching for some radios. I wanted those radios for two purposes only. I knew that our own radio telephone line would have a wave band able to be found on an ordinary radio, if the frequency was known. If selected longhouses were given a radio it could be used primarily for communications but also in adult education work. Kuching however could not help. Not wanting to be beaten I made an appeal to the Nuffield Foundation for a grant to buy fifty radios. By the time that the actual radio telephone sets had arrived, the Nuffield Foundation had approved the grant and we had fifty good quality radio sets. It is only right that the directors of the Nuffield Foundation should know that had we not got those radios, it would have been virtually impossible to use with any impact, the radio telephone sets that we had got from the Post-Master General. For months and in every conceivable way, at varying distances, and at varying heights we tried to make telephone contact with Saratok where we knew that a major control had been installed. All to no effect although we did know that each was calling the other. I became sure that it was the noise of the hand turning generator that caused the interference. It was at this point that the Nuffield Radios arrived. By careful tuning we managed to find the frequency and from that moment on, communications not only with a district office but between each main centre and every longhouse that had been allocated a "Nuffield Radio" as they came to be called. Many are still in use to the present day. Through those radios, Saratok used to relay important messages to all centres and to all longhouses at certain times each day. Indeed each day at ten thirty, everyone stopped what they were doing to come and listen in. Why not? There might be a message for them or for someone in their longhouse. As time passed and there was a tendency to misuse this for messages that were not really urgent, certain restrictions had to be made and the radio telephone network link limited to news of an educational kind, medical, or news that concerned the community as a whole. That the people used the radios to listen in to organised programmes forwarded to Radio Sarawak either by tape or letter was of course encouraged to the limit. Budu news and educational features were a mainstay at Radio Sarawak in the early days. So if it happened that we were in Kuching and wanted a canoe to meet us anywhere, this was just very easy now. A telephone call to Radio Sarawak and that night the news had reached the longhouse. We can never be too grateful to the Nuffield Foundation. It was a turning point in the whole project. Eventually, it was possible when the Iban Team Project had started to hold actual meetings of key personnel although each person was far apart. This was not only of tremendous help but it kept us all really in touch at times when we needed advice. So it was common enough that at a prearranged time, I would act as control at Ng Entebai and call in Entaih, Budu, Grenjang and Ng Budu. The fifth set was given me by the Police, not so much to help us but actually to help them. The Budu/Entaih radio link as it came to be called gave valiant service under security, medical administration, and education. When the new radio time call came in a year or so ago, the link had to be discontinued since it interfered with various frequencies in common use. It was fun while it lasted and prevented that feeling of being far from civilization. A later result of the Nuffield Grant needs also to be recorded. The Sarawak Government was morally forced to supply to other areas not just fifty but well over a thousand. At times I wasn't too popular but as I usually made conscience my guide, I didn't worry over much. The important point was that radio telephone communications had been proved to be possible in remote areas. This fact made many people determined to set up equal communications throughout the whole colony. Now it is possible for me at Ng. Entebai to speak with someone in Kuching should I desire to. This does not happen often though.

By 1958 the number of outboards that were needed to cope with the extent of business, not only at Budu, but at Grenjang, Ng Budu and Engkilili had risen from one to fourteen. The co-operative shops were also selling engines. It was essential then to plan not only for general maintenance but for full scale repair. Mac had been valiantly carrying the brunt of all this and while very able to carry out major repairs, costs of all spare parts meant that a considerable amount of money was "dead" in those spare parts. A fair number of trainees, under Mac's teaching were capable of doing a great deal by themselves with only the minimum of supervision. It happened also that at this time the Perkin's outboard made by Peter's of Peterborough, England, had just come on to the market. Both Mac and I thought that this was the time to start up our own repair and maintenance shop as part of the co-operatives at Engkilili, the last lowest down the river. So it was decided that I should approach the manager of the Perkin's outboards at Peterborough when I went on leave. This I did and explained the whole position. The Company became very interested and as a first gesture agreed to train four of the boys who were at Nairn, during their long holiday from school in the summer. This has proved a tremendous help indeed. There were also tentative proposals that Perkins would send at their cost, a fully trained engineer for a period of three years to set up this much needed repair and maintenance shop. We even got as far as meeting the lad who had volunteered. Robin was his name and he had himself become interested in the scheme through meeting our lads from Nairn at Peterborough. Both Mac and I were delighted at this possibility. Not only would it make us more independent of down river traders, but such a shop would provide a much needed service not only with our own agents but also with all the other engines that were being bought. The Perkin's Company were most generous also in that it would supply spare parts free till they were actually used.

I would that I could end this part of the story by saying that all went as planned. Short sighted policy on the part of a former Chief Secretary brought negotiations to an abrupt end, on the grounds that it was not the policy of the Sarawak Government to subsidise competition in business. I still cannot see just how Government was subsidising, since all costs were to be borne by the Perkin's Company. This was one battle I lost. There was actually no way on winning, since the Sarawak Government was normally bound to support Borneo Co. which also sold outboards. This angle of development had not occurred to me or to Mac. We were both very angry. Had we been able to establish this repair shop at Engkilili, it would have had a tremendous impact on the whole area. More important, from the point of view of development, it could have brought a real awareness of the need for technical knowledge. Other machines could have been gradually introduced, machines that would have helped to create a more enlightened form of agriculture.

It was natural almost, when it was found necessary, to establish a source of supply outside the country to ensure true and complete independence both in wholesale buying and in selling commodities, that we should turn to the Scottish General Co-operatives of Laidlaw Street, Glasgow. Nothing seemed too great a trouble for the staff there. Orders were fulfilled and despatched with promptness. Somehow they always reached us and throughout the years nothing was ever lost. Once or twice, however, through local mishandling, goods consigned for Budu or Entebai went to other ports, even to Hong Kong on one occasion. When it was known that no less than His Excellency the Governor would start the scheme off at Budu by officially declaring it open, I had the idea that he would not just like to eat from tin plates and tin mugs as we were accustomed to doing. The only glasses we had were as though they had been sawn from thick pipes. I quickly despatched an order to Scottish General Co-operatives for sets of good china, tumblers of good quality, cocktail and sherry glasses. The order was confirmed and there was ample time for all those things to arrive. As the day of His Excellency's arrival came near, there was no sign of this consignment. It had carried on to Hong Kong by mistake. As it turned out, the Governor thoroughly enjoyed eating from tin plates and using tin spoons. Perhaps he was just being polite but I do not think so.

The hidden help which Scottish General Co-operatives gave us was really because we could take our time in paying for the goods. Indeed we could wait till everything was sold. For a shop, starting on approximately one hundred pounds of share capital this was of immense help. To this day orders reach us although not too promptly. This is not the fault of Scottish General. One consignment particularly does deserve to be told in detail. Among other things that we needed I wanted two coffins. There was nothing morbid about the order. It just happened that from experience I thought we should be ready and in any case, things like coffins could well turn out to be a good selling commodity just like good biscuits. The idea of buying empty coffins from Scotland was I thought a bit of a waste and asked Scottish General if they would fill them with sweets or biscuits.

Never again, in my time anyway, will coffins be ordered to be despatched filled with sweets. Despite the bills of lading, it seemed impossible to convince Customs and Chinese launch owners that the coffins did not contain dead bodies. They must, both said, because of the weight. I myself had in the end to retrieve them and by visual means all the way up from the main port, convince the people concerned in loading and unloading that they were just boxes of sweets. Apparently Mr Lindsay, the manager of Scottish General, and Mr Lowe had had equal problems before they were finally shipped. When I was last at home they kept me in fits of laughter as they described their efforts. Phoning the coffin makers the answer was, "Of course we can make the coffins but Oh goodness me No, we couldn't possibly fill them with sweets!" Phoning the sweet manufacturers, the answer was, "Of course we can supply the order of sweets, but Oh goodness me, we cannot fill coffins with them!". So poor Mr Lindsay and Mr Lowe had in the still of the night to do it themselves. Such however was the service that Scottish General provided to us here. It was a most pleasant association right through. The staff, who might read this some day, were always giving us pleasant surprises. More often than not, goods were packed not with scraps of paper but good old Sunday papers like the *News of the World,* papers that we had not seen for years. It was very thoughtful of them and much appreciated. I remember opening one case and right on the front page of a recent edition of the *Sunday Graphic* the words Ng. Entebai in large black print caught by eye. "What on earth was this?" said I to myself and quickly grabbed up the paper to read all about it.

It was a full account of one of the strangest medical emergencies that I have ever been involved in. At the time it was written, we had had many visits from helicopters, some official, some purely friendly since Ng. Entebai had become a kind of haven of rest to tired pilots operating from Sibu. We knew all of them so well and how fortunate it was that this was so. However, one afternoon, Rabing came running to me and breathlessly told me that a young Dyak boy aged twelve had a spear right through his head. Naturally I thought he must be dead. "No", Rabing said, "He is alive and actually is able to walk!"

"Surely he must be joking" I said to myself and ran with Rabing back to the dispensary. Sure enough, although to this day it is hard to believe, there sitting quietly and quite unconcerned was the boy with the spear, a three foot spear at that, right through his head. They had been fishing under water and his friend had mistaken him for a big fish. For a moment I just didn't know what to do but acted on Arthur's maxim, that while there was life there was hope. On the radio telephone I got through to the Commanding Officer of the Squadron, 845 Squadron, and told him we had an emergency medical evacuation. "Could he help?"

Knowing me, I think he knew it was a real emergency and that night just on eight o'clock we heard the helicopter flying round and signalling for lights. We were in a near panic. I had never expected any pilot to try and get in to Ng. Entebai at night. Luckily I knew a bit of morse and sent up word to wait. Everybody dashed around lighting every conceivable lamp possible, all pressure lamps. Luckily too I had one of those rare flood pressure lamps and Jannga and Eddie were both competent to man it. Rain started to fall to add to my worry but crossing my fingers, I signalled "ready". Apart from a near landing on the roof of the school building, avoided at the last moment by quick thinking on Eddie's and Jangga's part, we managed to get him down safely. Cos was the name of the pilot and I knew him to be almost the best. Out jumped the co-pilot with a stretcher and shouting in my ear that they had to hurry because of fuel and weather we ran to the hut where Kumbang, the boy, was sitting quietly waiting. Seeing the pilot, Kumbang got up and even smiled.

"Is this the emergency?" he shouted. "What the bloody hell did you call us for someone who could walk?"

His eyes happened to rise to Kumbang's head.

"Good God."

"Yes", I said, "that's what I thought too." Carefully we shepherded him to the waiting heli and even more carefully managed to get Kumbang into the door by edging part of the spear in first. The co-pilot was visibly shaken at having this passenger but with thumbs up the signal was given and the heli lifted off to roar away into the darkness. Rabing and I were both emotionally and mentally exhausted and continued to sit watching even in the rain till the last light disappeared in the distance.

Yes, the heli arrived safely in Sibu and Kumbang caused equal if not more consternation when taken to the hospitals. The Doctors were quite naturally hesitant to pull it out since like everyone else, they thought that by doing so, Kumbang would just die. So for a day or two Kumbang was allowed to run about in the ward, still with his spear in his head. A red ribbon was tied to both ends. Interest in the case mounted to fever height. It was the nurses however that made action, any action, necessary in the end. He was a lovable looking boy, too.

The strain on the nurses became almost too much to bear and the doctors decided to operate. Kumbang didn't die. He was back at Ng. Entebai within a week, smiling away. A few months later, as a gesture of thanks, Kumbang presented to Cos the spear, suitably mounted, as a memento, at a very moving ceremony at Ng. Entebai.

Indeed 845 Squadron gave the helping hand in no small measure and always with a smile. A few weeks after this, one of the pilots, Nick Boyd, came to stay for his week's holiday from duty. He just wanted to read and fish. He also, however, was persuaded to help finish a new house I was building. Then disaster seemed to strike. Rabing had two deaths in as many hours and the dispensary was full of people who were vomiting and with diarrhoea. I think we both knew what the sickness was. Luckily Rabing had some saline and got busy. I went to find Nick and told him my fears. Within three hours we had evacuated three and had it confirmed, Cholera. I was near to panic as I had ever been, even over Germany flying through concentrated flak. Suffice it to say that by the next day, thanks to 845 Squadron, we had all the inoculations we needed and two teams from Sibu arrived with it. One team went up the Kanowit, one up the Entebai to Entaih. Rabing, myself, Jangga and Eddie took over at Ng. Entebai. When I think of those few days when the epidemic was at its height it is just a bad dream. I do remember Rabing telling me that in one day the four of us had inoculated 2,754 people of all ages. We had however contained the epidemic and no more died. When the Squadron finally left for home at the conclusion of its duty, Eddie on behalf of the people presented a hand woven Dyak blanket to the Commanding Officer, Commander Derek Levy. We still receive Christmas cards from many of the pilots and Tank Sherman often writes. He and Derek loved Sarawak and I am sure the Dyaks also. Nothing was too great a trouble for them if it was to help.

I think after the Squadron left, the idea, and it was just an idea at that stage, came to start up some form of river ambulance service. For years we had had to accept the sheer impossibility of helping remote Dyaks to hospital. The time that the journey took in those early days made it often unrealistic and useless, since even if we could have provided onward transport from Ng. Entebai, the patient would probably have died en route anyway. Even Arthur accepted it. By this time the road from Sibu to Julau was however nearing completion and this was going to make all the difference. Ng Entebai to Sibu and almost back was very possible if one was organised with canoes and engines ready.

Efforts were made to establish a river ambulance service through the Medical Department. The idea was appreciated but financially it was thought to be impossible. Once again I approached the Nuffield Foundation. The

Foundation was sympathetic but not hopeful. Nevertheless, after many months it was decided that an attempt to set up a river ambulance service would be worthwhile. The Foundation received a letter from the Divisional Medical Officer, giving full moral support to the project, and agreed to make a grant of £2,000. The grant allowed for the buying of four engines and canoes and provided running expenses for a year. When I received this news, I felt that a terrible weight had been taken from my shoulders and I breathed a silent prayer of gratitude. Gone would be the days when one just had to say, "Sorry, there is nothing one can do. Here is some aspirin which will help the pain." Gone would be the days when a radio telephone message from Entaih or Maong or Tappang would reach me to ask help to send down a child with a broken arm or someone who had almost cut his leg off, or a mother who kept bleeding after birth. We had of course helped when our slender resources could afford it. Now with the grant from Nuffield, there is an engine and canoe always ready at Entaih, Maong or Tappang on the ulu Kanowit. There were a few teething troubles at the beginning but for almost a year now the river ambulance service has been in operation. The Border Scouts stationed at those places help a lot. For one thing it was possible to train them in first aid. Arthur of course did this. We made our own stretchers from jungle wood and thongs. As each centre was high yielding rubber belonging to the Committee of Progress, it is possible to envisage this service continuing at any rate until the engines cannot be used any longer. As they are carefully looked after and only certain people can drive them, I have every hope that by the time the engines cannot be used, Government will have got round to creating this kind of service, country wide. It is inevitable and just as radios were provided country wide, so from this project made possible by the Nuffield Foundation, other rivers and other areas will receive this service which is so badly needed in remote places.

The tremendous help given by the United Kingdom Volunteer Service Overseas, started by Mr Alex Dickson need only be referred to in this chapter since the full story of this very worth while scheme as it affected Budu and Entaih can be read in another chapter. So also the V.S.A., the young brother of the V.S.O. but with volunteers from New Zealand. Offers of help often came from Peace Corps and the impact of this organisation was of considerable benefit in following up projects started by us. As, however, even with the best of intentions, this organisation rather tended to give too much without an equal share being given by the people we declined to have any permanently assisting at any one centre. As I have said at the beginning, great care has to be taken in giving anything, especially in remote parts. I always considered that Peace Corps workers would find their services of better value in more urban areas. All however were most pleasant to work with and brought a cheerfulness in their approach which inspired people to do what was asked of them. Chicken farms, vegetable growing, longhouse hygiene, building of minor bridges, helping to put in water supplies, construction of badminton courts, are visible evidence of the zeal the Peace Corps put into their work. Their greatest impact, however, has I think been in Secondary Schools since most were qualified with one kind of degree or another. It was just a different organisation to that of the V.S.O. in its conception and indeed in its application.

So by 1965, Malaysia had come into being and there seemed little or no possibility that any help would or could be given in the final phase of the project, namely the setting up of some form of Secondary School system to serve the Budu and Entebai areas. It seemed that almost all of the twelve years' hard work might come to nothing. That something would have remained is true, but for the continuation of real progress phase four was in my opinion vital. How could it be otherwise I argued to myself? The work of Community Development had created a situation where there was not only an awareness that education was the key to progress, but that without it, there could be no permanent progress. Fortunately the people, or most of them, were aware of the fact that not all could benefit from a secondary education but they knew and believed that some could. Those who could not would certainly form the nucleus, intent on learning new farming methods and applying them to the areas of their own longhouses. There was no evidence of the less clever being jealous of those who could go on in school, only an increasing determination that if they themselves could not, their children or their children's children might.

Although it seemed impossible to establish privately a secondary school of a vocational nature, I was determined to try. I hadn't much more to lose than I already had. By resigning from Batu Lintang I had in any case lost all pension rights although I certainly did not mind about this so long as I achieved what I had hoped to do. Phases one, two and three of the scheme were to a large extent successful. Most centres were running as they had been run by us, some better, some not so good. Rough calculations seemed to indicate that I would need no less than around $200,000. This figure in itself should have made me hesitate. The only thing I liked about it was the challenge. The situation reminded me of the time I had taken over an A.T.C. Squadron, just after the war when I had returned to civilian teaching. It was a squadron in name only, without Headquarters and little or no equipment. Within three years, the squadron had a fine well equipped pipe band, a band that even won a shield at the Cowal Games, a well equipped Headquarters complete with cinema and projector, our own transport and a fair balance of money in the bank. I make haste to say this was achieved not just because of the work I did but because of the interest that I created in the minds of the local people. Just as in Community Development work much could be achieved I knew, by simply stating one's objects and hopes, giving good reasons for them and perhaps by example proving that the boys in the squadron really earned the support.

So far from being persuaded that this needed $200,000 was just impossible to find I merely said to myself that somehow, some way it would be. Having decided, there was no question of being defeated. This may sound conceited and many who read this may smile scathingly but during the war I had learned the hard way, that to win through whether by a short head or just, there must be no thought at all of not being able to return. It is rather like the action of adrenalin. With right thinking one can and does create a built-in defence as it were, ready to meet the emergency of battle wounds. With right thinking one almost trains the sub-conscious to react by itself in times of great stress and the dangers are overcome. This does not mean to suggest that I was never anxious. Far from it. My very anxieties created the adrenalin that was to be needed at varying times. My very anxieties kept me training my subconscious to react correctly should things go wrong. I was always imagining that I had to forceland, always imagining that I had engines on fire, always imagining that I had fighters on my tail and so when all those things did happen, my hands used to take action before even I knew myself what I was doing.

So confronted with the task of finding this initial S200,000 I sat down to think, but chiefly I was trying to make myself afraid to begin even, in order that ways and means could be thought out and tried and to give the "subconscious" a chance to work. I had small reserves of money, around $10,000 of my own, saved over the years. I knew certainly this would have to be used at least initially and I was certainly prepared to use it. Having put it all into the kitty as it were, I then started to think of my old age with no money at all. I was, and am, much too independent to accept charity but the point of all this is that I was intentionally making myself afraid for the future knowing that my brain in consequence would work overtime to find a way that would perhaps save my modest reserves for use in my old age. The method seemed to work at least in the amount of paper that I typed and the number of letters asking for help that I sent out. I just could not allow myself to feel tired since much was at stake.

First results proved almost negative and even the answers I got, while sympathetic and understanding, suggested that I was really trying to do something that could not be done and that I should stop my nonsense and leave things as they were. It was rather like the time Jawie and Luke were refused admission to a secondary school in the early days of the scheme. I just became more and more determined. Then luck came my way. I had gone to Kuching on the odd chance that I might persuade the Education Department to give me books if nothing else. By the merest chance I popped in to see Allan Moore of the Schools Broadcasting Department since I thought I might get a free school radio. Luckily he knew about me and I knew about him so we got in famously from the start. He is a bit like myself and we both felt at ease pouring out our individual worries over a cup of tea. Allan was not only sympathetic but practical in his appraisal of the situation.

"Have you approached Asia Foundation?" he asked casually as though, of course I must have.

"No", I said. "I just cannot make contact". Alan grabbed the phone, dialled frantically and through his beard muttered, "If I can only catch Louis Cennick before he leaves today!"

After agonising minutes of "yes", "no", "all right right away", Allan threw down the telephone and more or less grabbed me by the hand and we both tore down the stairs into his small car. By the time he was in top gear I gathered we were on our way to see Louis but that we would have to hurry to catch him.

Louis was on the point of leaving for the aerodrome to catch the plane to Brunei. I had never met him before, but he knew of me and had long wanted to meet me. This was one good result from my policy of involving people outside Budu in some way or another. The work had become known. After we talked for a few minutes, Louis said he would postpone his flight till the next one in the afternoon. With Allan, we had a long session of what was needed, how much and in what way. Louis was very quick on the uptake and soon had a good picture of the situation. Finally it was decided that he, Louis, would write to the representative in Jesselton, Mr Cal Scollon, and explain the position. He himself was very hopeful that Cal Scollon could and would help since the project outlined by me was just what Asia Foundation help was meant for. Both Allan and Louis thought it would be a splendid idea if both of them could pay a visit to Entebai and see for themselves. I heartily endorsed this and sure enough in about two weeks' time both arrived and I was certainly pleased to see them. There was something to see and I intentionally let them visit both Entebai and Entaih by themselves so that they could ask questions that might have been embarrassing had I been with them. At Entebai they found the dispensary running competently. They found the primary school with around 100 children, the well stocked co-operative shop and the rubber gardens with terraced high yielding rubber trees planted neatly and thriving. More important they found a most pleasant attitude both from the staff and the Chairman of the Committee of Progress. Their visit to Entaih, with a night stay, was I understand most enjoyable and they agreed with me that Entaih had something. Henry and Enyang both being there and both being competent and happy lads I had had no fears that Entaih would not impress them. It is a commanding place and one feels its permanency and its importance to the people.

What doubts Louis had had, if any, were dissipated and he assured me that Cal Scollon would pay a visit very soon. This Cal did and from the moment he arrived I knew I was talking to a like soul. It made such a difference. Cal was direct and capable and was certainly interested in the people and was confident that help would be forthcoming. It did and very generous help it was too. Salaries of two teachers were to be provided for three years, science equipment, help in transport, help to buy books and agricultural necessities. Cal, with his immediate superior Mr Bill Filers, visited me the following year. They were very similar people in the sense anyway that they were both extremely interested in people and how they could be helped. By their help, almost half of what I needed was assured for the next three years. Indeed I have reason to be grateful first to Allan Moore for the introduction and to Asia Foundation through Cal and Bill.

A friendliness and a mutual trust exists between us to this day even though both have left Asia Foundation to do more responsible work in another country. I am sure too that they did like Entebai for its own sake and I would not be surprised if either appeared suddenly to visit me. This would be a pleasure indeed.

Confident at last that the school would open, I set about getting the accommodation ready. Once again, luck was with me. Murray Dickson, the then Director of Education, being himself very sympathetic with the project but powerless to help officially put me in touch with the Field Secretary for Oxfam. Alec Dickson, who happened to be well known to Oxfam from his own work, and who knew many of the committee, must have given me an excellent recommendation. I received word from Major Ackworth that a building subsidy would very likely be approved, spread over a period of three years. It could not however be definite till the Oxfam representative, a Mr Bernard Llewellyn, could visit Entebai to see for himself the position. When he did arrive soon after, I formed the same impression of Bernard as I had with Cal and Bill. We seemed to talk the same language and another friendship started. Bernard not only approved the building subsidy but having seen the standard of feeding that was possible in the school indicated that he would also advise a small food subsidy.   This food subsidy has been of tremendous value, especially during the months just before harvest when literally rice could not be bought at all by the pupils.

I was further heartened by a letter from Mr Taylor, Director of Scottish General Products, telling me that he and his co-directors had decided to donate to my work the sum of £500 and would I like it in actual money or in goods. I felt so grateful to Mr Taylor, whom I had got to know very well over the years. It was a most generous gift and within three months a consignment of bunk beds so badly needed for the school and a consignment of rain capes, haversack bags and biscuits arrived at Entebai. The biscuits were of course quickly eaten but the bunk beds remain the envy of even the more grandly built Government Secondary Schools. I was most touched to find in this consignment a few jars of thick Scotch marmalade for myself. I don't remember sharing this with anyone, but I am fairly sure that Mr Lindsay, who sent it, wouldn't have wanted me to.

Murray Dickson again gave me help by introducing me to Mrs Chan of the Catholic Relief Services. Indeed Mrs Chan wanted to help me. She had heard of the good work I had been doing and there would be no question of sharing in what she had to give. So from the Catholic Relief Services came periodic consignments of cooking oil, dried milk, bulgar wheat, oats and flour. Only those who have been in charge of a boarding school or other similar institution, when the stocks of food seem so low, can quite understand the tremendous sense of sheer relief when such consignments arrived. At least Mrs Chan must know that we are indeed grateful for this help.

Financially, the school was almost solvent and the only debts were to me. Several donations, however, came in from people who would wish to remain anonymous, but those donations meant a very great deal to me. It wasn't only the money. It was that there were people who believed in what I was doing and helped as much as they could.

My own personal money however was fast dwindling since from the opening of the school I just refused to accept any remuneration at all for the work that I was doing as Secretary Manager, the executive name that I gave to myself working for the Committee of Managers, the legal body responsible for the school. However I did not greatly worry. I still had a home in

Scotland, a reasonably comfortable flat which I owned and which had been used by the boys from time to time when they were in Scotland. This was one of the reasons for buying it. I had a car and a caravan and a few minor assets as well as my pension deposits held by the Scottish Education Department. As I had more or less made up my mind to make Sarawak my home, I knew all this would have to go anyway. The question was how to get home and back without having to pay out around £500, a sum of money that would keep things going at Entebai for a year at least.

Luck again was with me. The then Resident, Mr Donald Walker, having been asked to suggest a suitable person to carry out an investigation of that rare race of people, the Punans, thought of me and proposed that I should do this survey. Apart even from the fact that I had long wanted an opportunity to visit this little known nomadic people who were reputed to live in the heart of deep jungles, the remuneration was going to make possible my quick trip home to sell what I had. Naturally I accepted the assignment with eagerness although I knew there was a certain amount of danger to it and that living conditions would be even harder than I had already experienced.

The Officer Commanding, British Troops, Brigadier . . . was also intensely interested in the Punans. He felt that something should be done to rehabilitate the Punans whose way of life had been forcibly changed because of confrontation and their proximity to the Indonesian border. He had often visited me at Entebai, not so much officially as because he liked the peace of Entebai and could relax with me or relax by going up the river driven by Eddie. He welcomed that I had been chosen to make this survey and offered to put a helicopter entirely at my service. It would drop me where I wanted and pick me up when I wanted. To anyone who has travelled into the real remote parts of Sarawak, this offer could only be described as magnificent. To reach the Punans by ordinary means, foot and canoe would have taken some three to four weeks under probably the most uncomfortable conditions imaginable. Not only did the Brigadier arrange that I be picked up from Entebai but arranged various platoons of British soldiers to be near at hand should I need them. It was most thoughtful of him. Those same British troops I understand were lowered by wire from a large helicopter with instructions to prepare a landing ground for the smaller helicopter which was to bring me. The soldiers did a splendid job and I was most grateful to them. I had not expected such V.I.P. treatment far less consider that I was one. It was good for my ego anyway and certainly did indicate to the Punans that I was no ordinary visitor. That we nearly never found the spot is neither here nor there. Heavy rain came on as we approached the location marked on our map. Once again my own experience was to prove useful since I always revelled in map reading from the air. We kept circling the spot knowing we had arrived but could see nothing. Captain Thompson, a most capable and experienced pilot, was getting a bit anxious since he had to return and fuel was getting short. Just as we were about to give up, a bright green Very light appeared below but of a landing ground nothing was visible. Down we went to get a closer look and right enough there was a landing ground but down a tunnel of trees almost two hundred feet high. Any pilot could have been forgiven had he said "Sorry chum, no can do!" Not Captain Thompson. With almost exquisite manipulation of the throttle and controls down we went to land safely. More important still he got up safely too. A marvellous effort.

During the days that followed I made copious notes and observations and came to certain conclusions covered in the Punan Report. Some day I hope some action will follow since not only did I consider that something should be done to help the Punans but on being flown out, our helicopter had engine trouble and we had to force land almost two hundred miles from known habitation and help. Once again, Captain Thompson had to bring to bear all his skill to get us down alive even. He did, but he maintains to this day that it was possible only because I seemed to be unperturbed, as actually I was, having complete and utter faith in his ability, and because I had pointed out without thinking the only possible semi safe landing spot for miles around. Curious that subconscious action can still take over after some twenty-two years away from being used. We got down without injury and indeed apart from the blades being damaged there was no visible evidence that the helicopter had been damaged greatly. Safe we might be, but the next question was, "Would we be found?" The only comfort we had was that on the way down I also apparently had pulled the right tapes and the emergency signal giving radio for homing seemed to be functioning judging from the sound of pips.

Two of the trainees had accompanied me on this leg of the survey, Giman and Entebang. Being Dyaks they had brought with them their large hunting knives. Within no time they had hacked down enough trees near by to make possible a tiny landing ground for a helicopter should it happen that we could be located. Searching through the escape kit, we seemed to have everything except what we actually needed most. A balloon there was and twine but there seemed no way of getting it up into the sky which was our only hope. I was certainly looking for some cylinder of say hydrogen or helium, so was Captain Thompson. Away at the foot of the bag we did find some grey looking stones smelling vaguely of Carbide.

"Good God" I said to myself. "Are we expected to fill the balloon with hydrogen carbide?" Apparently this was the only possible thing to do. Off we all went to find some water, since although we carried the odd flask it was far from being enough. Captain Thompson had the better idea though. He had seen that the rain was about to come on and, taking one of the doors from the heli set it up to catch all that came off the roof. To cut a long story short, after we had literally burned all our fingers and hands, we had enough gas in the balloon to consider sending it aloft. We tied the blimp radio on the top and with fingers crossed set it free to go up. Slowly but surely we eased off twine. The balloon went higher and higher. It was a bright orange colour and as it went up it seemed to grow bigger. I found out later that this is actually what happens because of the change in pressure. Tying the twine to the heli I brought out the emergency rations which I seldom travel without. Tea, condensed milk, biscuits and a spirit stove a relic from camping days at home. We had just finished the tea having enjoyed it as one only can enjoy something like a cup of tea after either a harassing adventure or some equally exciting climb on rocks, when the sound of a large helicopter was heard in the distance.

"Would they see our balloon?" was the only thought in our heads, all of us. It flew on past but just as we were about to give up all hope we heard it turning round again.

"They've seen us!" shouted Giman. True they had, one of the engineers looking out back caught the orange colour in the light of the setting sun shining on it. It was too big to land on our emergency landing ground but a wire cable appeared to come down with the heli hovering above it. Obviously we were going to be winched up but we could take nothing with us, and certainly not my package of notes. Still life is sweeter than a bundle of notes even on the Punans and up we were all pulled into the helicopter to be whisked to the nearest base. Some weeks later all our possessions actually arrived safely and I was able to write my report. I must confess too that I accepted my fee with the feeling that I had really earned it, although I would have done the survey just for pleasure. The fee made it possible for me to make arrangements to go home and this I did. I realised all my assets and returned to Entebai with around $20,000 to provide the rest of the money required for the school.

The Punan survey, which I had started with Eddie and Sirai, was actually interrupted for about a week. I had taken Eddie to look after the medical side and Sirai to get the confidence of the Punans. Both were ideal for the job. In odd moments Eddie took tape recordings of meetings and Punan songs and took a number of the Punan boys to test their I.Q. We were busy working away when out of the blue came the sound of a helicopter. "It must be looking for us", said Eddie. We certainly had not expected one since we had several days to go at Long Wat where we were.

Down it came and landed with little difficulty since we had cleared a fair piece of ground. Out jumped Captain Thompson with a signal in his hand. As I read it, I could hardly believe my eyes. It read:

"In view of information from Resident that the Director of the Magsaysay Foundation wishes to meet you at Entebai tomorrow with a view to award you the annual Magsaysay award for Community Development amounting to $10,000, have arranged your immediate lift out and back to Entebai. Survey can be carried on as convenient to you and heli made available."

Brigadier . . .

I could hardly speak as I thought of this possible money of $10,000 American Dollars, nor of course could Eddie. It was a bit above the head of Sirai but he saw that we had had an important message which we quickly explained to him. My heart went out to the Brigadier for his thoughtfulness and his wish to help me and really I felt very humble in this remote part of Sarawak. Friends I certainly had, and I vowed that I would keep those friends.

Back we went to Entebai and hurriedly prepared for the visit. To save their time, the Brigadier had also arranged a heli lift for them from Sibu and back. "His goodness", as Eddie said, "was beyond expression of thanks." I would that I could say that I received the award. Apparently I just missed it by a hair's breadth. What a difference it would have made, had I been fortunate. I accepted the news, however, philosophically and carried on. I could quite honestly say anyway that I had been a runner up with this very important award for Community Development.

I got the impression from the Directors that the Magsaysay Foundation first knew of the Budu and Entebai Scheme from Mora Dickson's most interesting book, "Season in Sarawak". Both she and Alec had paid a visit to Budu as I have explained under the V.S.O. Chapter and she had allocated a few chapters to my work at Budu. Those chapters have certainly created a great interest and I often wonder if Mora knows just how much she helped me with her account so beautifully illustrated by her own drawings. The book was widely read as I certainly know from the numbers of letters I have received as a result of their reading. Possibly my unusual approach to Community Development made people feel that at Budu there was something different. As Mora has a most delightful way of writing the story, even to me it was extremely interesting. I am sure that it was Mora's book that made all the difference when Asia Foundation and Oxfam came to decide to help or not.

Andrew Burgess, a V.S.O. whose service in Sarawak was to end so tragically by his sudden death in a road accident, had also read Mora's book and in letters to his mother he had assured her that, so far as he was concerned, Mr Wilson seemed to be on the right track in the way he was helping the Dyaks. It was of course very sad indeed that this young man who had come to give a year's service should die and die so far from home. I felt intense sympathy for his mother and since then we have got to know each other through letters. In Andrew's memory, Mrs Burgess presented the Entebai School with money left by Andrew, saying simply that he would have wished it. So Andrew's name at any rate will live, inscribed on a very beautiful microscope in our science room.

As I looked back to the end of 1965 when there seemed not the remotest chance of fulfilling phase three I felt a humility which is sincere and full. Now in the evenings at dusk, I wander around the grounds of the school, see a substantial dormitory and messroom. I wander through the large classroom block and wonder at my luck. That we have not many pupils at the moment does not greatly worry me since there are hopes that the economic crisis affecting all ways of life in Sarawak with the fall of rubber prices, may soon change for the better. The school here is ready to take at any time as many as 60 pupils comfortably. Our numbers would be even smaller were not some being supported privately from friends and other sources. Perhaps the scheme started by Christ's Hospital School in England will multiply as time passes.

Graham Riches, one of our finest V.S.O.'s was a pupil in Christ's Hospital School before he came to help us here in Sarawak for a year. Always interested in how things were going on, he knew of my plans to open a Secondary School at Entebai. "Perhaps" he wrote, "Christ's Hospital can help you through their United Nations Group!" Various letters were written and Graham himself went down to the school to explain the position. Now each year a sum of £60 reaches me here from Christ's Hospital, subscribed by the efforts of the pupils themselves, to provide help to two boys in this school, boys who need help and who have possibilities. It is a kind of scholarship which helps this school to compete with the normal Government Secondary which in many cases almost wholly provides for selected pupils passing through the Government Secondary School stream. Were those schools not so academically bounded I would not mind so much, but believing that future prosperity for Sarawak must lie in the majority of schools giving more than just lip service and a week a year to Agriculture, I would that there might be a change of policy soon.

To provide free education at this stage of development is not one of my aims or purposes. To do so, the new generations might not accept the kind of life their fathers knew. Courage, ability, endurance and traditional pride, a product of the normal Dyak evolution could well disappear if too much is given free. The system which we used at Budu and Entaih and so far as money allows us here, by providing education in return for services to a community during non school hours, seems to be one which can retain the best of two kinds of worlds. Every effort must be made to guard against the paradox of our times, in that if life is made too easy, too comfortable, the pride and strength which made our fathers men can so be weakened. The final result, should safeguards not be there, could well be to export men and women as its major products. They would go because they must and because the new generation by giving too much help, could well not accept the kind of life their fathers knew. There should be no schools where parallel development within the family structure cannot also take place, and so ensure that the present day children will not be less than the men their fathers were.

A helping hand should always be there but if that hand is too often given, the child could well never develop his own confidence in his own physical and academic ability and a once strong virile race of people could well decline.

Jangga

178

CHAPTER TWELVE

CRITICAL INCIDENTS

During the days when someone near to us is critically ill, all else is given a second place and our uppermost thoughts are concerned only in helping that person to get well. When, as more often that not, the seriously ill person gets up from his sick bed, looks healthy and resilient, one begins to wonder why one worried at all and as the months pass one even forgets that the person has been ill at all and there is just a vague memory of some anxious days. In any home with a large family this kind of critical incident is commonplace and although anxiety is dulled through the passage of time the bonds of affection become very much greater because of the very anxiety that all passed through.

So it is with the critical incidents which took place throughout the years in the Budu and Entaih Schemes. In retrospect I wonder why we were so anxious at the time, I wonder why everything else seemed to be so unimportant as dealing with the crisis on hand. Yet, I am sure, that because we had those inevitable crises and there were many, so the team, the trainees, the people of the community, all equally involved in the efforts to find a solution, became a very close knit family, each with a gratefulness to the other that time does not erase. It would seem also in retrospect that such crises were almost necessary to produce this close knit family and almost because of them the scheme grew in strength.

It is of course not possible to relate them all and I intend only to relate those which affected the policy throughout the years.

When the shops had been running for some months and Mac had eventually established a system of buying the people's produce such as rubber, although the Co-operative Department deplored that it was not done under a separate co-operative with each member having a second share number for it, our capital reserves to buy produce were almost non-existent. After a great deal of discussion and thought, a meeting was held and it was proposed that the members should agree to accepting a small first payment and after such produce was actually sold, a second and final payment would be based on the price received on the market. The people readily agreed especially as there was a good chance of the final price being higher than the mean price chosen at the actual time of selling. Thus it was possible to treble, even quadruple, our buying potential. So much so that in order to lower costs of transport we decided that we would stockpile the rubber at Engkilili and when we had a hundred piculs we would take it all down to Saratok. This we did and one memorable day we managed to load five large canoes with one hundred piculs of rubber. Only the most experienced trainee drivers were used. Mac took his place in the leading one, driven by Chuk, with a 30 h.p. engine. I took my place in the last one. As Mac, the trainees and I were all for having a bit of "fun" it had been arranged that on the large open stretch of river a few minutes from Saratok our canoes would take up a flight formation with Chuk leading at the speed of the slowest canoe which had a 10 h.p. engine. It was a beautiful evening, that I can remember. For the first time I did wish that I had had a camera. The sight was impressive and the sound as though a whole squadron of aeroplanes were converging on Saratok. As we approached the landing stage, hundreds had run to the bank to see what it was all about. We had come a long way from the days when we had taken down around five piculs and both Mac and I felt a justifiable pride as we jumped on the river bank. No more would we hear in the bazaar that the scheme would not succeed, that it was impossible to organise Dyaks into a community for the welfare of all and not the individual.

So working with a will we all unloaded the rubber, had a wash and swim in the river and went to have food. We were all in grand humour and to celebrate the occasion we had a chicken killed and roasted. As we were spending the night in Saratok there was no hurry at all and Mac and I were indulging in the first bottle of iced cold beer that we had had for many months. We just felt on top of the world. Even the rather unusual District Officer did not upset us by insinuating that we had just become mere shopkeepers instead of Community Development Officers.

The first signs that all was not well came with news brought by some of the senior trainees who, having finished their food, had been wandering about in the bazaar tentatively asking the price of rubber. They came running up to Mac and me and said that the price seemed to have fallen twenty cents since the day before. Instead of the expected seventy dollars it seemed that we were only going to receive fifty dollars; total loss for the consignment was quickly estimated at around two thousand dollars. If this were true, there would be grave repercussions when we returned to Budu to make a second payment of even less than the first one.

Within half an hour both Mac and I had confirmed that there was no trader willing to buy higher than fifty cents a katy. It was obvious that there was collusion. Although very very angry I could not help ruefully thinking that our little "show off" had rebounded on us. We got all the trainees together and discussed what we would do. A few were in favour of just selling on the grounds that the Chinese traders had us in their power. Mac, I and the great majority were determined that we would NOT sell at that price. This was a test case. Lose on this one and in the future the traders could buy just as they wanted and at their price even though we knew from the radio that the fair price was around the seventy cents. By this time it was dark but the tide was on the turn. Even though we were all tired, having loaded the rubber at Engkilili and unloaded at Saratok, we decided to load the rubber back again on to the canoes and store it at Engkilili. This was a decision of the greatest magnitude. It was dark. The loading even would be fraught with danger not to mention the unloading again at Engkilili and the journey up river in the dark with five heavily laden canoes. Almost certainly at least one of them would sink and the loss would not only be in rubber but in a canoe, engine and possible injury to some of the trainees. I am sure the anger which we all felt stifled any fears we had and made us all the more cautious. I can still see the hundreds who gathered to watch in silence the reloading and the sheer amazement on the faces of the traders. None had expected this move. Talking only among ourselves we finished loading and each canoe set off with Mac again in the lead and myself in the rear canoe. By one in the morning we had by the grace of all good luck arrived at Engkilili and by three o'clock had finished unloading. Desperately tired we all just lay down where we could and slept, very conscious we had done the right thing.

Returning to Budu the next day an extraordinary meeting was held. Consternation there was when the news was told, but adversity brings its own rewards. Never had it been demonstrated so clearly the strength of the co-operative movement. All would rather have the rubber rot than have it sold at fifty cents a katy. All who had any money would immediately loan it to the shop to enable ordinary trading to be carried on and to enable us to buy what was needed from Kuching and not Saratok. The next two months were touch and go but there was still no weakening to sell the rubber in Saratok. Bills from Kuching were mounting and Mac and I were getting worried since unless we sold our rubber lying at Engkilili a month or so would see us bankrupt. No one had another dollar to loan. News, however, on the radio indicated that rubber prices were generally on the rise in Kuching and had reached eighty cents a katy. Advising the people not to sell rubber at all anywhere and especially in Saratok we made plans to hang on for another month and to sell our rubber not in Saratok but Kuching. Now this sounds easy but good staff work was going to be necessary for everything to work out. Alun, our friend in Saratok with his launch, had to be contacted and he agreed to load all our rubber at Engkilili, now some 200 piculs, take it down the river and tie alongside the Kuching launch, which would be anchored at a certain place and at a certain hour. A receiving agent had by this time been appointed in Kuching. All was set for the move and just three months after the loading and unloading at Saratok, our rubber went on its way to Kuching. The price received was ninety cents a katy. Everything we had done was now justified. The second payment to the people brought not only great joy but a sense of having won a long and hard struggle. Never again did the Saratok traders seek to cheat. Gradually there was a return to trading in Saratok since it was actually more convenient and to this day still exists on the understanding that fair prices are given for goods brought down and fair prices are paid for goods bought.

We continued, however, to buy certain things from Kuching but this brought on the second great crisis. Our sales of rubber had increased very considerably, a direct result of the Saratok episode, since almost every Dyak up river was now selling his rubber only to the co-operative shops, now well established at Budu, Grenjang, Ng Budu and Engkilili. It could almost be said that hardly a sheet of rubber was being sold outside the co-operative set up. Both Mac and I were delighted at the turn of events and thought most of our troubles were over. Unfortunately, the trader in Saratok kept running out of solid cash but was able to pay in cheque form on a bank in Kuching. This didn't worry Mac or me since we could pay our bills in Kuching with the cheques. This we did for many months until out of the blue came a letter from our supplier in Kuching, returning all the cheques to a value of seven thousand dollars, saying that they regretted having to do this but the Saratok trader had gone bankrupt and the bank refused to honour the cheques. The shock of this news to Mac and I just cannot be related. Once again bankruptcy faced us unless we could find a solution. While nothing could be proved it seemed fairly certain that there had been collusion both on the part of the Saratok trader and our Kuching supplier since the cheques had been sent not all at once but over a period of three months. Surely, Mac and I argued, had there been no collusion, the first cheques would have already been returned un-honoured. Also it was significant that the trader in Saratok still had plenty of goods in his shop. That we owed the Kuching trader over seven thousand dollars was indisputable and no matter how Mac and I examined the position it seemed that this was an attempt to put the Budu co-operatives into bankruptcy.

Once again an extraordinary meeting was called. Many were stunned with this new crisis and although seven thousand dollars might not be a great deal in big business, this sum seemed impossible to find at short notice and in the two weeks we had been given. Once again everybody was asked to loan every cent that they could and wonder of wonders, with Mac, Arthur and myself putting in every available cent and the Dyaks also, we had close on seven thousand dollars. As none of us could afford just to give what we had loaned, so Mac and I decided that we should go to Saratok, to the trader, and persuade him or otherwise to give us goods in lieu of the dud cheques which he had given us. Money we knew he had not or said he had not. So with a few older Dyaks suitably garbed in traditional war dress Mac and I went to do business with the trader. We had first, however, despatched the money by telegraph to Kuching and we at least knew that, temporarily at any rate, we had staved off the crisis. If we could get goods to the same value then apart from having money tied up in goods, nobody was going to lose much if anything in the end. It was all going to be a question as to whether the trader was going to allow us to take the equivalent in goods. If he was really bankrupt, then the chances of the Budu Stores getting a dollar a dollar payment for debts were very small and neither Mac nor I were prepared to wait and see. We needed the goods to begin getting our money back. So with some ten trainees, Mac and I went to interview the trader. By this time the three older Dyaks, acting on instructions, had seated themselves on the floor of the shop and were quietly but determinedly sharpening their large knives. There was no discussion. Of course we could take in goods the value of the dud cheques, plus of course, interest, Mac said, on the money we had borrowed to pay the Kuching debt. So this crisis ended as the first, with profits to the shop, since many were agreeable to be repaid in goods and the turnover during the next few months vastly increased. More important still, the trust between the team and people was now even more noticeable than ever. We had gained a great moral victory from near disaster.

Scarcely had we recovered from this setback when in rapid succession all the shops were broken into. It was our custom, although a stupid one in some ways to leave unused money for rubber purchases in amongst the rice in large earthenware jars. Often in the past, money which had been brought overland had got so wet that a lot of time was wasted in drying it. So the practice of leaving money at each store developed. First the Engkilili store was broken into and close on the equivalent of a hundred pounds was stolen. Although police from Saratok arrived on the scene soon afterwards it was not recovered although we know pretty well who stole it. A week later the Ng Budu store was also broken into and there close on a hundred pounds was stolen. Once again the police failed to catch the culprit. Mac and I were seriously worried and had the profits from rubber sales not been considerable during this period we would have been in serious financial difficulties. It seemed fairly certain that Dyaks were not involved in this for the very simple reason that everybody knew what everybody else possessed such being Dyak way of life. No Dyak, we argued, would be stupid enough to steal this amount and hope that he could hide his illgotten gains. Suspicion was there but nothing could be proved. When, however, a week later the store at Crenkang was broken into and a similar sum stolen firm action had to be taken. It seemed fairly certain now that the thefts were part of an organised attempt to break the co-operatives. Another extraordinary meeting was called. Once again it was clear that rather than the thefts creating a state of no confidence, the people were more than ever determined to protect what they certainly now regarded as their property. Some were all for an organised raid both to try and recover the stolen money and to indicate that this sort of thing had to stop or else. . . . Mac and I of course would not agree to this since two wrongs do not make a right. However, a kind of home guard was formed with all taking it in turns to keep watch at night at all the centres. Safes were bought for each store. There were, however, no further attempts and we recovered from these losses as we recovered from the losses in sunk canoes. There was just less profit to divide during this year but because all knew the reasons, the theft incidents rather strengthened than weakened us.

So far as was possible, the various crises were not allowed to interfere greatly with the academic study of the trainees nor even with the adults. Somehow one of us was spared to carry on with routine. Luckily we had intentionally developed within the minds of both the trainees and the adults in school that the responsibility of learning was theirs and that the teacher could only help. Often while Principal of Batu Lintang during examination of pupils in local schools had I heard the answer: "The teacher did not teach us that". It seemed to be the concept of the pupils in those early days of schooling in Sarawak that it was the teacher's responsibility to teach, not the pupils to learn, and if the teacher did not teach this or that the pupil felt quite justified in not bothering to learn anything outside the lessons. So at Budu I had made a point of impressing upon all that progress in real education depended entirely on what they learned by themselves. A good well equipped library was available, they had good and sufficient books, so what more did they need! I often cited my own grandfather as an example as one who never went to school at all but before he died he was a headmaster in a school and he had taught by a strange coincidence, Sir Duncan Stewart, the Governor of Sarawak. For my own part too, I was for ever telling them that I was alive today only because I had learned many things by myself. However, just for occasions such as the crises, I always had ready, prepared sheets of planned study, rather on the Dalton principle and it was surprising how quickly Dyaks learned using this method.

Study however was seriously interrupted one morning when a note was brought to me from the wife of one of the adults then supposed to be in school. The note asked that he return home immediately since his wife was seriously ill. Edwin was the name of her husband and apparently he had left home for school the previous Sunday. As he was not in school, the immediate question was, "Where was he?" When he had not arrived no one had bothered much since it was supposed that he was either sick or had important work to do which could not be left. Mac, Arthur and I were very concerned. Edwin was a real friend to us all and had given us a great deal of personal support in every way. As he had apparently left home and not arrived in school there was only one conclusion. He must have fallen and broken a leg or something and was probably lying out in the open. No time must be lost in organising the search for him. Within half an hour every trainee and every adult were going along possible paths from Budu to his home some five hours' walk away. Arthur and I were leading the group. When we had been walking about three hours we saw, just off the path, a small leaf roofed hut. As it was an obvious place to search we made towards it. Before we reached it we knew that if we hadn't found Edwin, we found something that was causing thousands of bluebottles to be flying around and a smell of rotten decay. Wetting handerchiefs and tying them round our noses and mouths, Arthur and I went nearer and climbed up the trunk of a tree at the door. Indeed we had found Edwin but knew he was past all aid. His body was bloated and the stench was appalling. I have never admired Arthur more. He was determined to examine Edwin's body and discover if possible what had caused his death. It could even have been murder. Difficult and all as it was owing to the state of the body, we certainly determined that there were no broken bones. Lying beside Edwin was a dirty coffee cup just beside his hand. From that we deduced that he had at least drunk coffee before he died. His face gave us more to think about. It was certainly obvious he had died in great pain and both Arthur and I concluded that he must have been bitten by a snake. Round his ankle we then noticed, tied very tightly, a rough tourniquet and sure enough just below this Arthur found the tell tale mark of a snake bite. Being slightly more suspiciously minded than Arthur, I was not so sure. Edwin was used to wearing sandals and always carried a stick. Indeed it was there lying beside him. The evidence of a snake bite could have been easily manufactured. Further extensive examination produced, however, no other evidence of death. As he could have been poisoned we took the cup which still had some liquid left in it, hoping that the contents could be examined pathologically. As there was nothing more we could do we paid our last respects to Edwin by closing his eyes and made off in the direction of his house to inform his wife. It was all very sad but we gave what comfort we could. By the evening his friends and relations had prepared a coffin from a large tree and left to bring his body back so that the last rites could be given to Edwin, as was the custom, in his own home, when the coffin lies in state overnight. Arthur and I remained as did all the trainees now gathered and many other friends and relations. I feared, as did Arthur, that the adults in school would take this as a sign or a portent that they should not carry on with school and that their Gods had indicated this very clearly with Edwin's death while proceeding to school. As it was customary for someone to say a few words before burial, with Arthur's help I emphasised that Edwin had always been one of the strongest supporters and that if other men and women were now afraid to return to school, then Edwin assuredly would not be at peace in his grave. I added in any case that it was not quite clear just how he died and that although there seemed evidence of death by a snake bite this was not proved. I did not need to say that there was a possibility of his being murdered since they were as aware of this as I was. "He had been not only a staunch supporter but a leading personality in the district." I ended with "If you all return to school and carry on, you will be doing what Edwin wanted you to do. Let him sleep at peace".

All of us breathed a heartfelt sigh of relief when, next day, school resumed as usual at Budu. I could not help thinking that when dealing with Dyaks in dangers or in crises clear statements of the essential truths were imperative and this very awareness brought once again the family closer.

Whether as a result of examining Edwin so closely, Arthur himself became seriously ill. His temperature kept rising and rising and nothing seemed to break him out in a sweat. The only thing we were sure of was that it was not malaria. Chundie and I never left his bedside, trying to keep him cool with sponges of cold water. By the third day his temperature had risen steadily to 105 degrees and Arthur was barely conscious of what was going on around him. If Arthur were to live I knew that we would need help and at Mac's suggestion sent off Chuk in our fastest canoe to Saratok with a letter to the District Officer asking him to telephone the Director of Medical Services giving details of Arthur's symptoms. The Director was to be asked to send his answer through Radio Sarawak after the seven o'clock news. Mac and I waited anxiously beside the radio that evening and sure enough the voice of our old friend came on clear and distinct.

"This is an important message for John Wilson at Budu. Your telephone message received. I have already despatched a fast launch to Saratok. Please make sure Thwaites is kept warm and bring him to Saratok earliest possible where the launch will be waiting to convey him to Kuching. End of message".

Needless to say, Mac and I wasted no time organising another fast canoe and this time I went with Arthur to ensure he was kept warm and left Mac to carry on as best he could, worried as well he might be. Going down one of the rapids Arthur got absolutely soaked. It had been unavoidable but I almost wept to see all Arthur's blankets, now a sodden mess. By this time it was early morning and bitterly cold. There was nothing that one could do except squeeze out the water bit by bit but strangely enough I knew that Arthur was slightly better through the soaking. His temperature certainly went down. When he returned to Budu two weeks later, looking well and hearty as ever, it was then I began to say seriously to myself that we should never worry. Nevertheless, this illness of Arthur's and the resultant action of the Director of Medical Services to help us even at Budu by sending a costly special launch did make us very thankful that help would be there if it were needed.

As though fate was determined to try us to the end, Mac himself became the next medical crisis, the only difference being that we knew what it was. Mac had been travelling quite a bit in connection with one thing or another and as usual carried his own haversack. Unfortunately a small sore which had developed on his back was not treated immediately and within days his whole back was a mass of tropical ulcers, deep relentless suppurating ulcers. He could not lie on his back and it was obvious he was in real agony although he complained little, except to shout at Arthur who every half hour almost had to wash and almost scrub before putting on the sulphanilimide powder which we knew as the only cure, plus of course penicillin injections. Mac was not evacuated but it was almost a month before he resumed normal duties and even then he had to be careful. All of us from time to time in those early days suffered from tropical ulcers to a greater or less extent. We discovered from personal experience that if the sores were washed vigorously with Lifebuoy soap and water about six to eight times a day with no dressing at all, the sores dried up much more quickly. In time too we developed our own resistance to them. A cure used myself with every success but frowned on by Arthur was to get Junei my dog to lick them. He was a clean dog of course and his little teeth used to bore almost into the hole to reach the heart of the ulcer. In no time at all the ulcer was quite cured. When Junei disappeared, Lassie took over equally successfully. When Lassie died, Little Brown Feet delights to lick out the sore. One can be cured by faith of course and indeed I had faith in Junei's method.

At the end of the first phase of the Budu Scheme, about ten per cent of the people had remained outwith and would not participate either to help in building the accommodation required, nor in buying a ten dollar share in the co-operative shop nor indeed help in anything at all towards progress. It was this ten per cent which prevented certain longhouses from penning in their pigs completely and so enabling sunk pit latrines to be dug. It was this ten per cent, just because they would not co-operate, which prevented in the early days, the planting of fruit trees around the longhouse. It was not only annoying but disheartening to have Dyaks coming to me complaining that the coffee bushes and other cash crop trees that they had planted were being uprooted by the unpenned pigs. At various times this ten per cent had been informed that they too could join although as late members on certain relatively easy conditions. They had been told that if they had not the money to buy a share, work would be provided to enable them to obtain enough money for this purpose. If the reason for not joining was that a certain family only consisted of a widow and children or old people unable to work then the head of the longhouse was given authority to certify that such families should be recommended to become members with no payments at all either in money, wood or work. Mac, Arthur and I, thought that the Committee of Progress had been as tolerant and helpful as was possible. So the day came when many of the original members began to voice the opinion that such people were not going to be allowed to enjoy the benefits which were now appearing. They were not for instance to be allowed to be treated at the dispensary which the members had built. Their children were not to be allowed to go to school. They were not to be allowed to buy goods in the shop or sell their produce. They were not to be given a share of the high yielding rubber stumps, nor indeed be allowed to come near any centre. The Medical Department ruled that since medicine was being given free, all people living in the Budu area were entitled to share this medicine even though they had not helped in any way to build the dispensary. Arthur, fully aware of his responsibilities not only to the medical profession but to his very alma mater which morally made it impossible for him to refuse to give treatment, was in a most difficult position. He steadfastly refused and both Mac and I supported him, that whether or not his patients were true members, seriously ill patients had to be treated. For a time there was much muttering among the members and some were openly saying that there seemed no point in being a member if medicine was to be given free to those who had not participated in providing the dispensary. Mac and I were actually sympathetic to both the members' point of view and certainly with Arthur's. Even Mac and I, when Arthur was travelling, treated seriously ill patients even if they were non-members. The only difference was that I think in our hearts both Mac and I felt that somehow this was not right either but we had not the moral courage to refuse. Sometimes, though, we did, when the patient didn't seem to be very ill at all. Conscience, however, always troubled us. So the time came when definite decisions one way or another had to be made. At the various monthly meetings of the Committee of Progress, more and more people put forward proposals that something had to be done about the non-members. As the committee were never very clear on what was to be proposed and were not receiving any encouragement from Arthur, Mac and me, it was possible to stave off the impending crisis. We three knew, nevertheless, that if we were to keep the majority of the people together with determination to continue on the lines of progress, something had to be done. Various decisions were then officially taken at meetings and all tried out. One of them, that non-members could enjoy all facilities of medical treatment if they were actually brought by a member and introduced. They then became honorary members by if I remember rightly, paying a nominal sum of fifty cents into the Training Fund. This worked well till we discovered quite by accident that the member before agreeing to bring the non-member had to be suitably reimbursed for his trouble either by a hen or some paddi. As this was morally wrong we quickly got a new rule passed. To cut a long story short, the rule that seemed to work best and which seemed to please everybody was that any non-member who was sick could be treated exactly as though he was a full member, providing somebody came with him who was willing to get five tins of sand which was always being needed to complete the cementing of floors. If he did not bring anyone, he could owe it and when well, get his five tins of sand. Careful records were kept and soon all the mutterings ceased. Ironically enough, Dyaks being the people they are, found themselves even as members, carrying up the five tins of sand for their friends who were not members. Possibly this taught them to be less sympathetic to the less enlightened. Perhaps of course the reverse happened. Anyway, generally speaking few if any are not now members.

Space does not allow me to write in detail of the many incidents which if not crises exactly, were diversions of the first order. I recall the night at Grenjang when at three o'clock in the morning we all heard wild shouts and screams. The rubber smoke house with around twenty piculs of rubber had caught fire. It was as fierce a fire as I have ever seen and only by every hand to a pail of water brought up from the nearby river, did we manage to save the longhouse being burned to the ground.

The main sport of the Dyak is cockfighting although football with no rules at all is a good second sport. For myself I did not like this cockfighting one little bit. It is a cruel sport and often leads to personal quarrels. Nevertheless I have never tried to stop them matching cocks, only advised them not to bet too highly if at all. Trainees were allowed to watch cockfighting but were not allowed to bet. As people gathered from distant places to take part, it was in many ways a social occasion and news was given and passed freely on cockfighting days. Usually betting was in groups such as the upriver group against the downriver group. So it was not unusual for open fights to take place between those groups. Although often called upon to try and stop them, I refused emphatically. It was their sport not mine and to interfere would have meant taking one side or another. Having several times had to spend Sunday afternoons stitching up severe wounds I was also emphatic, having warned them, that I would not continue to do this. Strangely enough, fights now are rare between Dyaks but occasionally still happen when other races arrive to take part.

Several times also during high floods all have responded to all night searches for children and older people who, having gone down to the river for their evening bath, slip in and get swept away usually to drown. I think these night searches exhausted me both mentally and physically more than anything else. It was seldom that the tragedy of drowning was averted and even on one or two occasions the attempt to save one, caused the death of two or three.

All four of us, Mac, Doc, Arthur and myself, have on more than one occasion been lost. It is not a pleasant experience either for those who are lost or for those who make a search. Snakes, leeches, mosquitoes, flying ants, midges, centipedes are all there in the jungle and more so at night. All having experienced this, we became very much more careful but even on the odd chance of being lost we usually were more prepared. We all carried, for instance, a cycling cape, a piece of equipment for jungle travel. We found it wise to carry a small mosquito net, a phial of potassium permanganate, a razor blade, matches in wet proof paper, salt for the leeches and for emergency rations a tin of corned beef. In addition I always took with me my little spirit stove, a tiny kettle and a tin of condensed milk. No, to be lost in the jungle especially at night is not an adventure to be sought. The experience is quite terrifying. When the thunder, lightning and heavy relentless rain adds to all the discomforts, survival depends just on remaining where one is at the time. I think, no, I am certain, that my estimation of the character of the trainees such as Luke, Eddie, Jangga, Jenuang and many others, was certainly confirmed during such escapades. Indeed, had Luke not, at great danger to himself, lifted a tree trunk under which I had been caught during a flood and at night, I would not be writing this now.

Dyaks, being generally uninhibited, do not normally go berserk. Their way of life just does not create the stresses and strains so common in more developed countries. If a Dyak wants to rise at three o'clock in the morning and in so doing, makes a lot of noise as he usually does, nobody seems to mind. If he wants to start playing gongs at midnight, that's all right. If someone wants to listen to the radio he does, and if he puts it on full blast this seems to be just fine too. I would that we Europeans could be equally tolerant. I suppose really this tolerance of the Dyaks to loud disturbing noises must have gradually come about through sheer necessity and have built up their own resistance to hearing such. That they have very keen ears is certain since often, travelling, the party has stopped because one of the Dyaks has heard the chirp of a bird which indicates the presence of an eagle. However that is all by the way. I have reason however to remember a Dyak called Salok. He was in the adult school at Budu. A very pleasant and hard working Dyak. Arthur was away at the time unfortunately, but that afternoon Salok just went berserk. He took his hunting knife and slashed all the posters we had hanging up on boards and with a mad look in his eyes began to look for more human targets. Luckily, a number of the older Dyaks were near and he was quickly trussed up and I was called. I gave him bromide and in a short time he went quietly to sleep. By bed time he had awakened and talked absolutely normally. Not being a trained mental nurse like Arthur, I asked Salok if we could untie him. He laughed and said that he was just fine and nobody need worry about him any more. Not being too sure, although we did untie his hands we kept his feet tied together and with Chundie on one side and myself on the other side of Salok we all settled down to sleep.

Whether it was because I felt slightly apprehensive that night, I lay awake for some time. Just as, however, I was about to drop off, I felt hands slowly but surely gripping my throat. Not wanting to wake everybody up I just cried quietly out to Chundie to help me. Chundie, however, was in a sound sleep and before I could shout to waken him Salok's fingers tightened round my throat and I literally could not shout. Luckily my fingers found my torch which usually I keep by my side and I battered this on the floor with all my might. In a second or two several Dyaks had come to my rescue and loosened Salok's fingers from my throat. Chundie still slept. Chundie was a splendid dispensary trainee but he could sleep soundly. Needless to say, I agreed to Salok again being tied up but I did not sleep much that night. Early next day, Salok had to leave under escort to be treated in Kuching.

Scarcely a week went by in the early days but we had canoes sinking with the loss of most things. We accepted those disasters philosophically and from them learned a great deal. One was particularly funny. Linsam was the driver with Jemat at the bow. The canoe was on one of the few straight stretches of river and travelling about ten knots. Jemat spied a monkey on a tree and shouted to Linsam to look also. Dyaks get very excited with any animals far less monkeys. Naturally Linsam looked and in his excitement he forgot that he was driving. Unfortunately just ahead of the canoe was a curled vine hanging from a tree and Linsam saw this not at all. He himself forgot about any monkey when he found his neck inside the natural loop and was literally pulled from the canoe. The canoe, with Jemat quite unaware that his driver was now suspended by the neck, carried on of course to come to a sorry end by completely overturning. As the river was deep most of the goods were lost. The canoe just broke up and its engine severely damaged. Nevertheless, despite the loss, the mental picture of Linsam hanging from the vine gave everybody a good laugh. When the laughing was over, we knew without saying much that this kind of accident would not happen again.

Floods at Budu as well as at Entaih caused havoc on more than one occasion. The real big floods somehow always came in the night. It is not a pleasant experience to rescue desks, stools, etc., that try to float out of the space where windows were planned to be. Nor indeed to rescue the pigs from their pens. When the floods subsided, I often felt like running away, such was the havoc. Mud alone took days to clean away. Still once again, such experiences with everybody working together, brought that comradeship so elusive in other spheres.

This chapter would not be complete without some reference to the many Dyak festivals that were organised throughout the years. Although not critical incidents in themselves, I recall none that did not bring forth at least one major crisis.

The Dyaks call a festival day a "hari besai" meaning simply a big day. When each centre has been established basically with a co-operative shop actually running, a dispensary or clinic in operation, the beginnings of the planting of cash crops in evidence with agricultural extension work started, adult education and primary education in full swing, the emergence of each centre was always celebrated by a hari besai. I make haste to say at their request. Not that I disliked the idea at all, in fact I thought it an excellent idea but somehow or another most of the organisation for it fell on me. Dyaks are very haphazard, rather a people who expect someone else to think for them. Typical of the Dyaks is a picture in my mind of several Dyaks setting out on a canoe trip even in flood waters. Everybody rushes around gathering his own belongings and all get into the canoe. The Dyak in the bow unties the rope and the canoe is immediately swept into the middle of river. Then and then only do they start looking for the paddles or poles and shout at each other asking where the paddles are. Of course usually there are none and confusion unbounded is apparent. If there are no goods belonging to me on it I just sit back and watch the fun. Often, too, with unlimited faith in engines, canoes are often untied before the engine is started. Still more often the engine doesn't start and the canoe has to be pulled back along the bank with the help of branches of trees. Needless to say, both Mac and I evolved strict rules for trainees in charge of canoes. The driver was by common consent the captain of the canoe and it was his duty to ensure that the various rules were carried out to the letter. If he didn't he was quickly reduced from driving to taking over the bow duties.

The first and most ambitious hari besai was naturally at Budu. It was a three day festival complete with Fun Fair, football competitions, concerts, dancing exhibitions and competitions, raffles for white piglets, outboard engines, sewing machines and an open air cinema, something that few, if any, at Budu had ever seen. The Fun Fair itself was an undertaking of organisation and "make do". We had a shooting gallery, wooden horse racing, coconut shies and almost everything that one would normally see at a fun fair at home. Mac with Arthur's help took this over. It was superb considering how little material we had at Budu.

To feed the normal one hundred at the Budu centre was difficult any time owing to distances from Saratok. To feed or ensure enough food for the expected two to three thousand for three days meant also a two month preparation. Crises came not just once or twice but almost every hour. In the football competitions the referee's decision was always questioned and being used to the custom of might is right each game brought football to an end replacing it with a melee of boxing and wrestling, all to the enjoyment of the spectators who rather liked it. In the end Mac had to referee all the matches. The inter school sports, and I am sure in retrospect Mac and Arthur would agree, were delightful with everything running like clockwork. Never have I seen so clearly demonstrated such differences between disciplined pupils and those who had had no schooling. It was actually a lesson to all and many of the older Dyaks remarked on it.

Crises came with the fights that developed from the cockfighting that was going on simultaneously. The knockout pillow fight on a greasy bar presented a comedy that few will ever forget, although it took me over half an hour to persuade them to start this contest. Arthur could rarely leave the dispensary day and night but somehow he coped with Rabing and Chundie to help him. Mac and I had fixed up electric lighting both for the stage and the fun fair by using small five hundred watt petrol engines. We even had spot lights for the Dyak dancing competitions. Between us we coped with everything except when it came to film time. To cover transport expenses only, since films, projector, operators were provided by the Information Department, we had agreed that a charge of fifty cents should be made for each person except school pupils and children. Here the Dyak had us quite foxed. Naturally enough when one considers pure Dyak attitudes at their stage of development, they could see no earthly reason to pay fifty cents to see the films when they could quite easily see them from branches of nearby trees and from the side of nearby small hills. So our films played to an "empty house" although some two thousand were watching them. I must confess that I did get a little peeved with Dyaks since we had hoped to make some money for the school fund. The concert was free but we had planned to pass round collection boxes, more to inculcate the idea of giving freely than by specifying a charge for entertainment. We made the mistake of not putting some coins in first. When the boxes were passed round the audience thought that the boxes were for cigarette ends and empty wrapping papers. Mac just couldn't believe his eyes. I think it was the first time that I saw Mac angry. Later we had a good laugh over it.

The Ng. Grenjang festival turned into a free fight between a party of Chinese visitors who had come for the cockfighting and the local Dyaks. The fighting cocks belonging to the Chinese were actually superior and trading on this they persuaded the Dyaks to bet much more than normal. Graham Riches organised the Grenjang one and apart from the fight, it was most enjoyable. As neither Doc nor Arthur were available, however, I found myself looking after the dispensary.

The Ng. Entebai one is remembered by all who came to it. It was the custom, while facilities to buy plates of cooked rice were always provided, that the people build their own sleeping accommodation of a small leaf hut, usually on the banks of the river. Unfortunately, heavy rain came on and within three hours every shelter was under water. It was quite a problem to arrange alternative shelter to some two thousand people. I remember going round about midnight. Round is the exact word since it was just impossible to go through any school or other building. People were sleeping on the floors, tables, desks and improvised attics. Luckily the next day was fine and Dyaks being as they are, quickly forgot the miseries of the night and proceded to enjoy one of the best festivals that had ever been arranged. Jenuang with a committee of senior trainees did it all with very little help from me.

The Ng. Maong festival, organised by Arthur, I remember for the magnificent Dyak dancing and almost perfect exhibitions of Scots Country Dancing. Both Arthur and his wife, Marjorie, were very keen dancers and had taught this in the schools. Arthur's influence in both singing and Scots Country Dancing is found at every centre even to this day. On one occasion a team was sent to give an exhibition at the Sibu Festival of Arts. Dyaks, I am sure, with the natural grace they possess, are superb and quite outclass average Scots boys and girls in this type of dancing. I felt very proud of them as they made their charming bow to this large audience in Sibu.

The festivals at Kadup, Ng. Budu, Tappang and Entaih were enjoyed by all with no outstanding crises to relate. Despite all the work involved, we are convinced that such festivals play a very important part in true Community Development. At them, people learn to give and take and to accept that every child cannot run at the same speed nor jump the same height. They give opportunities almost to teach organisation and the people learn that with a little self discipline, everyone can enjoy themselves. It would I think be true to say also that the festival days organised under the scheme gave birth to the idea of a Dyak Festival Day which is now held each year on the 1st of June, throughout Sarawak.

On the 31st of August 1963, Sarawak became independent within the Federation of Malaysia. Indonesia opposed this Federation although it was quite clear that the Sarawak peoples had agreed to it. Confrontation along the borders of Sarawak, infiltration of organised Communists, automatically meant that the loyalties of the peoples in the Budu and Entebai areas were going to be tested to the limit. Being the areas through which infiltrators would have to pass to reach their objective either from Indonesia or from the sea through coastal towns, much was going to depend on the very loyalties of the Dyaks and on the information which they were prepared to give of enemy incursions. I remember having long and important discussions with highly ranked military leaders, both British and Malaysian. It was an exciting time and much of the routine Community Development work had to take second place. It was as obvious to them as it was to me that the results of the Community Development work were going to be a critical factor in the defence of Sarawak itself. As, even before I commenced my work, it was my sincere belief that true Community Development is in itself a barrier to Communism, I felt confident that the peoples of Budu and Entebai would co-operate in every way. That they did so was an immense satisfaction to me since at least one of my theories had been proved. I was of course delighted to receive a letter in 1965 from a high official and in part of this letter he says: "Your work has shown its true value during the last two years. I am sure you can take pride from the fact that it has resulted in islands of stability in what otherwise might have been very troubled areas".

Since part of the defence system resulted in recruiting a completely new kind of unit, called the Border Scouts, whose main task was to be the "eyes and ears" for trained military groups always at the ready to come to any particular area threatened by infiltrators, it was natural enough that we were asked both to recruit, and to a large extent train, the Border Scouts in our areas. They proved not only useful but essential for the protection of the Country. It is to their credit that because of their very usefulness in helping the remote peoples in sickness, in carrying letters on patrols, in passing on important information towards progress, this group is still very much an integral part of the remote areas. Perhaps one day I might find the time and opportunity to write about the work of the Border Scouts. It is a story in itself, highlighted by Panggau, just returned from Nairn, being intercepted by six armed infiltrators and by a subterfuge, escaping to give the information.

Luke

SARAWAK WITHIN MALAYSIA
[1963 to 1968]

On the 31st August 1963, Sarawak gained its independence within the concept of Malaysia. In effect it became another state of Malaya as did North Borneo and Singapore. Brunei declined to become a state in this Malaysian Federation, since having separate treaties with Britain, Brunei was not obliged to seek protection from outside enemies within this federation.

Previous to August 1963 there were two schools of thought. One wishing to create a federation of the three Borneon states, Sarawak, Brunei and North Borneo, in matters of defence, trade and travel, leaving each state completely self-governing in all other aspects. The other wished to create a much larger federation with Sarawak and North Borneo as states of the federated states of Malaya, with limited self government.

The Cobbald Commission was convened to make recommendations to the British Government. This commission under the chairmanship of Lord Cobbald travelled widely throughout Sarawak seeking the views of the people and it can be said that anyone from the richest to the poorest in Sarawak was encouraged and given every opportunity to state their views to this Commission. When it became known that Sir Anthony Abel, a former Governor of Sarawak, a man widely known, widely travelled within Sarawak and highly respected and loved by the many different races of Sarawak, it was generally felt that Britain was endeavouring to obtain an honest picture of the views of the peoples of Sarawak comprised of approximately 350,000 Dyaks, 300,000 Chinese, 25,000 Malays, and 20,000 other indigenous races of Muruts, Kayans, Kenyahs, Kelabits, Melanaus, Dusuns.

In due course the Cobbald Commission's report was published, widely read and discussed. It was and is an excellent report. Briefly the Commission recommended that, in view of the economic conditions within Sarawak and the need for a comprehensive plan for its long term development obtainable within the concept of Malaysia, Sarawak should be granted independence as a State of Malaya in a new federation of states to be called Malaysia.

The Commission, however, in recommending this, laid down vitally important safeguards and conditions. It was clear from the report that the Dyaks generally were apprehensive of becoming a minority race within Malaysia and at Kapit, a small town in the interior of Sarawak, all Dyak chiefs met to decide by themselves the conditions under which they would agree to the Independence of Sarawak within Malaysia. Twelve points were finally agreed on at this very important meeting. These included that no decision regarding the National Language was to be taken till 1973 and until then English was to be used as a medium for all government departments and in Secondary Schools. Approximately a fifth of the Europeans were to be retained in executive positions within the general administration of the country. To the Dyaks this was a vital issue in that by laying down this condition, they were in effect protecting their own long term interests. It seemed essential to the Dyaks and to many others that if a proportion of Europeans were not retained for ten years, government for all practical purposes would be in the hands of Malays and Chinese. Only since 1949 had the Dyaks been given facilities to educate their children in any significant numbers and a minimum of ten years was still needed to produce well educated Dyaks able to play their part in the government of Sarawak. As most of the interior of Sarawak was owned by the Dyaks under customary rights it was stipulated clearly that there would be no change in the land laws which gave considerable protection to ownership of Dyak land. The Dyaks felt strongly also that since Britain would only protect her frontiers if she accepted Independence within Malaysia, this should not absolve Britain from ultimate moral responsibility towards the self determination of her peoples, should Malaysia tend to confuse and confound state interests to her detriment and for the sake of national issues and national prestige of the Federal Government whose headquarters would be in Kuala Lumpur.

Under this cloak of protection and to safeguard the rights of the majority race in Sarawak, the Cobbald Commission recommended that Sarawak be granted independence within the Federation of Malaysia. It was in effect an agreed cession of the colony of Sarawak to become a self governing state within Malaya and almost similar in every respect to the cession of Sarawak as a colony in 1946 when the then Rajah ceded Sarawak to Britain with similar protections for the indigenous peoples.

So as the 31st of August 1968 approaches, just five years after the Federated States of Malaysia came into being, it is right and proper that an objective look be taken at affairs within Sarawak and in so doing estimate the guardianship of the Federal Parliament for this unique country whose indigenous peoples are perhaps the best loved and admired of all Asian peoples. No one who knows the Dyak and this includes both the sea Dyak and the land Dyak could but agree that this race of people are probably the most polite of any race. It is such a natural politeness that one is hardly aware of it. It is not effusive yet there is a charm in it that warms the heart. They ask for nothing in return for the hospitality that is given to any traveller and indeed would be offended if such were offered. As their children are their most treasured possessions it is enough that the visitor makes friends with those children and in so doing is privileged to become almost a member of the family. The Dyak does not cringe nor bemoan his fate nor the poorness of his standard of living. What he may desire, he desires not for himself but for his children. For himself, he care not for the comforts that the more modern civilisation can provide but for his children he cares a great deal that they may be able to share in the good things of life. For his child the Dyak will give all and prays that his child might grow up with more than he has had, in an economy which will provide the day to day necessities in a more permanent and lasting form. It is perhaps this tremendous love that exists between the Dyak parent and child which almost prevents the very stable economy so much desired. Seldom if every would one hear a Dyak father asking his son to do this or that, and the child is allowed to join in the work of the farm as he feels inclined. Up till a certain age, the Dyak child is given without question the best of what there is. When it is considered that he can play a man's part, only then is there no difference between what is given to him and what is given to the father to eat. Without words he is expected to share in the work of the family but no one would dream of forcing him to do so.

So in this acceptance of Sarawak independent within Malaysia he was naturally apprehensive that a way of life that he had enjoyed under the Rajah and under British Colonial rule might change under Malay rule. They are not a people who can be forced to do anything that they do not want to do yet they are willing to be led to do things which will be for the ultimate benefit of their children. There were many who remembered the tales told by their fathers and grandfathers of the era of Malay rule when the then Sarawak was part of Brunei, and remembering were apprehensive as to what the future would hold for them.

All were agreeably surprised when with the advent of Malaysia everything seemed to go on much as before. A few changes were immediately apparent such as the introduction within the schools of rules relating to the flying of the State flag of Sarawak and the National flag of the Federation. Both had to be flown and every school was given the flags free. As the average Dyak loved flags of any sort this pleased him andhe did not much worry about the significance of this rule. On the radio, it is true that they could no longer listen to the British broadcasting items of news or entertainment but as reasonably good programmes were broadcast in their place the Dyak was quite content. News in Dyak, Malay and Chinese was broadcast in absolute fairness. A few, however, of the more thoughtful Dyaks were outspokenly alarmed when even Dyaks began to be addressed in the Malay form of "Inche" rather than"Mr". As this was discontinued, so natural fears were put to rest.

Soon too it was obvious that the Federal Government were going to waste no time to put into action their five year development plan. Divisional development committees were formed and were of a form that certainly did bring considerable representation. Members from remote areas were selected to take part in the discussions. Over the radio almost daily came the news that many millions of dollars were to be allocated for development with particular attention to the rural peoples. Large land development schemes were to be started and roads and bridges were planned connecting all the main towns from the capital Kuching, to Simanggang, to Sibu, to Miri, indeed from North to South. All primary school fees were abolished and this enabled many children to go to school. It certainly seemed that a kind of Utopia had come about in Sarawak since she had become part of the federation. The fact that Indonesia periodically sent infiltration parties over the borders into Sarawak didn't seriously worry the Dyak. On the contrary since Britain had agreed to defend Sarawak in the event of outside attacks, confrontation increased the numbers of Europeans in Sarawak. There were many European soldiers. Hotels and shops were busier than ever before. There seemed to be helicopters by the dozens and as they were often used to evacuate sick people from remote areas, landing almost at the very door of the main hospitals in Kuching, Sibu or Simanggang, few Dyaks at that time would have elected to become once again a colony of Britain. Indeed the Dyaks felt that they were enjoying the best of the two worlds and the future looked bright and more secure. Even those Dyaks who had openly opposed the concept of Malaysia began to feel that they could have been wrong. Nevertheless there were still many Dyaks who while admitting that considerable progress had been made reserved judgment and said very little. Possibly they could not quite rid themselves of an inherent distrust of Malay rule even though all seemed to be well.

It was certainly true that when Singapore very suddenly declared her complete independence by withdrawing from the Federation many Dyaks, especially those who either lived near towns or worked in the main towns, began to wonder a little. Subtle changes had taken place and most of the higher executive positions in government had been taken over by Malays, many of them from Kuala Lumpur. By 1966, where there had been many Europeans, there seemed now only to be a very few left, and as each week passed there seemed to be no doubt that, rather than the State of Sarawak having independence, she was being governed almost entirely from Kuala Lumpur. It was true that Council Negri still sat and passed laws but no one seemed to be able to do anything except on orders from Kuala Lumpur. Since the radio was completely controlled by federal authority, the explanation of Singapore deciding to separate from the Federation was calmly explained. Likewise newspapers in Sarawak, under threats of closure, were very conservative in their news regarding Singapore. Only through newspapers from Singapore did the true picture emerge and it seemed certain that Singapore had declared her own independence because she opposed the very policy of Malayanisation that was even then infiltrating into government circles in Sarawak. The small nucleus of Dyaks in government circles in Kuching began to take stock seriously. The then chief minister, Mr Stephen Kalong Ningkang, a Dyak with support from his ministers took positive steps to oppose the policy of Borneanisation. In other words the Sarawak Government would no longer tolerate any further reductions of Europeans holding executive posts in government. Reaction from Kuala Lumpur was speedy and on a pretext that the Chief Minister Mr Ningkang was unfit because of his own personal life, he was removed from office by Federal Government orders. Constitutionally this was wrong, indeed very wrong since the political party of whom Mr Ningkang was head had not even been consulted. Most of Mr Ningkang's ministers resigned in protest or if they did not actually resign they refused to work under the new Chief Minister Mr Tawie Slie, who had been selected by Kuala Lumpur. One again this seemed to be impossible under the constitution of Sarawak since Mr Slie had certainly not been elected by the party in power. Within a few days, however,

Mr Slie had managed to form a government and although there was considerable disquiet and a growing concern, it had all happened so speedily that there was little that anyone could do about it. Only one man had the power at this stage to bring to light this abuse of the constitution of Sarawak, Tan Sri Temonggong Juga, the paramount chief of all the Dyaks and the Minister of External Affairs for Sarawak. For reasons of his own he became the puppet of the Federal Government in Kuala Lumpur and declared his support for Tawie Slie. There were few Dyaks who did not feel that their own leader had not betrayed them. An uneasy calmness settled throughout Sarawak, although some wanted open rebellion. Rather than risk this, Mr Ningkand declared his intention of bringing a lawsuit against the Federal Government for unlawful dismissal. Most people, believing in the justice of the courts, felt it was only a question of time before Mr Ningkang would be reinstated as Chief Minister and the crisis of open rebellion was averted.

Development schemes continued to make progress, roads became finished and bridges built. More and more Europeans seemed to be leaving and their places taken, if not by Malayan Malays, by ill-trained, ill-educated Sarawakians under the complete control of the Federal Ministry. All waited impatiently for the case to come to court. Delaying tactics were employed quite openly by the Federal authorities since it was a foregone conclusion that Mr Ningkang would win his case.

So after many delays, judgment of the court declared for Mr Ningkang and that same day, he, with his own loyal ministers, returned to office and once again took over the reigns of government. To those who knew what was going on, it seemed incredible that such things could happen in these days of democracy. Despite the fact that Radio Sarawak gave little importance to the reinstatement of Mr Ningkang as Chief Minister, one sensed rather than saw a deep relief throughout the length and breadth of Sarawak. The Dyaks, who even in their own family circle would decline to force an order of authority and believing fundamentally in the self determination of the individual openly expressed approval that Mr Ningkang had won his case. It was apparent however that the seeds of distrust in the Federal Government had been sown by this episode.

Federal action was again swift in that by the next day an extraordinary session of the Federal Parliament was convened in Kuala Lumpur with the sole purpose of amending the constitution of Sarawak, giving the Federal Government powers to remove once again Mr Ningkang from office under an emergency law for the security of the State of Sarawak.

Exactly five days after reinstatement Mr Ningkang was removed from office, this time forcibly by the Commissioner of Police acting on direct orders of the Federal Government. It seemed impossible that such a thing could happen and overnight a major crisis was sure to develop. That Mr Ningkang's loyal ministers followed him, only added to the conviction that much was now wrong. Once again Tan Sri Temonggong Juga, with the principles of democracy at stake, gave his support to the Federal action and hourly on the radio his voice could be heard voicing his complete and utter loyalty to Tawie Slie who again found himself installed as Chief Minister. It seemed certain that open rebellion would now follow and bands of angry Dyaks began to gather in all parts of Sarawak. British military authorities, still in Sarawak but concerned and committed only in the defence of Sarawak from outside enemies, politely but firmly declined to order British troops to man and take up defensive action on all access roads to Kuching. Luckily however for the Federal Government there were considerable purely Malay forces stationed in Sarawak at that time and these were deployed at strategic points with orders to shoot. News of this quickly was spread and since to fight machine guns with knives would be a useless effort, the Dyaks returned to their own villages and longhouses but with a deep anger in their hearts, a complete and utter distrust of Malay rule and a feeling of shame against their own Dyak chief who had allied himself with autocratic authority. There seemed little that anyone could do against authority, however illegal, backed by machine guns.

The few remaining Europeans were blamed for the crisis and within weeks many more had been asked to leave. Contracts were torn up and although compensation was given in some way or another it was very evident that Federal Authority was now supreme and the State Government had no governing control whatsoever. Within weeks, confrontation mysteriously ended, thus making it possible for all British troops to be asked to leave Sarawak. This was completed in record time leaving military control almost entirely in the hands of the Malay regiments.

All this time considerable progress had been made on the land development schemes. About twenty throughout Sarawak were near to completing phase one. Each scheme comprised approximately 2,000 acres. Basically each scheme was the same. A certain piece of land was examined as to whether the land was suitable for the planting of high-yielding rubber. If so negotiations began to alienate the land from the Dyak owners either by compensation or by agreement. Theoretically the land was then divided into 200 blocks, each of ten acres, and in each block eight acres of terraced high-yielding rubber was planted under either direct agricultural department control or by direct contract with the agricultural department supervising. Two acres in each block were to be left for other cash crops such as pepper vegetables, hens, pigs. At this stage applications were then to be invited and from those applications two hundred families of approximately one third Dyaks, one third Chinese and one third other indigenous peoples, would then be selected and to each family a ten-acre block was then allocated under provisional title. In each scheme houses, shops, school, dispensary, lighting, water and sewage would be provided, centrally placed within the 2,000 acres. After the initial planting had been completed and all accommodation ready, families would then be allowed to take possession. Each family was then responsible for maintaining the rubber by keeping the terraces weeded and by giving the due amount of fertilisers at definite laid down periods. When not looking after his eight acres of rubber, he could go ahead and farm his two acres by planting any crop which would give a quick cash return. As normally rubber takes anything from six to eight years before tapping can begin, it was possible for each family to receive a cash loan to be repayable with interest after seven years. At the beginning thousands applied since it appeared that they were to get a great deal for nothing. The rights and wrongs of the scheme were not discussed nor was it made clear that in the event of loans not being repaid, ownership of the land would revert to crown ownership and blocks re-allocated or sold. Nor was it clear just how Dyak families, uprooted from their normal locations where at least a subsistence living could be obtained, could live. That a loan was available for this very purpose was true but even Dyaks felt that to mortgage their land at so early a stage meant in the end that such loans could never be repaid and because of this. their ten-acre block would cease to belong to them. Chinese families being much more able to gain a living from the two acres and in any case having cash reserves of their own to tide them over welcomed such schemes and feared not the future and feared not that they would in the end lose their ten acres. Families, however, Dyak, Chinese, and other races began to move in with what possessions they had. Beginnings of unrest however were quickly apparent when it was realised that the two empty acres in each block just were not there and in effect only eight acres of planted high yielding rubber were allocated. Someone seemed to have forgotten about the need for the two acres of empty land. In some cases empty land was allocated but quite some distance from their eight acres of rubber. Dyak families began naturally enough to move back to their original longhouses leaving their eight acres of rubber to be looked after as was possible from time to time during non-farming periods. It was soon realised that only those with large families could survive and be able to retain on permanent ownership those eight acres. Many families find it impossible and ownership or temporary lease of those eight-acre blocks are more and more being allocated to Chinese. Indeed it is openly being stated that all land development schemes begun under Malaysia are just a means to enable the many Chinese families to gain a foothold in Dyak land and territories. It is hard to believe this can be true but ... What is true, is that many Dyaks feel that they have been cheated and resent very much that the land they used to belong to is now being lived on by the Chinese whom they know to be much more clever than they are and feel that such families having now gained a foothold will make further incursions and in time take over more and more land from the Dyaks. This is of course possible, very possible and already there is a growing resentment within the hearts and minds of the Dyaks. Trouble is almost certainly going to develop since the Dyak will not acknowledge the new ownership purely because they will feel they have been cheated and being so they will feel justified in taking such steps as required to regain title or ownership. The Chinese, knowing the character of the Dyak, will live uneasily on such land. With rubber prices being as low as they have ever been and without much prospect of those prices ever rising again, even the Chinese might well evacuate such land. It is difficult to understand why no thought was given when planning such schemes to the proven fact that generally, people whether they be Dyaks, Chinese or any other race, will never in any case feel a sense of real ownership for something that somebody else planted.

Concern is growing also regarding the real purpose of the roads which have now been built. Economically it is cheaper to transport goods by sea from Kuching to Sibu than by land and will for many years be so. For one reason since the roads are not tarred speed is not possible and indeed, because of the constant heavy rainfall, are often dangerous. Dyaks are beginning to ask why those roads were built. They could not have been built for them since not one Dyak in a thousand could ever hope to own or even control a lorry far less a car or even a bicycle. Such marketable goods as the Dyaks have are still much more easily taken to market by the traditional canoe powered by an outboard engine, the cost of which is within the Dyak economy to buy. As more and more land adjoining such roads is being bought by Chinese to begin small holdings and pepper gardens, substantially built houses are beginning to appear, while Dyak longhouses become more and more dilapidated. It may be asked why, if the Dyaks feel so strongly about their land, are they selling it? The answer is simply to survive through this present period of economic recess brought about by the very low price of rubber. It may be asked too why the price of rubber is so low at this time. One school of thought believes that Malaya stockpiled rubber in the hope that high prices would materialise, forgetting that if they did this, synthetic rubber might gain the market in its place. This is in effect what happened. Stockpiling was possible a year or so ago since there was no adverse balance of trade and large concerns were not in immediate need of money for normal day to day running. Manufacturers, having tried synthetics and finding this to be equally good are certainly not going to buy natural rubber at high prices. Whatever the reason, Dyaks are having to sell their land as their only means of survival at the present time. Needless to say there is growing resentment against the very roads which were hailed at the beginning as the way of progress. Even the less intelligent Dyak is beginning to realise that roads may be another snare to take their land from them. The Dyak in his simplicity of thought argues that if the roads had not been built, the Chinese would not want to buy the land adjoining. Many Dyak leaders, while understanding the reasons for the land being sold but realising that if this is continued, in time the whole future of Dyak survival would be in serious jeopardy and even acknowledge that the Dyak could become the coolie on the very land they once owned, are entreating, cajolling, assisting where possible, that no more land should be sold. There is almost a hate growing for the very roads which were to help so much. It hardly seems possible that the building of the roads was an expedient to exploit the Dyak and yet . . . , normally roads are only built either to take produce out or transport necessities in, unless there is an ulterior motive.

In schools there is an equal if not more disquiet. Coming to light also as a reason for the removal of Mr Ningkang is the undisputed fact that Mr Ningkang opposed strongly the introduction of Malay as a second language in place of English. It is a fact that as from the beginning of 1968, Malay is a compulsory subject in the secondary school curriculum. It is a fact also that civil service vacancies are being filled only by those who are fluent in Malay. Intelligent Dyaks view this with considerable apprehension since even at the best such a procedure puts them ten years behind other races. Dyak children will in effect have to learn two languages instead of one, English. The Malay in his ignorance of both the fundamental Dyak language and Dyak customs, quite wrongly believes that there are little differences. Nothing could be further from the truth. No Dyak living in a remote or even semi-remote region could understand Malay. That numerals and more modern words are common to both is true and this is the reason why the misconception has arisen. Basically there is as much similarity between English and French as there is between Malay and Dyak. As to customs it would be hard to find even one that is common to both races. To the Malay the pig is an unclean animal, to the Dyak an essential and important part of his life. In religion the Dyak is still essentially pagan while the Malay is a Muslim and to imagine that Dyaks will cease to eat or rear pigs is to imagine that the sun will not rise. That there is a similarity in forms of dress is true but this arises from convenience and because it is a comfortable form of dress for a tropical or warm country. Indians and even Europeans dress on occasions as the Malay dresses.

No Dyak will believe that advanced education will be possible through learning Malay and since this is basically true, he will oppose the teaching of Malay to his child even although that child will not be accepted into the civil services or other government departments. Inevitably, therefore, the percentage of Dyaks in government service will steadily decrease not increase as the years pass. That the Federal Government is determined to compel the use of the Malay language and acceptance of Malay as the national language much earlier than as agreed under the terms of independence cannot be questioned. That there are still quite a number of European teachers is true, but they teach under arrangements of the Colombo plan or the volunteer service for overseas. There are few Europeans left in established positions and by August this year, almost no European as headmaster in any government or aided secondary school. Such facts speak for themselves.

By law, there must be a general election no later than August of this year, just five years after Sarawak gained its independence within Malaysia. There is hope in the heart of the Dyak that the present pro Malay government will be replaced by a government which will play its full part as a true State Government, a government which will adhere to the conditions laid down by the Cobbald Commission. The great majority of Dyaks are quietly waiting to see what emerges from this general election. They hope that the election will be conducted and arranged in a way that will allow for a true and honest expression of opinion and popular demand. They will accept the result providing that it is possible for every Dyak, irrespective as to whether he has an identity card or not, to register in his vote his own thought and opinion. Many fear however that the arrangements for elections will not allow for the distance and cost factor that the average remote Dyak will have to face before he can actually vote. If remote schools are used as voting booths and properly compiled electoral rolls for the areas in which those schools are, are used to determine which Dyak can vote or not as the case may be, then the results of such an election could be regarded as a true expression of majority opinion. If however voting is restricted to those in possession of identity cards and venue of election only in administrative offices of each area it will be economically impossible for the average Dyak to register his vote and the result could be a travesty of self determination.

It is felt in many circles that Britain has at least a moral responsibility towards the peoples of Sarawak. She could reasonably at the end of this five year stage pend final decisions on the amount of help to be given to Malaysia to offset the economic results of complete British withdrawal from Malaya in 1971. It would not be unreasonable for Britain to receive assurances that such help as is decided to give in arms and other military equipment, should not be used to oppress minority groups within Malaysia. In no other part of the world is there still such a respect for the British than in Sarawak. Perhaps even the time has come when Britain should cease to bow her head and raise it to inquire into the guardianship of territories which she in all good faith and in an honourable manner has agreed to grant complete independence and severance of British influence. Perhaps the time has come and events in many parts of the world would indicate so, when the United Nations Assembly should pause and take stock on the very policies that this assembly has sponsored. Neo colonialism can and does exist and with it a virulent disease which can and will destroy the faith of trusting peoples in all that stands for honesty and decency.

Is the British lion now destined to remain in its corner of shame and never again roar or can it rise again, shake its mane, and be once again the protector of the free?

Postscript

The following letter written by George Edinger, Leader and Feature Writer in the *Straits Times*, 1953-1956, and President of the Singapore Trade Union of Journalists, 1954-1965, was published in the *Guardian*, 25th June 1969.

Borneo and free elections

Sir,—The abandonment, not postponement, of free elections in North Borneo (Sabah and Sarawak) after the setback to the Kuala Lumpur Government in the last elections in Malaya is a melancholy postscript to the long and tedious war that British troops fought in the Borneo jungle to establish the authority of Kuala Lumpur on a people whose enthusiasm for such a rule was always more than dubious: particularly since, with the secession of Singapore from Malaysia, the whole purpose of this dubious union, formed to outvote the Chinese population of that city, ceased to exist.

We have heard some highly disquieting stories of Indonesian rule in West Irian, though at this distance of space and knowing the positively pathological attitude of press and politicians in this country to the Indonesians, one must approach the situation cautiously. But at least there is to be some sort of an election in West Irian. In Borneo there is going to be none.

It is the more melancholy to reflect that at one stage immediately after Mr Enoch Powell's courageous statement on the advisability of keeping British garrisons East of Suez, the Indonesian Government of the day were prepared to negotiate with us on the basis of free elections in West Irian in return for a free vote in Sabah and Sarawak. This I can vouch for, Sir, having been myself an intermediary in this approach. At this distance of time I can supply you details and the names of those involved, in confidence.
—Yours faithfully,

George Edinger.
4 Raymond Buildings
Gray's Inn.
London WC 1.

4 Raymond Buildings,
Gray's Inn,
London W.C. 1.

23rd July 1969.

Dear Mr Wilson,

Many thanks for your letter of 22nd July.

I shall be extremely honoured if you use my *Guardian* letter as a postscript to your book. I have long known of your selfless endeavour and all you were accomplishing in your lonely struggle for the peoples of Sarawak.

I did not know you had been banished from Sarawak (but you are in good company) until I had your letter and the news came as a great shock, though not unhappily as a surprise to me. Please call on me for any help that I can give.

Yours sincerely,

(signed) George Edinger.

PS. Have you thought of asking David Steel (M.P. for Roxburgh and Selkirk) to ask in the House if it is British policy to give military aid to countries that deny a free vote to their peoples?

BOOK II

WHAT ARE THEY LIKE —

THE DYAKS ?

208

Plate 1

Only a few of the Sea Dayak (Iban) people live anywhere near the sea and some have never even seen it, but in the old days their head hunting expeditions sometimes involved a sea trip from one river mouth to the other and Merchant Sailors have told the world of their ferocity.

Sea Dayak longhouses are built on the banks of rivers in the interior of Sarawak and *Plate 1* shows a man by the name of Baling walking through the forest. Though the Iban may be carrying a heavy load and be quite tired, this will not prevent him from smiling and stepping off the path to give you the right of way.

How would you answer these four questions from an absolute stranger whom you happened to meet on a public footpath?

"Where are you going?"

"What is the purpose of your visit?"

"Where did you spend last night?"

"What are you carrying in your bag?"

If your encounter was with a Sea Dayak on a forest path in Borneo then of course it would help if you could speak his language. It would also be appreciated if you recognised the Dayak courtesy prompting these queries and gave him factual information instead of telling him to mind his own business!

In any case he will be making his own visual assessment of you whether you speak Iban or not and the odds are that he will decide to be friendly towards you. This is the same friendliness and interest which is shown when the Dayaks ask you to pause in your journey and climb up the notched log into their longhouse.

Some logs have good deep steps cut into them and others are worn and difficult to negotiate; in all cases it is unwise to lean upon the flimsy handrails provided. Longhouses are built on stilts and the higher ones may be thirty feet off the ground so a sense of balance is needed when entering or leaving, and once inside it is as well to tread warily. Many floors are made of split bamboo instead of hard-wood planks and it is advisable to walk where the bamboo lies directly above a supporting beam lest the slats break.

Iban longhouses are built where there is enough suitable farming land and clean water to drink. The bird omens and other auguries are assessed when choosing the actual site, and then gongs are beaten continuously as the main posts are raised, lest unfavourable bird calls are heard and that site has to be abandoned.

Belian (iron wood) is the timber of choice for posts, planks, and roof shingles, and such timber can be used over and over again in subsequent rebuildings. However the availability of durable materials varies and many houses are built with soft wood, roofed and walled with leaf thatch, and either split bamboo or tree bark is used for the inside walls.

It is common for anything between eleven and thirty families to join together under one roof but smaller or larger houses are not rare. The Tuai Rumah (headman) builds first and he is usually at the centre of the house. It is his lot to construct both walls dividing his bilek from that of his neighbours then all other families need build only one such dividing partition. In fact the

a. the bilek or family apartment.
b. the tempuan, a narrow storage area.
c. the ruai, main street + banqueting hall.
d. the pantar, where men sit and talk.
e. the tanju, an open-air drying platform.
f. the sadau — storage loft for rice etc.

Thwaites.

dividing partitions do not reach the roof and many have doorways leading into the next bilek, thus all normal conversation can be heard in the bilek each side and raised voices can be heard two or three doors away.

Running the whole length of the house is an outside verandah called the tanju and this is used for drying clothes, rice, etc. Inside the house there is another long verandah or gallery and this is divided into three parts, the sitting area, the main street and a narrower storage area where rice pounding equipment and extra forewood are stored. The fighting cocks are tethered here too and often such pets as hornbills, monkeys, etc.

Though the large inner gallery stretches the length of the house, each family is responsible for its own section, stores its lumber outside its own bilek and sits down with visitors on its own section of the ruai. However the families do not keep only to their own territory but wander up and down visiting each other and joining in anything of interest which is happening in somebody else's section (*Plate 2*).

During busy farming seasons one can enter a longhouse and find it practically deserted. However, it is almost certain that there will be at least one man left to look after things and usually there are old ladies and infants too. In *Plate 3* a solitary man is seen rolling a cigarette. The human skulls are well in evidence and most Sea Dayak longhouses have such a collection unless they have been destroyed by fire or the people have changed to Christianity and been asked to bury their skulls.

In the olden days a man proved his manhood by lopping off the head of another man and many Kayans and Kenyah people, and even other Sea Dayaks from different rivers, have lost their heads to this cause. The heads were carried back in triumph to be made much of by the ladies who wrapped the gory trophies in hand woven cloths and paraded them up and down the ruai, no doubt to music. Even in those days there were probably other reasons for girls agreeing to marry one man and not another, but to have provided a head for the longhouse certainly gave a man a tangible advantage in the marriage stakes; even today there is one rite which should be performed by a man who has killed someone else.

However, headhunting was strongly suppressed by each of the three White Rajahs in turn and though there were sporadic revivals of the Art during World War II at the expense of the Japanese force of occupation, the likelihood of you or your friends losing your heads to Sea Dayaks is somewhat remote.

The smoked heads, they are not shrunk, are occasionally fed ceremonial meals of rice and sometimes they are even taken down and paraded around the house. However this is not done without due cause and certain rituals must be performed before the heads are handled. At all other times the dusty skulls are not even noticed as they gaze sightlessly over the longhouse cycle of routine and pageantry, and this traditionally fierce people have channelled much of their energies into farming and "Development". Indeed I suppose that it is just possible that one could now live amongst the Iban for quite a while without ever discerning the steely yearnings of warrior lust which are still there.

Plate 3

Plate 4

Plate 5

At other seasons of the farming year, and certainly most evenings, the longhouse is a very busy place with groups of people sitting around on the mats and others moving here and there on various ploys.

This drawing was done in December when the weeding was finished and equipment was being made for the coming harvest. The lady in *Plate 4* is weaving a basket whilst two friends next door are making mats, one of them holding her baby the while, and the dried leaves used for these coarse mats are seen hanging in coils on flanking posts. Finer mats woven in intricate designs are used for sitting upon but many of these coarse mats are needed too. They are used to line simple granaries in the farm huts and into these is poured the golden streams of warm sun-drenched padi carried in from the surrounding fields. More mats are needed to cover the ruai when the padi has been carried back to the longhouse for threshing: more mats are needed when drying the padi on the tanju, when winnowing and when preparing it for storage in the attic.

The young man partly hidden by the nearest post is taking time off to carry his fighting cock down to the river to wash its glossy white plumage; the man with two strings of flowers tattooed down his back is making a conical fish trap, his wife is preparing strands of rotan for him, and it is their baby which is cradled in the sarong hung from a spring suspended from the rafters. A girl of six carries her wee brother on her back nearer this end of the longhouse and other folk can be seen doing a variety of jobs all the way down to the other end of the house. On the right a child is seen emerging from his bilek and through the open door we can see three plates in racks near the unseen hearth and beyond that some large storage jars standing on the floor at the back of the next bilek beyond that.

A stranger visiting the longhouse for the first time should first call on the Tuai Rumah (Headman) and his section is usually to be found in the centre of the house. Other men sitting on their own sections will invite the visitor to sit with them but nevertheless it is courtesy to go and sit with the Tuai Rumah first. Mats are spread for him to sit upon and he is expected to ask for water if his feet are muddy and then to sit down lightly upon the mats. A foreigner who clomps wearily down the ruai and throws himself down upon the mats with a heartfelt sigh and a resounding thud will not see anyone laughing at him but amongst themselves the Iban do not demonstrate exhaustion.

The bilek on *Plate 5* is a rich one both in size and furnishing. Whilst a number of people have bought a four-poster bed from the Chinese traders, the majority of Iban still sleep on the floor; most people sit on the floor to eat too but a new table may well be produced for the use of a visitor. A mirror-fronted wardrobe is now almost a social necessity and if the lady has a sewing machine and uses it adeptly then that is another status symbol. A man who has an outboard motor outside his bilek, and enough money to buy petrol for it, saves himself hours of poling on the rivers and these engines and transistor radios have become fairly common now in the longhouses. However, Iban have few possessions really and what they have can usually be hung around the walls or stored in large earthenware jars. A bilek where there are a number of jars and a set of gongs is considered rich to this day.

Hanging from the beam is a collection of charmed articles including an empty medicine vial and the little figure painted on the piece of wood at the bottom is there to repulse evil spirits. The finger daubs on the nearest post record the taking of some medicine, and there were in fact other charms hanging up in the other corner of the bilek. The man and the two boys are eating their rice and wild pig with their fingers and to do this circumspectly is more difficult than it appears.

Since headhunting was stopped the Iban have found other ways to outshine their neighbours. Consistently growing enough rice to last the whole year though other families run short, to have fought with the Army or been in the Police Force; to have a Government job as a teacher, hospital assistant, agricultural assistant or clerk is pretty good. To be a Tuai Rumah (the head of the house), or a Penghulu (area head of a number of houses), or to be a "Komiti" member of the Local Authority is also prestigeous. Literacy is becoming increasingly important and though few up-river adults can read or write in any language, nearly all their children now attend school. In fact, to be able to persuade the local authority that their first school in a new area should be near one's own longhouse instead of two hours' walk away near another house is considered a fine achievement.

Short hair is now common amongst both men and women and modern European clothes have reached far above the places where they can be worn to advantage (!) though this is not always realised until the purchases have been made. Nowadays a young man still wears nothing but a pair of cotton pants as he negotiates streams and slippery logs on his way to a feast. But he is more likely to be carrying leather shoes, white shirt, long trousers and unnecessary spectacles than his own traditional costume. In fact, I see increasing signs of opulence at the feasts I attend, and I expect that it will not be long before all these finely proportioned people will hide grace, symmetry and tattoos beneath the anonymity of European dress. Mind you, I do think that the ceremonial dress which the ladies wear encumbers them instead of accentuating their line and form; they are never so elegant and unhampered as when wearing the short or the long sarong to go about their daily work, and I don't find it surprising that they prefer modern party dresses to the heavy ceremonial attire which effectively prevents them from sitting down or moving their heads freely.

Normally, the family and any female guests sleep in the bilek, whilst bachelors and any visiting men sleep outside on the pantar. At feast times all the men sleep on the pantar and as the day's ceremonies extend to the night's carouse many men sink into sleep wherever they happen to be and some bodies form pillows for other heads. The chances are that your hosts will have no intention of letting you go to sleep anyhow; in fact they are not above sending two or three of the girls round to get the men up again. Indeed it is a sound sleeper who can sleep through the shrieks of the dancers and the vibrations of the gongs, especially when one is apt to be shaken at midnight and again at 4 a.m. to come to eat and at other times to have another drink. However, if you are one of those people who like to have had some sleep before working or walking the following day, then you would do well to earmark a certain spot and get your blanket, pillow and sleeping mat ready to be rolled down there.

Because many longhouses have been burned to the ground some Iban now build separate kitchens a little distance from the main building; however, most people still cook on a clay hearth in one corner of the main bilek. This hearth is at floor level and the ladies either squat on their heels or sit on a low stool as they cook. Stacks of firewood are dried on racks above the fire and everyone knows what a fire hazard this is. Just a few of the ladies still know how to make their own cooking pots. They beat the white clay into shape with a patterned wooden beater, and do not use a wheel of any sort, nor a kiln either. In fact they bake the pots in an open fire and the lady I was watching told me that she had had a number of pots ruined by firewood collapsing on top of them. Many of the old folk say that rice cooked in an earthenware pot tastes better than that cooked in a metal pot, but the clay utensil needs careful handling and nowadays most Iban settle for buying thick metal pots from the bazaar. Another handy cooking utensil which adds its own pleasant flavour to the rice or fish cooked in it is a section of hollow bamboo. A couple of these are visible behind Mayang as she sits by her fire. One end of the bamboo is closed, the other is plugged with a leaf, and the cooked food is then easily carried in its portable container be it to a distant farm or on a journey.

Boiled rice is the staple food of the Iban and it is eaten in large quantities. Hand pounded fresh hill-rice has such flavour and such an appetising smell that it makes an enjoyable meal even though there may be nothing at all to eat with it save a little rock salt. Maize, which is planted at the same time as the padi, ripens early and boiled or roasted it is a welcome substitute at a time when many people have no rice left. Job's tears ripen late and take second place to the newly harvested padi but it is quite nice made into a sort of sweet porridge. The root vegetable tapioca can be eaten throughout the year and sago is another uninteresting standby if the rice supply fails.

Water for cooking is carried from the river in gourds, and many folk now boil all their drinking water. Hanging over Mayang's fire are two pairs of tongs with which she moves hot things around. The wooden spatula will also have been fashioned by her, or her husband Kaba but the metal slice and the spoon will have been bought from the bazaar. Hanging above the hemispherical frying pan on the near side of the firewood is a string of fruit skins and these provide a kind of soap when thoroughly dried. Cleaning the kitchen is a pretty rapid chore because of all the gaps in the floor, and I haven't yet seen anyone painting or washing down walls which are made out of tree bark or split bamboo; before there are altogether too many cobwebs on them they usually need replacing anyhow (*Plate 6*).

Access to the attic is by way of a small almost vertical log leading from inside the bilek. Lengths of rotan, extra mats and carrying baskets are stored up there when not in use, as well as clusters of gourds and a variety of clutter. However, the main thing up there is the padi bins, and a man who has enough padi for his family to eat three rice-meals a day for the whole year is

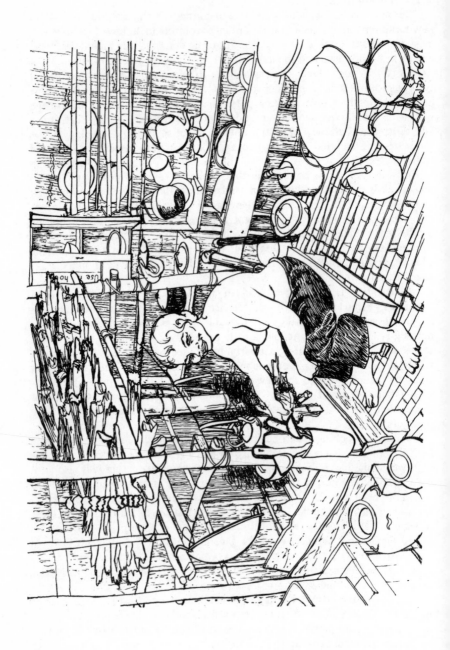

218

Plate 6

Plate 7

Plate 8

fortunate indeed. In *Plate 7* three baskets of padi are standing next to one of the bins and another basket is being carried up by the man whose head and shoulders appear at the top of the log. The lady watching him is standing in the bilek below. One of the young men is frankly getting his breath back and the other is preparing an offering (piring). At this stage all can see the best and the worst of the harvest, the number of baskets is easily counted, nevertheless it is believed that offerings, supplications, oblations and libations (and rice wine all round) will induce the Rice Spirits to favour these bins so that, however much padi is taken out, the amount remaining does not decrease too rapidly.

Should rice be spilled when transferring it from one container to another, or scattered on the mat when eating rice with the fingers, then a great show is made of carefully scooping it up again lest the padi Spirits feel themselves to be slighted and decline to help the family again. Because your Iban hosts may well offer you whatever they are eating with their rice and you may not necessarily like fried red ants (which have a sharp taste because of the formic acid), or monkey (don't look into the cooking pot first), snake, squirrel, grubs or roasted grasshoppers, it is as well to know how to refuse food. It is so simple! Just touch it lightly and say nothing at all! The Iban believe that all things have a soul including inanimate things like food, and if you don't touch it but merely say, "Thank you very much but I do not want any more, thank you", then the soul of that food may well feel offended and arrange for you to be bitten by a snake or fall down and break your leg. Your Iban host would feel responsible if a calamity such as this befell you because he had unwittingly offered you something which you did not want; therefore you might well like to adopt this custom of touching proffered food which you don't want if only for his sake. If tuak (rice wine) is being proffered and you are handed only a small amount with much gesticulation, it may well be that you are required to pour that lot through a hole in the floorboards for the Gods, and accept the next glass for yourself.

Plate 8 shows one lady husking padi in the wooden mill her husband has made for her and two young ladies pounding padi to remove the remaining husks. Power-driven rice mills owned and operated by a number of longhouses do this sort of job far faster and save the women much labour but the hand-pounded rice is far superior in flavour and in Vitamin B content. There are many different kinds of rice. The up-river Iban plant dry hill-rice and of this there are quick and slow growing varieties; long, short and medium sized grains; ordinary and glutinous kinds, all of which require their own method of cooking. Also there are different colours of rice including red rice and some which is almost black. The black rice when it is cooked is the colour of blackcurrant jam.

Sea Dayak women do not speak up at meetings; they eat what is left of a meal after the men folk have finished theirs; carry water; tend the children; cook and do the washing; they also do weeding and other backbreaking jobs on the farm which, naturally, most men will not do. However, their influence on affairs is more than at first appears, and the amount of conviction which *does* make the ladies form and voice an opinion on something which concerns

Plate 9

them, is often enough to release a verbal missile lethal enough to stagger the men momentarily. Iban grannies' tales to their five- and six-year-old charges give a pretty comprehensive account of the differing functions of men and women in longhouse society; a roused Iban woman tends to give tongue to a detailed harangue on men in general and rather personal observations on the culprit in particular, so that all present hear a considerable amount of the female point-of-view in a short space of time.

Not all is bitterness however. Some of the funniest repartee I have ever heard was at an Iban wedding where the visiting ladies from the bridegroom's longhouse said what they were prepared to do to make the evening's entertainment a success, and the men of the bride's house offered their wives to provide similar services for the visiting men, with certain injunctions which hindered no one but sounded very funny indeed. And yet it was not lewd. Dayaks are neither seedy nor secretive about these matters and I rather think that vice rings could not flourish up here because participants and the general population, of all ages, would discuss all the details of these surreptitious thrills with such candour and humour that they would become ridiculous.

Visitors to the longhouse are often welcomed with ceremony. Placed on the mats for each to help himself are the essentials for preparing a chew of betel nut and rolling cigarettes of the strong, dark red tobacco. A hen is waved over the heads of the guests and the appropriate incantations made. The chant of welcome tends to be rather long, but after first counting slowly up to six and positively lingering on the seven, the duty host gabbles the rest at a positively furious rate, pausing only for breath. The hen squawks and flaps as it is waved aloft, then its throat is cut and a couple of its tail feathers dipped into the blood and dabbed on the foreheads of those sitting round in order to minimize the effects of any evil spirits which may have accompanied them into the house. (*Plate 9*).

There is an even more impressive ceremony if the visitor is an expected V.I.P., or if many guests from surrounding longhouses have been invited to attend a big feast. With bold tattoos on throat and thighs, and long hornbill feathers soaring out of their hats, the men of the house stride magnificently down to greet their guests. Silver amulets flash above elbows and calves and clashing coins almost sweep the floor on the ends of brightly coloured loin-cloths. Yards and yards of cloth are used for these ceremonial loin cloths; one end is passed between the legs and the other is wrapped round and round the trunk as high up as the lower ribs. One end falls to the ground beneath great loops, like a bustle, and in front the other end hangs straight and smooth to below the knee, heavily encrusted with beads and embroidery and coins. More bangles encircle the wrists, and necklaces swing from the neck; ornate knife scabbards are lavishly decorated with bells and feathers, and hand-woven jackets cover muscular chests.

Beating gongs and waving flags, they escort their guests from the water's edge to the ladder where a pig is trussed abaft a pole. With a spear or a knife the chosen guest despatches the pig more or less adroitly (the tender hearted should neither watch nor listen to this rite) and at the top of the ladder a

Plate 10

bevy of ladies are lined up to greet the guests who then pass down this line in single file.

Dressed in handwoven skirts covered by a corset of old silver coins, their breasts covered by bead collars or narrow lengths of embroidered cloth, the ladies have high, tinkling combs fluttering above the crimson hibiscus in their glossy black hair and, much bedecked with bangles and anklets, each lady holds a glass of rice wine in her hand and has a helper who replenishes the glass as each new guest arrives in front of her. If it should be that you are doubtful of your ability to drink so many glasses of tuak in quick succession without thereby missing all the later excitement, then you may elect to sip no more than a mouthful from each glass and hand it back to the girl to finish for you. This ploy is not very popular with the girls. If there are a number of drink-shy guests in a long line they may have to drink a considerable amount, thus it is up to each man to strike his own happy medium between chivalry and self-preservation (*Plate 10*)

"Many years ago we Dayaks were literate too and had committed much knowledge to paper; however there came a great flood, and each race had to swim to the summit of a mountain for safety. The white man was wearing his topee and he kept his documents high and dry under that. The Chinese gentleman did not have a hat so he put his writings into his shirt pocket and though they got sadly wet and the ink ran somewhat he was still able to decipher what he had written (even though no one else could nor can to this day). The Sea Dayak, however, wearing nothing but a loin cloth, tucked his writings into his waist band and got them absolutely soaked so that by the time he reached dry land most of the writing had been washed clean off the sodden wedge of paper. Nevertheless an attempt was made to preserve what remained by spreading the papers to dry in the sun, but the birds swooped down and flew off with the papers so now we are dependant on the birds to tell us a lot of the things we need to know."

This story, and variations of it, is often told by Sea Dayaks. It allows a man to learn from other races without lowering his self esteem and also it links up with a vast bird mythology which is of paramount importance in Iban thought. Some of the most powerful gods are believed to have assumed the shape of birds and the opinion of these birds is diligently sought when any major undertaking is being considered. Indeed many decisions will be held up until a certain bird call has been heard coming from the correct direction, and if the wrong call is heard then previous decisions may well be reversed. I have known a man discard two months' work on his farm and hurriedly start working another area all because a bird had forecast bad luck if he had continued.

Quite recently a headman called Balai and his wife, in the ulu Kanowit, counted seventeen hawks wheeling high in the sky above their newly harvested farm; he says that there were more but that they were only able to count seventeen with absolute certainty. Because hawks are usually seen singly or in pairs up here, Balai took this visitation to be a very special sign from the gods and though he did not know its portent he arranged for his

Plate 10 a

Plate 10 b

Plate 10c

Plate 11

229

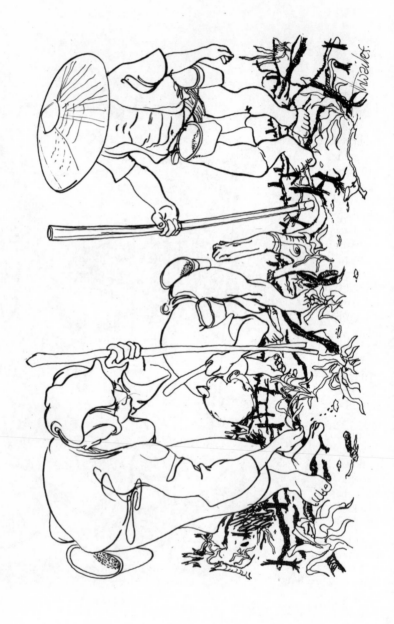

Plate 12

longhouse to hold a big feast in honour of the supernatural appearance. The feast was held on the open tanju where all the birds could see and attend.

This picture *Plate 11* was drawn about 9 o'clock in the morning when the sun was already shimmering fiercely as it climbed into a cloudless sky. A row of bamboo posts, festooned with palm leaf plumes, has its top fanned out to receive the offerings to be made. One man adds a final blanket to the line of red and brown weaving watched by a friend sitting on one of the gongs. Most families have already put out their plates and bowls ready to be heaped with food for the gods but an old man in the foreground finishes putting a banana-leaf lining to the baskets which are to be hung right up on the roof ridge, whilst another man essays a wee dance to himself. Most of the other men had already retired inside to greet their guests and pour more and more tuak into them, but each family kept one sober enough to kill its pig and two or three guests mellow enough to arrange its offerings. This was a gay party, most Iban gawai are, and you can probably imagine the noise of gongs and laughter and the aroma of new rice and roast pork pervading this intensely colourful scene.

On *Plate 12* I have drawn a weird collection of sinister figures which are to be found in the gloomy interior of a roughly made hut at Nanga Maong. For years the land at the mouth of this cold forest river had been guarded by one crocodile carved out of compacted earth. Five feet long, with gaping jaws moulded onto hardwood shingles, it is forever menacing, vigilant and evil. At least once a year and more often if the growing padi or the Spirit/human relationship was threatened, there was a ceremonial feeding of the crocodile. Flags were planted and the awesome reptile ritually fed with rice and tuak and a piring offering, drums and gongs were beaten, and against the expiring squawks of a hen, the crocodile was exhorted to fulfil its purpose of repulsing evil spirits.

Last year the crocodile acquired a wife and both were moved closer to an anthill which also is invested with supernatural powers. To prevent domestic pigs from grubbing up these sacred relics Kaba built a hardwood fence around them and put a roof over the lot. By the time I saw them again, many roughly hewn men and earthenware jars had been ranged round the crocodiles, and baskets had been hung on the wall. Plates left on a rough altar and shrivelled banana leaves placed near the jaws had no doubt contained food some few days before, the bottles would be full of tuak, and I suppose that the blackened tins in the ashes had contained some delicacy. As I understand it, the peculiarly evil wooden figures are decoys deflecting upon themselves the wrath which spiteful spirits aim at humans and indeed the figure with outstretched arms like a cross had been dressed in a man's shirt. However, it is difficult to see at all clearly in the darkness and the dread aura of a strange spirit world permeates the very air, discouraging unnecessary exposure to such malignant forces. The sharp stakes in the bamboo staves are there to impale unwelcome intruders and I personally am only too glad to leave these brooding malevolents in their eerie gloom and step back into sunshine.

In fact, the quality of light in Sarawak is remarkable. The sky is a glorious blue and beneath it everything has a rare clarity of outline and

Plate 13

texture. The tiny pink tip of an emerging fern is quite separate and distinct from the downy blade of grass next to it, and instead of there being just a patch of green there is a magnificent variety of shapes and shades of green; they may intertwine or overlap but each shape is specially discreet in this clear sunshine. Dayak skin is not just honey-brown, it is highlighted with a translucent sheen, and one can see that it is going to be like satin to the touch. The aquamarine and turquoise of a butterfly's wing positively glows where it shades into the vandyke brown at its edge and the darting dragonflies become iridescent. Royal blue, emerald green or velvety black with chestnut brown, these two inch dragonflies light up the green jungle like jewels and once I saw three different red dragonflies all hovering over the same pool together; scarlet, crimson and cerise.

Plate 13 is a drawing of a dampa, an extended farm hut housing six families. Because the slash and burn method denudes the steep hills allowing the rains to sweep the top soil straight down into the river, it then takes anything from seven to twelve years before that piece of land has regenerated sufficiently to grow another crop of padi. This "shifting agricultural" is wasteful of land and effort; each farmer needs lots of land (practically all of it lying fallow until it regenerates) and every year he does a major clearance all by hand. Often three or four families will farm close together at a place where there is enough land for each of them to farm two or three years using different land each year. Because this area is likely to be a couple of hours' walk from the longhouse it is worthwhile building a more substantial farm hut and some of these dampa are quite palatial. In fact they look like small longhouses with a bilek and a ruai and much of the equipment normally kept in the longhouse itself.

Invariably situated near water, some of these dampa are beautifully sited, and that includes the one that I have drawn which is up the Maong river overlooking a thundering waterfall. The water is deep and clear and cold after ·its long journey through the high forests and to fish its pools or stand under its battering white spume is absolute joy; whereas the tumultuous roar, the sheer power of the rushing water when the river is in spate, is awesome indeed.

Because the land is not flat, the up-river end of this dampa is a mere couple of feet off the ground, whilst the end which I have drawn here is at least fourteen feet up in the air and access is by a log which seems to go up and up for ever. Personally I have climbed longer logs than this one. I can think of one longhouse which is thirty feet off the ground, but this one at the dampa is of soft wood with notches that are all but worn away, and the hand-rail is not only too fragile to support any weight, it doesn't even give a false sense of security. In fact, if you are the slightest bit apprehensive of your ability to walk up a practically smooth tree trunk, nineteen feet long, set at an acute angle without a safety net, then you would probably be better to use the four foot log at the other end of the house and walk back along the ruai to the downriver end. Off the picture but behind the partition on the extreme left, is the bilek and at the end of the ruai is the top of the log leading down to the ground. The end wall of this dampa is no more than a few sheets of tree-bark and elsewhere the leaves of the surrounding trees are clearly visible; in fact one has a sense of actually living up in the tree tops on a sort of roofed platform. Hanging down in line with the main doorway are loops of cut rotan, and other lengths of creeper used for mat-making or tying up canoes etc. can be seen coiled on the floor or suspended here and there. A new water-gourd is hung up to dry out after the inside pulp has been soaked out of it.

A young father can be seen taking his ease after spending the latter half of the night and most of the morning fishing. At his side is a newly completed fish trap which will be secured with its large open end up-stream in a shallow gully where the current is full and fast moving. Fish funnelled through the inside cone into the larger chamber cannot return against the force of the incoming water and so remain quietly feeding here until the fisherman comes to lift them. The baby is crawling across a partially made mat, his mother is threading a needle, and the dog is not dead but sleepeth. Near the dog's paws and next to the upturned rice mortar is a durian fruit. Most Iban love the foetid smell emanating from these large spiky fruits and they chop them open with relish to eat the luscious flesh enveloping the chestnut-sized stones inside. There are also kinds of soursop, jackfruit, mango, lychee, rambutan and a variety of lesser known wild fruits ripening between November and February (alternate years seeming to produce bigger crops). Varieties of pineapples, melons, papaya, bananas and thin-skinned citrus fruits are grown successfully too. Few Iban know how to preserve fruit so a glut is met with gluttony, and most years most Iban gorge most fruits to excess with predictable results.

Rice farming is not only an agricultural procedure to the Iban. It is a religious cult and a way of life. In each longhouse one man is chosen to co-ordinate the efforts of all the individual families. This man should not be argumentative nor allow altercation on his ruai, he should know about bird auguries and estimating planting time by the stars. Each family farms for itself but may well decide to farm close to another family for company; certainly sparrows and rats will steal less grain if the planting is synchronised and the fields ripen simultaneously. Each family stays where it intends to farm and if the present harvest was a bad one they may well start off with a ceremony to bless the earth. Offerings to please the good spirits are buried, put in the river, and hung on poles flanking the main path to the new farm, together with sharpened bamboo spikes to spear the evil spirits. Winnowing baskets are dragged through the house and each family laughingly throws in spent and useless articles for "the Greedy God". His share is tipped out onto the ground beneath the house and he is told not to come looking for more. Most longhouses celebrate the Gawai Batu or feast of the whetstones before starting to slash their new farms. These whetstones are the ones which will be used to sharpen the bushknives and they are respectfully carried up into the longhouse and paraded round about before being ceremonially washed in water containing charms. The stones are then oiled, a piring offering is made over them and after being paraded again they are put inside the wooden troughs used for rice-pounding and the lemembang begins a long chant. Early next morning another hen is waved aloft and a procession carries another offering down to the river, returning to hold a short session of cock-fighting on the ruai before breakfast. Fresh mats are then put out for the expected guests, and they arrive late in the morning or early in the afternoon whereupon the tuak begins to flow. Meanwhile the host ties up a sacrificial pig on his tanju, and the whetstone, in its trough, is placed at the foot of a bamboo pole to which has been tied bunches of betel-nut, a kind of lily, and the straight bushknives with ornamental hilts and scabbards, some of which are decorated with the human hair taken from a severed head. During the afternoon there are more processions with flags and gongs to mark the ceremonial combing of the sacrificial pig and then to honour those men who will kill the pig and pronounce on its liver. Other rituals are performed here, then boys scale the steep roof to plant offerings and flags on the very roof-ridge where the gods will see them, while the whetstones are carried in to the ruai. A piring, a bushknife, an axe, and maybe some porcupine quills are put next to the whetstone, a circular wall is made of a strong mat, and the whole lot covered by a handwoven blanket. Each family has its own altar and after the evening meal the lemambang takes up his chant again, slowly pacing along the ruai, circling each altar and occasionally turning to coach the two or three men who follow his chanting the choruses. The slow, rhythmic thump of the staves and the high, sustained notes of the chant repeatedly toppling down in a descending cadence of half notes, will now continue throughout the night (*Plate 14*).

Piring offerings are made on each family's ruai and hung around the posts, then later there is a most colourful procession when one man and one lady from each bilek don ceremonial attire and parade three times round the house to encourage Sempulang Gana, the god of the soil, and other great spirits to attend the feast. At midnight another meal is eaten on the ruai and there is dancing and drinking, gossip and laughter until the pre-dawn breakfast is served, and the prominent guests who have kept all-night vigil at the altars sit up straighter ready for the visitation. Just before dawn is the time when Sempulang Gana and his retinue enter the house and the humans parade with all ceremony to lead them in. The Lemambang announces the arrival to the men, waves another hen, and at this stage another procession forms to kill the pig. One lady feeds the pig with offerings, another scatters roasted rice on it, it is ceremonially washed and combed, and then speared. The liver is "read", and if the gall bladder is full then a good harvest is anticipated. After a second breakfast the human guests return to their longhouses and the Spirits are presumed to return to theirs, leaving blessings behind them. The Lemembang then has a lot to say to the women of the house.

After the Gawai Batu the whetstone is taken to the farm and more ceremonies are performed there until, after one week, the length of time spent slashing has increased to the whole day and both men and ladies work hard cutting down the grass and bushes. At 4 a.m. the ladies have already lit their cooking fires, the whole family eats rice before the dawn, and the workers set off for the farm at first light, carrying small children with them if

Plate 14

there is no one left to care for them. Some years the farm is five minutes' walk away and some years it is two hours' walk away and sometimes it is necessary to go by canoe part of the way. Work is pretty constant all day with short breaks for a smoke and a longer pause for lunch. Most people finish work about 4 p.m. and by the time they have walked home, bathed themselves and the children and cooked the evening meal, it is 7 p.m. and dark again.

Usually a farm hut is built at the bottom of the hill, near water, and slashing is begun at the bottom working upwards to leave a fringe of trees on the crest as a fire break and so that the Spirits have somewhere to sit. Severe cuts occur frequently at this stage of the farming and even more so when saplings and enormous trees are chopped down. Felling trees is the men's job and it is a fine sight to see two Dayaks simultaneously chopping down a great giant of a tree, one on each side of the massive trunk. They work five or six feet above ground, balancing on the flimsiest scaffolding made out of three or four pieces of bamboo, yet, when the tree falls, they manage to skip around to the safe side, only rarely losing their footing or being struck by the bucking trunk. In virgin forest there are trees 150 feet high and over, with hardly any undergrowth beneath them. In overworked land there are no trees but a heavy crop of ferns and coarse grass; such a farm will require to be weeded twice and even so will not yield a good crop of padi.

Cutting the grass and bushes first allows them time to dry out before the trees are felled on top of them, and once the felling is completed, the farmer hopes for a week or ten days of dry sunny weather to dry everything ready for burning off. Sometimes it happens that, whereas one more day of sun would have been sufficient to give an adequate burn, it rains instead and the whole drying out process must start all over again. To burn a scarcely dry farm in case it rains the next day results in a poor burn and hours spent restacking and reburning the logs and branches which have been left; but if one waits too long the dry spells get shorter, green grass begins to grow again, the rainy season arrives and there will be no rice farm that year (*Plate 15*).

Planting padi on the burned hillside is a slow and thirsty job in the full glare of the sun, so most people cover as much of themselves as possible and wear huge sunhats. It is the responsibility of the farmer's wife to choose which kind of padi grain is to be planted where, and she is careful to arrange that no quick-growing strains are entirely encircled by slow maturing varieties. It would not do to force a passage through the Spirits in the unripe padi in order to harvest over-ripe grain in the middle: such a planting blunder would be the talk of the river. The men dibble two-inch holes about 18 inches apart in the ground with their long dibbling sticks and the women follow behind flicking five or six seeds into each hole. Dexterity varies, sometimes as many as fifteen seeds are flicked instead of five, and occasionally the seeds lie on the lip instead of going down into the hole. If there are not enough women then an older man will help with the planting; sometimes a man will both dibble and plant as he goes along. However, families join forces to plant each other's farms in turn, so that it is usually possible for the men to maintain the normal division of labour. Wrists and arms must ache after thrusting and twisting the dibbling stick for hours, but that is preferable to

238

Plate 15

Plate   15 a

240

Plate 15 c

241

Plate 15e

244

Plate 15 f

the stooper's backache, and a really large hat can shield much of an upright body. Planting is followed by weeding, harvesting, carrying home the harvest, threshing, winnowing, and storing the padi in the attic. Weeding is obviously women's work, it is so tedious, so the men take over the baby-sitting if necessary and expedite their fatherly duties by acquiescing to their children's every whim, or they may go off to the forest hunting for food or making a canoe.

While the women are weeding the growing padi, the men may have to find food if the last harvest was a poor one, and then it is a staple food that is needed. Most farmers plant a few sago palms beside a stream on each year's farm, and when hunger threatens they force a way back through the secondary jungle to see if any of their palms have matured. Sago is not a good substitute for rice. Dayaks neither find it palatable nor can they work hard on such a diet, but it does fill a void in the stomach. On the right-hand side of this drawing is a sago palm: it is the largest trunk there and in real life it looks as though it has been carelessly wrapped around with ragged old hessian sacks. However, its long fronds of dark green leaves are spruce enough and a number of these can be seen arching up from small sago palms behind the men.

Tuai Rumah Belayong and his men had already spent two days working on this job, so that when I joined them on the third morning they had already chosen a twelve year old palm, chopped it down, sawn it into six-foot lengths, and removed its tough bark with an axe. The stream meandering near the selected palm was only small, nevertheless the men had dragged a canoe up there and moored it securely by driving flanking staves firmly into the bed of the stream. Immediately down-stream from the canoe they had then constructed a dam by making a fence of staves across the stream and facing these with large leaves (indeed there are some large leaves in Sarawak: I can think of one variety, shaped something like the oak leaf, which is all of three feet in length). The dam collected enough water for washing the sago through the mat and also floated the canoe off the stony river-bed. Over the boat a platform of split bamboo was erected and covered with mats to form a treading-out platform, and beneath the platform was slung a piece of material to strain pith out of the flour as it went through (*Plate 16*).

Two logs form a trestle and in the hollow between them is laid a sago log which is then rasped by two men pulling and pushing a nail-studded plank across it. Two piles of coarse shavings collect at the feet of the men and this is scooped up in baskets and thrown onto the threshing platform. Here two men are treading out the pith, forcing the starch out of the wood, whilst a third man splashes pails of water over the sago so that the starch will be swished through the mat to collect in the bottom of the boat. As the day wears on more and more white sago flour settles in the bottom of the canoe and the water, which is now yellow, fills the canoe and overflows back into the stream. At the end of the day the surplus water is ladled out of the canoe and the white, wet, sago flour is scraped off the bottom with wooden spatulae and divided out into equal shares. The pith which does not pass through the

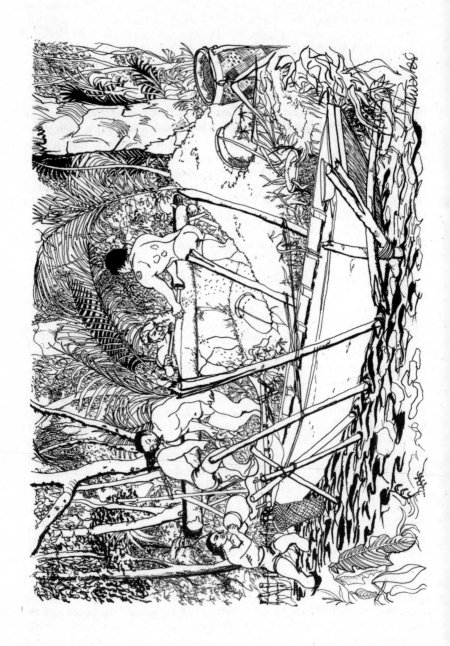

Plate 16

mats and the finer pith strained out by the cloth forms quite a pile, and this too is stuffed into sacks and carried home to feed the pigs and the hens.

If there is no mature sago and the men are needing food then there are two more palms with edible stems and the inside layers of these are quite nice when cooked with something of a good flavour, though there is even less food value in them. Tapioca is another standby and this can be eaten when it has been boiled, or it can be boiled first and then fried in a little pig fat or vegetable oil. The tapioca is a root vegetable about the size of a large parsnip, and the leaves on its thin segmented stem can be eaten too. Tapioca can be pulled and eaten throughout the year, though if it is left too long it grows even more tough and stringy. In fact it takes a lot out of the soil and certainly is not a good intercrop to put on terraced ground because pulling up its tubers tends to break down the terraces.

Most men enjoy leaving the womenfolk behind and going off on a hunting trip. They may stay out in the Primary jungle for a week or only for a couple of nights, and they may go alone or in a group. In any case there is likely to be a lot of gear to carry in a basket on the back, and it is fortunate that the Dayak knows to invert his wedge shaped load so that the smallest part fits into the small of the back and the widest and heaviest part is well above the shoulders. This simple reversal of the bulging rucksack makes a man stagger forwards if only to keep his balance instead of being dragged backwards at every step, also it allows the use of a head-band and the powerful neck muscles thus help too. Equipment usually carried includes a shotgun and ammunition, a waterproof and a blanket; paraffin, matches, rice and a cooking pot, salt for preserving the catch, and of course a duku (bush knife).

Walking quietly through the cool rain forest beneath towering trees is very pleasant indeed, and, though the hills tend to be steep and the small land-leeches a nuisance, there is hardly any undergrowth and the going is easy. The best shots go first and the others follow at a little distance, ready to freeze when the leaders stop. Most of these up-river Dyaks are good trackers and some of them can imitate the calls of birds and animals most skilfully.

Edible animals found in the forest include somewhat ferocious wild pigs, grey gibbons with their bubbling calls, woolly-coated red-monkeys and two or three other species of monkey including the sophisticated "Bejit" with soft orange fur on its underparts and sleek black evening gloves of longer fur. There are large sambhur deer, the middle sized barking deer such as the one in this drawing, and the tiny mouse deer whose delicate hooves skip through so many Iban folk tales. The black honey bear is worth avoiding when she is annoyed, and an unarmed man who is close enough to see the golden V on her chest as she comes towards him would be wise to run down hill away from her claws. The scaly anteater can reach a length of three feet or so and is good to eat, and there are two species of porcupine, one of which is quite large (*Plate 17*).

Fairly common is a harmless lizard which can be over three feet in length: clumsy on land, I once saw one cornered, and it climbed along an overhanging bough to dive into the river with scarcely a splash to remain

Plate 17

submerged for ages. Further down in the tidal reaches there are crocodiles, and though I seldom went down so far, I remember seeing one large specimen lying in the mud and displaying a most convincing array of teeth as we passed by. We had an 18 h.p. outboard engine and the tide was behind us too, but there was never any thought of going nearer to look at that fellow. If you prefer to be scared by something which will not in fact harm you then it is worth looking at the "flying lizards". Only six inches long, they look like little dragons as they snap out their semicircular "wings" and puff themselves up. Their camouflage is good and you may have difficulty in spotting these lizards unless one happens to glide across your field of vision on its way from one tree to a lower branch some feet away. Another rather smart lizard has a lime-yellow underside shading through emerald to a row of dark green spikes along his spine, and near his eye is a patch of pure Sevres blue. He is able to change his colouring to even brighter greens or into dull greyish greens but does not have the independent eye movements of the true chameleon.

Maybe only the cold blooded amongst us can enthuse over snakes but I have admired some of the Sarawak snakes, especially the "flying" Paradise tree snake. Most snakes get out of one's way as quickly as they can, though I must admit that I personally never argue the right of way with a king cobra or with any other Elapidae for that matter. The python has no poison but can incise rather conspicuous gashes in your sun tan: thus I was interested to see a group of seven-year-old school children performing dental extractions on a small python that they had found. One child held the snake's head whilst another continually presented a piece of rough towelling until it struck, and then suddenly jerked away the towel with the teeth still embedded in it. And after this they brought it into lessons with them.

This drawing was done on the first evening of a hunting expedition. A number of the party cleared the camp site, built a shelter, and gathered firewood before the guns returned with a large wild pig and a rhinoceros hornbill. The pig was cleaned and quartered and is here having its bristles singed off. Three of the men turn the pig and attend to the fire whilst a fourth fans the blaze. The young man who shot the hornbill drinks a mug of coffee before plucking his bird; another man carries in more firewood, and the man who has cooked the rice in the pot suspended over a small fire has boiling water on another fire behind him ready to cook the fish.

In fact the hornbill is now a protected bird and certainly the Bornean species are most impressive as they go flapping over the forest canopy on their enormous wings. Their nesting habits are remarkable and as well as prizing the white and black tail feathers of the real birds for ceremonial wear, the Iban make wooden effigies of these birds and honour them as gods. The tail-feathers of the argus pheasant are also sought and there are other birds which have really brightly coloured plumage, some as small as the diminutive honeysucker and some as large as the domestic fowl. Many of these birds are unremarkable songsters but bulbuls sing a glorious song, two or three of them taking it in turns to sing short phrases in a long continuous paeon of sound (*Plate 18*).

Plate 18

However, though a man occasionally brings back a bird for his child to keep as a pet, it is not the songsters that are chosen, or the talking mynah bird, but the love birds or one of the hornbill species, and these latter make an absolutely hideous noise clamouring to have more balls of cooked rice pushed into their gaping beaks. Monkeys, and gibbons, porcupines and large tortoises are fairly common pets and just occasionally one sees a family keeping a honey bear or a sambhur deer, a civet cat or a slow loris. The slow loris is not exhilarating company; during the day it tucks its head well into its tummy, rolls forwards onto its shoulder blades and sleeps. But if you prod it often enough it will eventually open its enormous close-set eyes so slowly and so sleepily; and yet if it did find your finger with its needle sharp teeth it could be long enough before you were free again. The tarsier is also to be found in Sarawak but personally I have never seen one never mind kept one to study its habits. More fun than the loris were two black civet cats which had white tips on their long tails and brownish patches on snout and chest. They grew to be so playful and adventurous that they quite ruined the psyche of the cat who had mothered them, and their habit of returning from the jungle at 4 a.m. to chase each other up and over my mosquito net did something to my psyche too. Also in the forest are a kind of otter and the clouded leopard which is no bigger than a domestic cat, but the ones I saw were dead. The Dyaks do not go out to look for pets but to shoot the protein food which they need. A few men still use the spear for hunting pig and on rare occasions a man will use a blow-pipe to kill birds silently without. frightening away other game. However, most hunters use shotguns and with a bit of luck they shoot enough to feed well in camp and have plenty to take back to their families. As well as nearly all the living things mentioned so far on these last two pages, squirrels, flying foxes, and freshwater turtles are also eaten and that portion which is to be taken home is cut up small and well salted. In fact, by the time everything has been singed, skinned, chopped and diced it is not always easy to guess what one is eating. Most meat is either boiled for an inadequate length of time or fried in a little vegetable oil, but the hunters usually put a few hunks of meat round the edge of their fire and these roasted titbits, all blackened and charred, are very tasty indeed. Sarawak has its share of spiders and insects (one fat grub and some grasshoppers are commonly eaten), and the shape and colour of some of these spiders and the noises made by the nocturnal insects are quite fascinating.

If Dyaks are walking fast for long distances they seldom drink because too much water slows them down, but if they need a drink yet are far from a stream they may find a thick liana which contains free water in its hollow stem. A three or four foot section is cut out of this long creeper, first cutting the top end, and then as soon as the bottom cut is made the severed piece is held high so that the water gushes down into the open mouth.

During the busy farming seasons there is no time for the men to go hunting and seldom any cash with which to buy anything to eat with the rice. This young man holds a few of the ferns he is collecting for food and the other one has just laid down two bamboo shoots in order to cut free another shoot. Men, women and children all take their turn foraging for jungle

254

Plate 19

produce and they take reasonable precautions not to touch the bigger bamboo stems with their irritant fur, or get bitten by a snake nesting in the clump. Certainly the fresh bamboo shoots are worth eating. Cut longitudinally they are boiled twice, and the first lot of water is thrown out because it will be bitter; then the shoots can either be eaten as they are or fried in a little pig fat with maybe a clove of garlic and a dash of soya sauce.

Cultivated vegetables also grow well and cucumbers, marrows, pumpkins and ensabi (which tastes like spinach) are planted along with the rice in the fields. A few Sea Dyaks also prepare small vegetable plots in which they grow such things as long beans, loofahs, aubergines, chives, Chinese cabbage and the changkok manis with its sweet green leaves. The longhouses do not have refrigerators so food is eaten quickly whilst still fresh or else heavily salted, or occasionally smoked, but in the next drawing it will be seen how Masil has solved a meat problem by penning three of the tortoises he has caught into a shallow pool in the swamp opposite the longhouse. He feeds them on cucumber and vegetable scraps and will kill them when he runs out of other food (*Plate 19*).

Engkebang, pepper and rubber are the three cash crops which give the Iban a little money to buy salt, dried fish, sugar, and tinned milk for the babies. Engkebang (illipe nuts) are a wild crop growing on tall trees along the banks of the rivers. The big trunk on the right of the next drawing is in fact the base of an engkebang tree and like many such it is entwined with lianas, and supports many parasitic growths. It is not every year that there is a good engkebang harvest, in fact a good engkebang year is the exception rather than the rule; also the nuts ripen at the same time as the early padi is ready for harvesting, so even when there is a glut few farmers have the time to collect this cash crop. The easiest way to collect the nuts is to sit in a canoe down-river from ripe trees and collect the windfalls as they float downstream. Not all the nuts drop into the water however and much time is spent searching around the base of the trees and then staggering back with heavy loads to the canoes. A man and a girl are here seen hitting the nuts to separate them from their winged sheaths and they will then be dried over a low fire or spread out in strong sunlight for three or four days. In the evening when the harvesters have returned from the rice fields and fed themselves and the family, they will join the few people who have been collecting engkebang to work far into the night sitting around a small lamp and telling stories as they split open the dried nuts and put the good kernels on one side to be dried again ready for sale down-river. Engkebang yields a nut oil which is of good quality and does not have a strong flavour, and the Chinese traders sell it in bulk to European companies who crush the nuts and use the oil in manufacturing chocolate and soap. The Dyaks also pound small quantities for themselves and make a kind of margarine which is rather nice melted onto cooked rice. Because the amount of the engkebang crop varies each year and so does the price obtained, some Iban who want a steadier cash crop and are prepared to spend money on fertiliser and hours on weeding may plant a pepper garden.

Plate 20

up-river bazaars. Boxes of tinned goods and clothes, tins of paraffin and a hundred and one other things will be stacked shoulder high, almost meeting the great bunches of vegetables hanging from hooks in the bulkhead, so that it is often difficult for passengers to find a place to lie down when tied up at some mid-way bazaar overnight *(Plate 20)*.

Now new roads are being pushed through to link the main towns and transport is far quicker though more expensive. Isolated longhouses, previously hours away from the nearest bazaar by winding rivers, now find themselves on a main trunk road with their land opened up for development and an economically valid reason for growing more cash crops. But to make the most of the low price being paid for natural rubber it is necessary to plant rubber trees at the optimum distance apart and improve the methods of processing the latex, and because soil erosion is such a problem in these hilly areas, a deal of heavy manual work is entailed.

The next drawing shows one man slashing the secondary jungle followed by another man who is making level terraces along which new high-yielding rubber is to be planted.

The longhouse children do not have toy cupboards: on occasions I have seen a child floating a toy canoe, or pushing a wheel in front of him made from a tin can loosely nailed to a stick. But usually they don't play with toys, they scream until their parents take them along with them to do whatever they are doing. Down they go to the river, out they go to the farm, off goes the infant tied on to his mother's back while she does a hundred and one jobs. When grandma goes for a quick gossip about what she heard last night then the wee one will be there to hear it all; baby sits cross legged inside father's crossed legs at the meeting, and when father smokes and drinks baby may just decide to have one too. He will be told not to play with the sharp knife, but he will usually do just that in the end. Parents love their children, also, if the young ones are alienated in life, they will leave home as soon as possible and then who will help the old folks when they can no longer farm for themselves.

In fact the girls are employed at five or six years of age helping to carry water and minding the baby, and it won't be long before they are doing some of the cooking and the rice pounding too. Boys are a different matter, when asked to do something they may simply say "I don't want to". In the farm hut younger sister minds the baby, prepares the vegetables and scares the birds away by shouting at them and pulling on the strings of the rustling paper which stretch to the far corners of the ripe padi field. Older brother idly glances at the other bird-scaring devices his parents have constructed; he may even go to look at the bamboo one fixed on a pivot beneath the tiny waterfall, because it empties and rings a little bell every few minutes, but his heart is not really in it. He is more likely to be scheming how to stay awake very late so that father will take him to watch for wild pigs which would trample down the padi at night. He would enjoy climbing up to the flimsy hide perched precariously over the field and he might even hold the gun for a short while. In fact the boys do not involve themselves in the dreary business of farming unless it is absolutely essential, and when they are old enough they

259

Plate   20 a

Plate 20 b

261

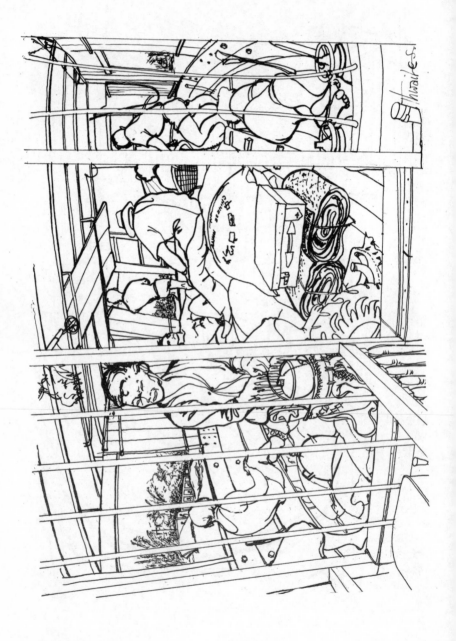

Plate 20d

Pepper vines have been planted for years by Sarawak Chinese and they have got good crops from vines trained to climb up nine foot poles 6 feet apart. Now a few Iban are trying the hedge-planting method in which the vines are trained along the rungs of a fence only six feet high thus obviating the need for step ladders when harvesting, whilst still hoping for good crops. As each three-inch long cluster of berries ripens it changes from dark green through yellow to red. When the red berries are dried in the sun they turn black, and if the farmer is prepared to put his berries in a loaded sack and soak them in the river for a few days he can then sell them as white pepper and get a higher price.

Rubber is another cash crop which has been planted by many Sea Dyaks. A collection of old, badly tapped rubber trees with scarred trunks are a common sight around the longhouses and their owners rise early in the mornings to gouge off another sliver of bark and let the latex drip into bamboo receptacles whenever they need to buy something or other. In the middle of the morning the white latex is collected in a bucket, poured into tin moulds with a small amount of formic acid and allowed to set. The sheet of rubber is then rolled out with a rolling-pin and put through a mangle which squeezes it still thinner and in the process impregnates a design into it. Few Iban smoke their own rubber sheets, so when they have been hung up and dried the sheets are ready for taking down-river in a canoe, where the trader weighs the bundle, assesses its grade and haggles over the price he is prepared to pay for it. The Iban then leans on the counter and looks around him at all the goods on sale. If he is in a small village shop up-river then there will not be very much to tempt him, but if he has gone all the way down to the bazaar the Chinese trader will have lots of things in his shophouse and there will be much bargaining and slander and threats to buy elsewhere until a compromise is reached and the shopowner may well treat his customers to a cup of coffee. This coffee will be served in the thickest crockery you have ever seen, the cup will be overfilled and much coffee will be slopping around in the saucer because an Iban does not like to be given short measure! For those who are prepared to pay for them there will be little rolls of glutinous rice wrapped in leaves, small egg buns, dry sponge cakes, long batter buns and violently coloured sago cakes on the round marble-topped tables; and it says much for the health authorities that these will usually be individually wrapped or kept in a glass box. At night the customers sleep on the floor of the big room above the shop and use a hearth to cook their rice without expecting to pay for this lodging, and early next morning they will load up their canoes for the long return journey then make last-minute purchases of some of the things they had declared were far too expensive the previous evening.

Two or three times in a lifetime the up-river Iban will go even beyond the bazaar and board a Chinese launch which slowly chugs down the long river to the coastal town. In my drawing there are two small bundles of sheet-rubber beneath the suitcase and the rest of the cargo is mainly Iban padi sewn into sacks which have previously held Chinese rice. On the return trip, however, the launch will be heavily laden with a proliferation of goods to be sold in the will want to travel to a distant part if only to claim the distinction of having travelled when they return. Meanwhile both boys and girls do seem to enjoy an idyllic childhood. Everyone makes a fuss of them, and I have seen one child of five lovingly adopted by the people next door and he settled readily enough though he could hear his own family conversing normally through the dividing wall. Mind you, the foster parents had done the job properly with the correct gifts and the Lemembang going into a trance in which he sets out to visit the heavenly hill and carefully uproot the tiny plant of the child and transplant it into the clump of its new family *(Plate 21)*.

These days more longhouse boys and girls go to school and you may like to compare the rather restrained speech days in European schools with the opening ceremony of a new school built by the Iban for their children. Ferns and hibiscus are tied to the main post of the classroom, a large pig is trussed up where the classroom door would be if there was one, and thirty six-year-old children sit on the forms driven into the earth floor. The new pupils are dressed in brightly coloured cotton dresses or shirts and shorts bought specially for the occasion, some of the girls have borrowed make-up from goodness knows whom and I notice that one of the boys is wearing a charm necklace of very old beads which he will probably retain even though he gets fed up of wearing shirt and pants. One half of the Reception Committee are dressed in white shirts and long trousers and the other half in loin cloths and feathers and bangles and they look very smart indeed, as they wave their flags and beat the gongs. The school teacher kills the pig and leads the School Committee and the visiting celebrities in to stand in front of the children. Two young ladies in traditional costume give each man a glass of tuak on the way in and every man standing at the front has to make a short speech exhorting the children to learn hard and the parents to help the school teacher with school gardens, roof repairs or anything at all that the teacher cannot manage alone. Parents and sisters cannot all crowd into the small school but they lean far in over the low walls encouraging their offspring to pay attention to the words of wisdom flowing over them and some of the speeches are drowned by the men cooking the pig on the river bank who seem to be whooping it up a bit. Finally, the speeches are over and the young men take off their fancy shirts to go and play barefoot football on the pitch they levelled so arduously, and older men make piring offerings closely watched by the mothers who want to ensure that the individual offering made for each child will give it the best possible start on its academic career. Rice wine circulates freely and by the time the roast pork is ready for eating Iban joy and high spirits have invaded the schoolroom and all the pupils are being urged to gobble up the edible parts of the offerings made on their behalf and only the tobacco and betel nut, etc., finish up in the rafters for the Gods. In fact there is a great danger that some of the more inebriated folk will not get their due share of roast meat and everyone knows that will lead to endless trouble. Don't underestimate the resourcefulness of your friends if they are Sea Dyaks. The servers put all the chopped up pork into two buckets and all the chopped up chicken into another bucket and ricocheting around the classroom they dole out a scoopful of meat into every right hand they can see:

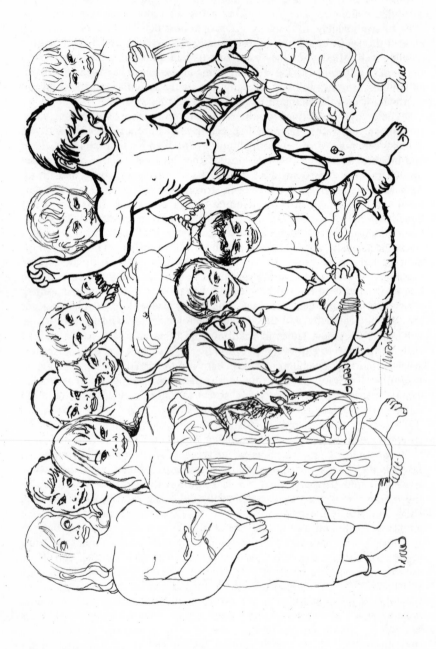

Plate 21

behind each server there follows another man and he daubs a white paste on the recipient's ear or chin to keep the servers right as to whom they have fed and whom they haven't.

It is a gay and noisy crowd who board the canoes for the short ride back to the longhouse or walk along the path and wade across the river. After a bath and a feast on the ruai there is music and dancing and a little more rice wine until a very late hour and thus the new school is well and truly honoured by the men who have built it and then brought it to life.

When an Iban dies unnerving hysteria sweeps the house as men and women wail and weep, and the largest gong is struck again and again to announce the sad event. Once I was called to visit a dying woman whom I had never seen before and I was not long in the house before she died. Whereas custom decreed that I should stay, I had to return to another patient, and so made my escape, and that uncontrolled wailing and the frenzied tolling of the gong is all I have seen of the funeral rites. On enquiry, I hear that the body is washed and laid out on the ruai, surrounded by walls of handwoven blankets. Some of the deceased's cherished possessions are put on one side for him and these will ultimately be buried with him or placed on the grave. While the body lies in state the women sit around and weep, and an appointed mourner sits on a swing and sings of the deceased's achievements in this world, and of the passage of the soul into the next world. The corpse is taken to the graveyard in a canoe and some of the company stay near the canoe to sacrifice a hen and cook a meal, whilst the other men go forward to dig a grave, and to hollow out a tree trunk coffin if this has not already been done. Before digging the grave, rice is sprinkled on the ground, and care is taken that no green leaves are buried under the coffin lest the spirit returns to haunt the living. Once the grave has been filled the men cut forked twigs which they place on their shoulders to hook back their own soul from the awful brink of the next world. When they return to the canoes again they reverse the hooks and plant one or more of them into the ground to prevent any of the graveyard spirits from following them back to the longhouse. All the burial party have the blood of the sacrificed hen smeared on their toes and eat the cooked hen and the rice, then they return to the longhouse. Before entering they first wash themselves very thoroughly and are careful to see that no particle of graveyard soil is taken in by them lest sickness result. The close relatives of the dead seclude themselves in the deceased's bilek, and it is not until the third day that other longhouse folk go to them with a duku and an offering of food. The duku is used to push open the window, which has been tightly shut, and the food is thrown out for the dead man to eat. The relatives eat with their friends and return to work but there is still a mourning period of a week or a month or even longer, fixed by the relatives, and during that time any wireless in the house must remain silent, voices are subdued, and any adult who momentarily forgets and laughs or shouts loudly in the house will be required to pay a fine. The end of the mourning period is often celebrated by the men going off on a hunting trip and on such occasions I have seen them charge the last few yards to the crest of a hill, plant staves decorated with fronds around the summit whilst calling on the Gods for

Plate   22

favour, and have a haircut there and then. Their smart appearance on re-entering the longhouse and the fact that they have brought some of the frivolous fronds with them announces the start of a return to gaiety without saying so in as many words. But the dead are not forgotten, some Iban hold a feast for their dead every five years or so, others wait thirty or forty years and then have a really big feast for all the people who have died since they last celebrated this Gawai Antu *(Plate 22)*.

These are not sad occasions but great parties, to which so many visitors from so many surrounding longhouses are invited that it is often necessary to strengthen the floor, and the spirits of the dead are invited by name to join in the merriment with the humans: food and drink are put out for them and cockfights organised at which only they, the unseen guests, are allowed to place bets. At the close of the celebrations, in which the dead have been so lavishly honoured, small wooden huts on stilts (called sungkup) are taken to the graveyard and erected over the grave. Inside are placed tiny bamboo replicas of all the goods and chattels which any Iban could possibly need in this world, and the souls of these inanimate things are said to wing their way to the soul of the loved one and equip him magnificently in his Spirit life. Often the sungkup itself is decorated with designs and a fretwork of mythical beasts rears up from the roof ridge.

The grave which I have drawn here is not remarkable to look at, it doesn't have little hinged doors on the hut (which holds crockery, a clock, and a Quick Quaker Oat tin in which the deceased may well store his tobacco in the next world). There are no designs either, just a corrugated iron roof, and the flags, which mark this spot on a vantage point overlooking the river Entebai, are limp and faded now. But this is in fact the grave of Asun, famed among the famous headhunters: and on the left is his son, Tuai Rumah Nyawai, who can tell the exciting story of his father's defiance of the Rajah's ultimatums, of the punitive force which razed Asun's empty longhouse to the ground, mowed his growing padi, and felled nearly all his rubber trees; of the fury of his father when he returned and saw his burned-out house and how he and his incensed warriors installed themselves on a mountain called Bukit Setulak.

Courtship amongst the Iban is a robust affair. The young men visit the girls at night and, if they can talk themselves into being accepted, are admitted inside the mosquito net. The girl's parents are aware of their daughter's visitors (they are sleeping in the same room), and though they like to know that their daughter is being sought out, the father will let it be known that a certain man should declare his intentions if he visits constantly. The young man will then ask his own father to arrange a marriage for him, or else he will take the hint and visit elsewhere. The Iban night is lit up by young men criss-crossing to different longhouses with torches in their hands.

If a pregnancy is started before a marriage has been arranged the girl can either name the father or not name him, just as she wishes; in any case the Iban make no difference between children born in or out of wedlock and a girl who has proved her fertility has a good point in her favour. Acquiring another man's child along with the bride is rather fortunate; children are

270

Plate 23

loved, they are also economically vital, and there will be couples who would love to adopt and bring up a child as their own. However, a girl who is pregnant without having named the father will probably be blamed for any bad weather and her parents won't like that very much. On the other hand, if she names a father when actually there is some doubt about it then the named gentleman may well stand up in the Penghulu's court and ask if it isn't possible that the real father isn't in fact Mr A or Mr B, or maybe Mr C?: and if he can actually supply names then the litigants tend to drop the case rather quickly. Where this sort of accusation cannot be made to stick the father may accept responsibility but pay a fine rather than marry the girl, or he may marry the girl but then sicken her by being bone idle, etc., until she divorces him. Divorce, for this and other reasons, is easily arranged but the many rules pertaining to the division of property are strict and unfavourable to frequent remarriage. In fact, most Sea Dyaks marry in their late teens and stay together through good times and bad until death takes one of them in their old age *(Plate 23)*.

Before a marriage is performed the parents and their cronies meet to recite their respective family trees to make quite clear that the marriage will not be within the forbidden degrees of relationship, then the headman of the girl's house marries them by waving a sacrificial hen over the heads of the bride and her maid and the groom and his friend, and finally daubs all foreheads present with hen's blood. Also there is a ritual of eating betel nut. The bride's father then promises that the incoming young man will be afforded support and, if necessary, the help and advice of the longhouse; and the visiting folk reply pledging similar facilities to the girl when she stays in their longhouse. Drinking, eating and dancing follow throughout the night.

Next morning the visitors leave to return to their own longhouse but the new son-in-law will stay in his wife's house for a few days before taking his bride on a return visit to his house. His prowess in man's work will be noted at this time and it pleases many of the parents to have their new son-in-law go out and collect firewood. The young man will want to find good wood which burns well and can be chopped to a good shape and he will want to carry it nonchalantly back in enormous bundles without showing any fatigue and stack the wood neatly and impressively outside the bilek door. If he is from another house he is likely to take another young man with him to show him the best firewood areas and to give him moral support. Sometimes they use an axe for chopping down the trees and my drawing shows how, sometimes, they just use a bushknife and lop off the branches first.

They both know that it is going to take a lot of firewood to impress anyone and that it just won't do to gasp along bent double under the load and collapse in an untidy heap of scattered wood and groans immediately inside the door. Fourteen years ago, when I had newly arrived in Sarawak, I saw a girl of eighteen or so returning to her longhouse with a canoe load of firewood which she had had to collect herself because her father was ill. Naturally I paddled over to her to give her a hand, but I couldn't even lift one of those bundles, and the girl roared with laughter as she swung a load up

Plate 24

onto her shoulder and stepped out of the wobbly canoe to walk with ease up the slippery bank and the ladder into the longhouse.

When the bride pays a return visit to her husband's longhouse she will find that her mother-in-law has contrived a shortage of pounded rice thus she will be encouraged to help the older lady to pound more rice, wash clothes in the river, mind the children, etc. There will probably be farming jobs to do as well, or the collection of such things as wild fruit and freshwater molluscs. Women's work inside the longhouse includes mat making and weaving, but weaving patterns are carried in the weaver's head and it is unlikely that any young girl could take over anyone else's skill. Leaves are wrapped around that part of the pattern which is to remain the natural off-white colour of the cotton and then the whole of the warp is dipped into a bath of red dye. When thoroughly dyed it is taken out, dried, and more leaves wrapped around all those parts of the warp which are not dyed black. The whole of the warp is then submerged in a black dye which has been made from leaves. When this second dye has dried and all the leaves have been unwrapped the required pattern stands out boldly in white and black on a dull crimson background. The hanks of cotton which are to be used for the weft are dipped straight into the bath and dyed red throughout and ultimately this thread will be woven backwards and forwards across the patterned warp. Blankets, ceremonial jackets for the men and short skirts for the women are made in this fashion, and because most of the women can only do a little weaving each evening after returning from their farmwork one blanket may take anything up to twelve months to complete. It is made in two longitudinal halves joined together one above the other and, when separated, the two halves are roughly tacked together with stitches utterly unworthy of the lovely designs and the craftsmanship involved. There are certain strictures and superstitions affecting the choice of patterns; for instance, only those who have been granted permission in a dream may weave patterns representing human beings, otherwise sickness or other serious misfortune is said to result (*Plate 24*).

In this drawing you will see how the weaving is done without a fixed loom. The tension of the warp is maintained by the weaver's body exerting counter traction as she leans back against the harness. Tie dye weaving is a dying art amongst women who are doing so much work on the farm. Much of the Sea Dyak women's work is hard work, but like the men, they do not make a fuss about physical effort. In fact, any Dyak who is so unwise as to show physical exhaustion in everyday tasks causes intense amusement, and it is only rigorous control and impeccable courtesy which prevent Dyaks from laughing when they watch other races actually stressing tiredness. Clumsiness, falling, and many kinds of accident, including even some calamities cause spontaneous mirth, and the details of exactly how a person slipped, his position on the ground, and how long he took to get up again are noted with glee by onlookers and all those people who will be told about it later. These things are so funny to the Dyaks that, if they don't laugh at a man's downfall they are treating him as a stranger and not one of themselves. Some of their own names send them into fits of uncontrolled laughter whenever they are

273

274   Plate 25

pronounced though it may be noticed that the owner of such a name or the victim of such an accident does not always laugh quite so heartily as the onlookers. (I remember a schoolgirl pointing out somewhat acidly that one of the boys had laughed at her so long that his teeth were dry) but the victim doesn't seem to suffer from any lasting trauma and the ability to laugh at the next man's downfall seems to remain unimpaired. It is questionable whether a European can ever quite see drollery in other people's mental deficiency, blindness, deafness or other physical disability; the mental subnormal Dyaks I have seen were obviously used to watching their own longhouse folk doubled up with laughter at them because they would ask him questions and then shriek out at his attempts to answer till they were limp with laughing; but such a man remained in the community doing whatever work he was capable of doing and whoever noticed when he was stumped would help him complete the work. Certainly I would say that the Dyaks have a strongly developed sense of humour. I once attended a school concert where soldiers from another country had sung a popular song and one of the group had been dancing from side to side to put some life into the performance. Later I asked the girls why they had spent so much time with bowed heads laughing themselves silly and learned that one of them had wonderingly blurted out that the dancer looked exactly like a crab caught in a fish-trap. Indeed it was an apt observation on that particular modern dance where the dancer scuttles from side to side getting nowhere.

This is a drawing of Moa Hari. The edge of his circular fishing net is weighted with a metal chain and he has the knack of twisting round and flinging the net far out in front of him without overbalancing and falling out of the canoe. A cord from the centre of the net is secured to his arm and he hauls on this to pull up the net from the bed of the river. A longer and stronger net is sometimes stretched right across the river: occasionally this catches the huge "Empurau" fish, and sometimes it catches the propeller of a passing outboard engine and then feelings run high. In the smaller streams I have seen ladies fishing with a net about 4 feet square. One lady stands motionless holding the submerged net whilst another lady pokes around with a stick and drives the fish towards her friend who then jerks her net out of the water as the fish are swimming over it.

Most boys and a lot of men also fish with a rod and line: they stick the rods into the river bank and return later to see if they have hooked anything. "Bubu" fish traps are also positioned and left, in fact they may be left for days, and unless the catch is eaten by marauders, it will remain quietly feeding itself from the inflowing water. There are some large frogs which are edible, some crayfish of a dark metallic blue speckled with gold, and also freshwater turtles. Large turtles measuring 2½ hands across the shell are not uncommon but it can be extraordinarily difficult to catch them in the deep pools, and even when the great silhouette passes over the pebbles in shallow water it is not every man who will rush forward and risk being bitten.

Nowadays many men are swimming underwater and catching fish with homemade harpoon-guns, the sharpened metal spike being shot away with a piece of stretched rubber. This rubber is usually part of an old bicycle

Plate 25 a

inner-tube sold by the traders though few of the men have ever seen a bicycle much less know how to ride one. To go with the home-made harpoon gun the traders also sell underwater face-masks and though most of these have a single oval window the earlier ones have two windows placed too close together and passing canoeists are now quite used to seeing grey, shivering men popping up out of the river and squinting at them most horribly (Plate 25)

The most exciting fishing to watch is the "nubai" and it is a pity that this is also the most destructive and wasteful method. The chosen river has two or three dams built across it then tubai (derris) roots are pounded and thrown into the water upstream. At a signal from the appointed organiser scores of men dive into the water to spear the stunned fish, or lean far out of canoes paddled by their friends and stab the fish as they drift past. It is a noisy, festive occasion enjoyed by a couple of hundred folk as they race to grab the largest fishes. The divers rather quickly assume a mantle of pallid goose-flesh, but the girl paddlers dress in their best sarongs and what with the colour and the gaiety it is reminiscent of an August Bank Holiday on Hampstead Heath in London. What a great pity it is that this kind of fun denudes the rivers of fish for years afterwards.

Other riotously coloured fishermen are the kingfishers which flash over the sparkling chiaroscuro of frothing rapids into the dark green tunnel of trees overhanging the motionless opacity of still water. Sometimes a heady scent causes passing boatmen to look up at a cascade of white orchids hanging down amongst the aerial roots of great parasitic growths, or fragrant tree-blossoms drift down on the quiet stillness of dark pools. Some mornings the rising sun lights on dense white mists swirling up from the rivers, whilst the afternoon sun illuminates the water so brilliantly that a distinct layer of dust can be seen spread out on the surface of the river like an irridescent layer of gold dust. On a really hot day it is rather nice to opt out of the sunshine and wander along a stream at the edge of one's farm because the gurgling of the tiny waterfalls and the cool, damp shade of moss covered trees is balm indeed. So when a man descends from his longhouse to join a friend waiting for him in his canoe he knows that poling upstream can be hard work and paddling downstream rather slow, but neither of them are likely to be racing against time and there will be plenty to talk about on the way.

The average Dyak has considerable respect for the "Tuan" who sit in offices and can even afford to buy meat for their dogs however bad the harvests may have been, but their own life, with all its hardships, has much to commend it.

EPILOGUE

On Friday, 24th May 1968, exactly at four o'clock in the afternoon, in an atmosphere tense with drama I was served with Banishment Papers. I was informed that it was a Federal Government decision, the order of banishment being signed by the Deputy Prime Minister. The papers had come direct from Kuala Lumpur since apparently the Sarawak Government had declined to serve them through the normal administrative channels.

No reasons were given but it was common knowledge that my influence and affection for the remote Dyak peoples was considerable although I had been most careful to remain quite neutral in all things political. I had also consistently refused despite considerable pressures to use that influence in the political issues which were due to be settled in the General Elections to be held in August 1968. There seemed no point in appealing against this decision but it seemed a strange reward for almost twenty years' service in Sarawak.

To enable me to remain at Entebai for the twelve day period of grace allowed before I had to leave Sarawak for ever, I gave my promise that there would be no demonstrations on the part of the Dyaks as a protest against my expulsion. Being very much aware of the intense loyalty of the Dyaks, their sense of justice, I was above all apprehensive that they might try to take the law into their own hands and create a situation which could not but end in tragedy. Ironically enough it was my influence which had prevented a critical situation developing when the Federal Government expelled from office the chief minister, himself a Dyak. Only those who had to know were told of my banishment and as a cover for my departure I merely said that I had to leave earlier than planned for a short visit to London to discuss the book I was writing.

I was not concerned about the continued running of the nine centres opened up under the Community Development Projects. They had been handed over some years previously to the respective Committees of Progress. It was true that one or two centres were not doing as well as had been expected but some, particularly Entaih, had proved beyond any reasonable doubt that the Principles of Development had been sound. Since January 1966 I had only been concerned in establishing the Entebai Private Vocational Secondary School which seemed then, as it does even now, the obvious end of a Community Development Project within a remote area, to ensure that it was possible for continued progress to take place.

As it is more than likely that there will be a sequel to this book, I need not dwell on the dramatic events which took place at Entebai during those short twelve days. I think I remained calm, almost detached even as though it was someone else being banished. Curiously enough I felt no bitterness, just a deep sadness that I could no longer remain in Sarawak. All that I could do I think I did. The Committee of Managers of the Entebai Private Secondary School met in solemn session and authorised Luke with Eddie to be joint secretary managers during my absence. All necessary mandates were signed and witnessed. I felt a deep pride in the bearing of both Luke and Eddie at this momentous meeting. The many thousands of dollars held in trust by me for and on behalf of the Dyaks had been most carefully handed back. The final parade of the group of Border Scouts which I commanded had been held and Sgt. Moa Ari had taken over. I had been very proud of this loyal, efficient and well disciplined group and I knew it would be a very long while before I forgot the last salute from Sgt. Moa.

Making my last preparations to leave, I comforted myself with the thought that we, the team, had given of our best and perhaps it was right that the Dyaks should be allowed to meet their own destiny and take what steps they felt fit to guard their own heritage and in so doing ensure a reasonable prosperity for their children.

So the time came to leave and early on the morning of 4th June 1968, I asked one of the boys to take Brown Feet, my dog, up the river in a canoe as though she were off on a hunting trip. I wanted above all else to spare myself the harrowing sight of her swimming after me. Giman, immediately she was out of sight, got my own fast canoe ready and accompanied only by Arthur, Luke and Eddie, I left Entebai almost unnoticed, a day earlier than the local people expected.

I was accorded every courtesy by the British High Commissioner and as I walked to the very steps of the aircraft with him I felt proud at that moment to be British. I was on my way to New Zealand where in the company of wartime friends with whom I had flown many hours over the darkened skies of Germany, I knew I would find a welcome and perhaps begin to heal the wounds. I wanted also to spend some time with Jangga, one of my adopted sons, studying in the Auckland Technical College.

It was difficult to remain calm and unmoved, however, as the sounds of the convulsive sobs from Luke and Eddie reached my ears. They had until that last moment of departure been so splendidly cheerful.